Library of
Davidson College

# PYGMIES
# AND
# Dream Giants

KILTON STEWART

HARPER COLOPHON BOOKS
Harper & Row, Publishers
New York, Evanston, San Francisco, London

A hardcover edition was originally published by W. W. Norton & Co., Inc. It is here reprinted by arrangement with the author's widow, Mrs. Clara Stewart Flagg, 144 East 36th Street, New York, N.Y. 10016.

PYGMIES AND DREAM GIANTS. Copyright © 1954 by Kilton Stewart. All rights reserved. Printed in the United States of America. No part of this book may be used or reproduced in any manner without written permission except in the case of brief quotations embodied in critical aricles and reviews. For information address Harper & Row, Publishers, Inc., 10 East 53d Street, New York, N.Y. 10022. Published simultaneously in Canada by Fitzhenry & Whiteside Limited, Toronto.

First HARPER COLOPHON edition published 1975

STANDARD BOOK NUMBER: 06-090423-2

75 76 77 78 79 80 10 9 8 7 6 5 4 3 2 1

*To my parents, who had to accept the Negritos as part of their family because the pygmies made me their brother and because I insisted that I myself, and the other members of the family— that all men—are pygmies, except as their stature is increased from day to day by the dream giants.*

# Contents

| | | |
|---|---|---|
| 1 | The Whirlpool | 3 |
| 2 | The Egg in My Past | 15 |
| 3 | Juan of Bataan | 29 |
| 4 | Spirit Cave on Pinatoba | 39 |
| 5 | Hunting-and-Gathering Magic | 59 |
| 6 | Olan | 71 |
| 7 | Funeral Feast and Betrothal | 82 |
| 8 | Courtship the American Way | 89 |
| 9 | Nomads of Zambales | 97 |
| 10 | Typhoon | 114 |
| 11 | The Sopot-Sopot Demon | 120 |
| 12 | The Head-Hunters | 132 |
| 13 | Hymns and Head Dances | 148 |
| 14 | MacGregor and the Enemy | 159 |
| 15 | Bontoc | 170 |
| 16 | Journey into Ifugao | 191 |
| 17 | The Rice Terraces of Ifugao | 197 |
| 18 | The Rice-Increasing Ceremony | 212 |
| 19 | Lost among the Gods | 225 |
| 20 | Spiritualism in Ifugao | 238 |
| 21 | Spirits of the Mountain | 249 |
| 22 | The Trail Back | 260 |
| 23 | Universal Man | 271 |
| | Index | 285 |

# PYGMIES
## AND
## Dream Giants

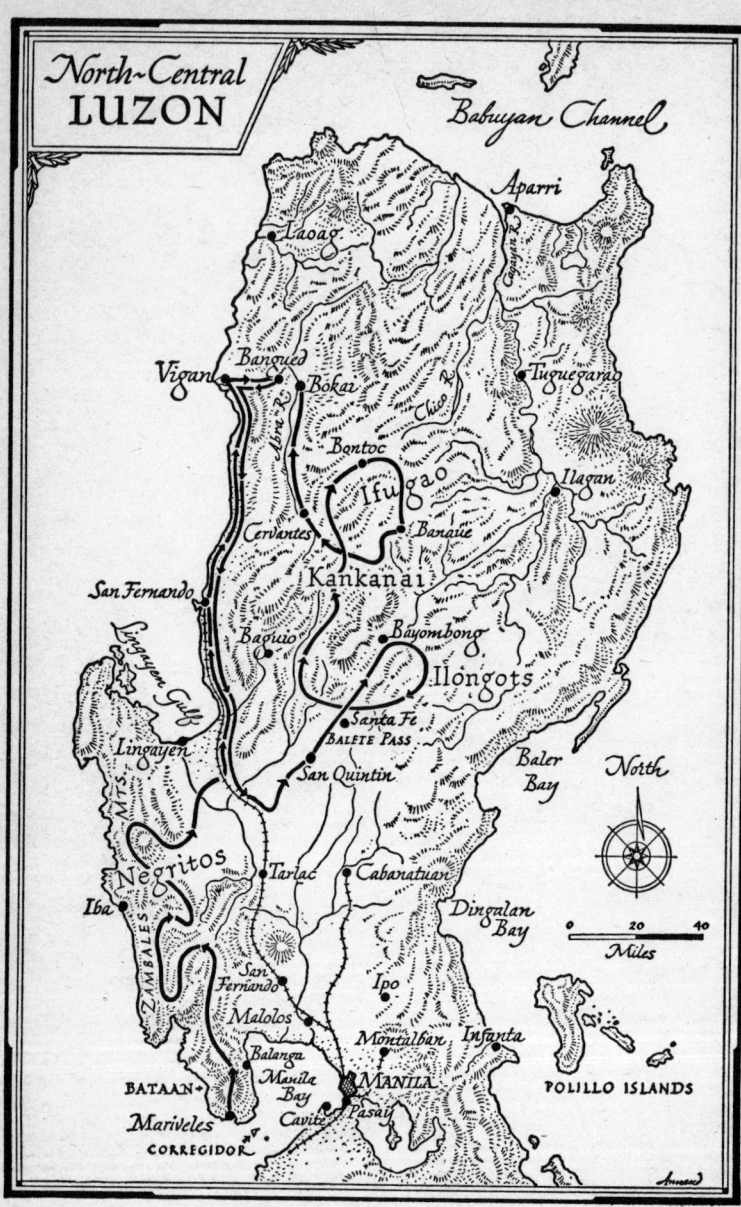

# ONE

# The Whirlpool

THE Abra River, which I had seen as a brook at its source, was now a raging flood that poured from the Philippine jungle, turned at the base of a giant granite crag, and roared through a deep gorge past the little village of Bokai.

The granite cliff was the first thing I had noticed as I approached the village from upstream. I wondered how the mountains and the river country through which I had passed would look from its peak. It would be a difficult climb in this rainy season, but since I could remain at Bokai only two more days, I persuaded the two sons of the house where I was staying to arrange for an expedition along with some of the village boys.

In order to arrive at the river's brink by sunrise, we started at midnight, using torches of pitch pine to light our way. The thunderous vibration from the gorge filled the air and shook the earth underfoot. Behind a rhythmic, surflike booming, came the roar of a Niagara.

When at last we topped the crag at the upper end of the gorge, I was able to see the reason for the pulselike roar. A half mile above, the meandering island-dotted river broke into straight, steep rapids. At the top of the rapids, the water formed a smooth, glossy sheet, but toward the bottom it broke up into deeper and deeper furrows, as though the pressure from above wrinkled its surface at the lower end. Just before reaching the cliff, the furrows curled and broke like ocean waves into clouds of spray. The vast, pulsing sound was said to proceed from the vitals of a water fairy so fierce that no man or beast had ever lived while traveling through the turbulent waters of her domain.

After striking the cliff, the boiling water slithered along the gorge another half mile in an unbroken chain of whirlpools, until it reached the abrupt end of the cliff and emptied out into a wide bubbling pool, only a short distance from the village. The natives called this pool the Mother of Fountains. From where we stood, it looked like a tremendous well.

The boys explained that not even the biggest raft could survive the whirlpools. If it was not smashed to pieces at the top, the water fairy would suck it under like a straw. As we watched, a floating hardwood tree buried its broken branches in the cone of one of the whirlpools. Lifting its knotted roots slowly into the air, it sank vertically out of sight. The lads beside me turned pale, and making some trivial excuse, retired to the other side of the cliff to wait for me.

Terrified at being alone, I called to them to rejoin me. The twisting gargantua below filled me with panic. While it was still black, the water had abounding life. Now, as the sun tipped the horizon, it was becoming crimson. At first only the foam on the crest of the waves glinted red against the shadows. Then, as the red tips of spray grew pink, the whole river turned scarlet. This was not the birth of a day; someone had slit the jugular vein of night.

I turned from the scene and joined the boys. They were discussing a cave, whose black mouth the sun had revealed a few miles up the river. From where we stood it looked like a tiny speck in the face of a white cliff, but judging from the distance I knew it must be immense. They were talking about a snake, the mythical father of all snakes, which lived inside it. The uncle of one of the boys claimed he had built a fire on the back of this snake, thinking it was a log, and had been carried by the snake into the gloomy interior of the cave. The lads who had been to school doubted that the snake lived there. They were especially skeptical of the old man's story.

The cave was too far away from the village to frighten them. They said that the old man had been dreaming in the woods because he had drunk too much rice wine, and they were not inclined to give his nephew credit for being related to the only living man who had actually seen the monster.

As I listened to the discussion, I realized that I must explore the cave. It spelled adventure and possible treasure. Ancient Chinese traders used huge jars, exquisitely made and decorated, as containers for rice and other merchandise sent to the Philippines. Some of the mountain people exchanged rattan for the jars, which they used as caskets when they buried their dead in the caves. A cache of those Ming jars is worth a fortune, to say nothing of the ancient carvings and ceremonial objects which were buried with the dead.

The boys knew of no one who had explored the cave. The people of their valley were afraid of the mythical snake and gave it a wide berth. Because they knew that strangers would ask to be guided there, they never spoke of it to them.

If I could take advantage of the braggadocio of these Filipino boys, who had expressed their disbelief in the snake, so that they would lose face if they refused to accompany me, I knew they would guide me there even at the risk of their lives.

"Why are you boys so much afraid of the things you don't believe in?" I asked them.

"Afraid of what?" one of them asked.

"Afraid of the snake in the cave, for instance," I answered.

"We are not afraid of the snake." The insult made the boy turn pale.

"If you are really not afraid, you will take me to it," I answered. A movement like the wind playing in a clump of reeds ran through the group.

"Of course, we will take you if you want to go," one of them answered, "but you will wish we hadn't. In the rainy season, the trails are overgrown with thorny creepers of rattan. We will have to cut our way through every foot to get there. With the help of the farm hands we can do that, but the mud will cling to your feet at every step, and before you have gone a mile, your legs will cramp. The trail leads along the old river bottom. Even a horse would be exhausted by the trip."

"I've been in your mountains for months," I answered. "I know what your mud's like. I want a good day's workout. Let's get under way."

Without a word, the boys pulled out their bolos and we began the journey. Soon I had to admit to myself that they were right. A hundred times I wished the lads were Americans and I could suggest that we turn back without losing face myself. No treasure on earth could be worth the torture of perpetually pulling my feet from that clinging mud.

Six hours later we crept into the mouth of the cave, more dead than alive, to find shelter from the torrent of rain which had been beating down upon us since an hour after sunup. The boys had shown no mercy for me along the way, and had pushed on relentlessly, without addressing a word to me. The only sounds had been the endless hacking of the bolos and the gradually fading roar of the rapids.

We found no hint of smoke on the walls, no sign of cave paintings, none of the discolorations which would indicate human occupation. Millions of bats poured out of the gaping mouth as we entered, and a few small snakes darted into cracks in the walls. The stench of bat manure was stifling.

The boys walked calmly around the cave's gloomy interior with me, as if too exhausted by the grueling journey to feel their former dread. With their long knives they willingly dug into any corner which I indicated, only reminding me that there was a long trail back, and that no pines were available for torches. After a half hour of digging, it stopped raining and we made ready to return.

Now the boys would not have to cut their way, and I knew that my legs would never stand the quickened pace they would set. If we went back the way we had come, my need for repeated stops for rest would keep us on the trail all night without food, and we had had little to eat since morning. By swimming down the river to the head of the rapids, however, we could escape the clinging mud of the bottoms. I had gone swimming with the lads before and knew that they were like fish in the water. There was the danger of crocodiles, but the boys were adept at avoiding them.

We could make the six or seven miles in an hour or two, and land at the head of the rapids fresh for the remainder of the journey. We could then pick up the trail of the morning and be home by sunset.

"If you boys were not afraid of the crocodiles," I said nonchalantly, "we might swim down the river and have a refreshing afternoon of sport instead of a dreary tramp through the mud."

The boys looked at one another with astonishment. In the rainy season no one ever wished to swim in the river above the rapids, unless bewitched by the water fairy and marked for death. I learned later that they could not tell me of this belief without arousing the fairy's wrath against themselves, so they would have to swim with me.

They argued awhile in dialect, and we started for the river. It made a wide bend through the bottoms. The bank at our side was a morass of mangrove swamps where swimming would be impossible. We would have to swim over to a chain of islands in the center and skirt them until we had passed the swampy shore, well down toward the rapids. We could then wade across a broad shallow arm of the river, back to the left bank at the head of the rapids.

As we descended, they pointed out the swamp and the shallows to me on the maplike landscape below. Along the mangrove fringe, the crocodiles would be dangerous, since they could dig their feet into the mud or roots and lash out with their tails. They would not usually attack a man swimming in deep water, let alone a group. If we followed the central chain of islands we would be in little danger from them. As we cut our way down to the river bank, I found the boys stealing sidewise glances at me, half in wonder and half in dread. They sang native songs as they hacked away, and the spirits of the party rose noticeably.

At the bank of the river I took off my shirt and boots. The boys thought I had better leave on my breeches—which had been shortened and reinforced since my arrival at the village—as protection against snags and rocks in case I fell in the shallow water. All the rest of our things were given to the laborers who had come along in the morning to bear the torches and help cut the trail. Wild horses could not have dragged one of them into the water. They did not have to maintain face or share the burden of the master class. Since they could not hope to keep up with us along the trail, the boys told them we would meet them at the village.

No suspicious-looking logs floated in the little creek which formed the cove at our feet. In his left hand each of us carried a bolo, holding it by the sheath so that it would not cut the hand, but could be easily drawn should a water snake contest our trail or a crocodile attack us while swimming. We were ready to leave, but each time I looked at the brown water something held me back. I could not call it intuition. I would not admit that it was fear.

Letting go of the bank, I pushed off into the stream. What a blessed relief it was to feel the water supporting me and the current taking the place of my will.

"Swim straight across for the islands!" someone shouted. "But don't fight the current!"

For two hours we passed strings of islands without difficulty. It was easier than trudging through the mud. Each time we stopped to rest, the boys examined the currents below. Their feeling for the power and danger of the water was uncanny. Repeatedly they warned me away from a suspicious eddy and told me where my feet would find a sandbank or when to be careful of rocks I could not see.

It was an exhilarating journey. Excitement grew as the roar of the cataract gradually became louder. Finally we rounded the bend which put the swampy territory behind us and brought the head of the rapids into view. Up to the point where they broke, the land looked as level as a table, and from our position in the water, we could see nothing beyond. We seemed to be approaching the edge of the world.

Now we were on the last long fingerlike island, which reached over toward the left bank, where we were to land. The island, which had appeared so small from the cave, proved to be nearly a mile in length. The ribbon of water across which we must wade was some quarter of a mile wide. On the sandy upper point of the island we stopped to rest and discuss this last lap of our journey. The water, less than waist deep at the upper end of the island, looked the same all the way across.

"If it gets deeper toward the shore, we will have to walk upstream," the boys cautioned me. "If the going is too difficult we will have to walk back to the island and try it from the next one above."

So far the journey had been easy and pleasurable. I only half listened to instructions. The increasing roar and vibration had acted on me like a stimulant, and the ribbon of shallow water ahead seemed puny.

The water exerted a steady pull against my legs, but it was so constant that I soon failed to notice it. Walking was simple enough, except for the pain on the soles of my feet caused by the rocky bottom. I decided to seek relief by swimming a ways. Before I had taken a dozen strokes, the lads called out something about the water fairy. I stood up again and was astonished to see how far above me they were. The swift water had been forcing me downstream, and it was getting deeper again.

Pointing off diagonally toward the bank, they motioned for me to walk upstream. It had become obvious to them that there was a channel on the extreme left side and that we would have to walk upstream a bit further.

I could hardly hear what they were saying, but it was apparent from their gestures that they were filled with panic. Suddenly the rock on which I was standing gave way, and before I could find a foothold, I had lost another fifty yards. The water had increased in depth and swiftness. I noticed also that the current at the bottom was much more rapid than at the top, as the water on the bottom was sucked out over the smooth lip of the rapids below.

I tried to walk upstream, but to my astonishment I made no progress. Under my feet the whole bottom of the river was moving with the water toward the rapids. The footing on the stones was too unstable to permit my pushing against the stream. I could not go straight up toward the boys. Nor could I walk toward the bank. The water became deeper with every step.

I turned and made my way back toward the island. This was easier because the current at the bottom was now with me. When I looked up, I was shocked to find how much smaller the boys appeared. I could no longer hear a word they were saying. Half of that fingerlike island had mysteriously slipped by me. For each step I took toward the island, I was being washed down two steps toward the rapids.

If I lost my footing once more, I would have no chance. I must swim back in the direction of the island. On the surface I might escape that wrenching undercurrent. The distance rapidly diminished as I swam, but the nearer the trees approached, the more quickly the island slipped away from me. Finally, it disappeared from sight.

I had reached a point squarely on the brink of the rapids. The water was still shallow, and my feet found the bottom. But here the rocks underfoot were like feathers. I could not stand on them.

They seemed to be floating into the rapids. Not more than fifty feet separated me from the last great root, which projected off the end of the island and stretched out through the foam toward me. Leaning against the current and treading on the shifting rocks, I was able to approach that root inch by inch. If I could keep my balance I would reach it.

I felt like a squirrel running in a wheel. At last I could see the wrinkles in the bark of the root. A step and I would be able to grasp it, but my foot found no bottom. Too late I realized that I had stepped from the shelf on the shallow side of the island. The current from the other side grasped my feet. The roots and the trees disappeared; the island above me moved up and down; I was over the edge of the universe. One last glimpse of the human specks in the river at the head of the island and then that upper world was wiped out.

Now I was floating, with nothing to do for awhile but look at the cliffs where I had stood at dawn, watching them grow rapidly larger; nothing to do but slip down the glossy sheet of water between the freshly washed green hills toward the inferno. The rocks, which had refused to support me, were clashing against each other with quarreling, sobbing sounds, as they were hurled along beneath me by the frenzied water. The sobbing, grating sounds filled up my head, as though the water in my ears had solidified into a metal chain stronger than the current. The chain tightened. I no longer seemed to move. I relaxed and prepared to die. I gave up. There was no chance. That sobbing chain of sound held me in place while everything else in the world slipped away. The clouds on the hills became white caps on green waves, the trees at the river's bank, clouds of emerald spray. Even the granite cliff had lost its solidity and was blowing toward me.

Directly above was one cloud which, like myself, failed to move with the rest of the world. It was head-shaped, with shaggy edges like hair. The face of the head was somehow connected with the sobbing. My mother's eyes seemed to gaze down at me. Now the rest of the face was becoming painfully clear. It was a young face, white and sad, much younger than my mother's when I had last seen her. It seemed to say, "Why do you hurt me by being reckless and wasteful?"

"Wasteful," echoed the mournful sob from the grinding rocks. In a few seconds that rapidly growing black storm cloud below would break over me and life itself would be wasted. Faced with the whirlpool, which I accepted as death, I had no fear of dying, but only nausea, guilt, and self-loathing, a sense of sin so deep that I felt my body losing tone and warmth, and all its customary inner feeling and action.

The rhythm of the sobs moved more slowly. Now the face moved down out of the sky and hovered before me until I could hardly see the world moving by. The sadness in the eyes was unbearable. The rhythm stopped.

The face was beginning to swim before me. It was like a picture in a black frame, and as the image became more vague, the frame grew wider. So this was death—blackness closing on a picture. Only the eyes were clear now. They had taken on the impish look of Olan, the Negrito girl to whom I had been betrothed by the rites of her people. Now the face was filling with wrinkles, and the eyes with the desperate urgency of the old Filipino woman trying to express her gratitude because she believed I had saved her son from black magic. The recognition was like an explosion. The eyes were conveying a message to me: "Not all bad, but good and bad."

Blood suddenly flowed in my veins again, sweeping away the ice that had frozen my heart and contracted my mind, dissolving the lump in the pit of my stomach, turning it into exaltation, which bubbled up as laughter. I was full of blood, full of a life that felt like fire. I would not submit to death in that senseless brown water. Beneath that black cliff, which was now almost over my head, was only the struggle, life.

By now I was in the middle of the river, well down the rapids toward the canyon, where from the crag I had seen the smooth surface of the water beginning to wrinkle in the red light of the morning sun. The roar from below was deafening, and I felt rather than heard the pulsing rhythm of the waves breaking on the diagonal granite cliff that blocked their path.

Now the water about me was rapidly dividing into waves. The little one I was riding became a leisurely moving dowager whale. It had been especially created to carry me and it kept expanding to give me a better view. My arms sliced the puny water like blades, as though a powerful and cunning fish brain inside me had taken over the simple function of swimming, leaving my mind free to drink in the blue of the sky, the gleaming crystals of the wet, black granite rising up before me, the towering height of the cliff, and the red of a flame tree which clung to a deep scar in its battered face.

The whale-wave violently hunched its back, swelling rapidly upward, and I was lying on a curling, silver fin of water which broke away beneath me. Dropping through space, I fell into a world of foam which let me down and down. Then suddenly it was gone. I had struck a rock, which bit into my flesh. Flat and smooth where my leg and foot had hit it, there was a sharp edge at the upper end which tore the skin over my ribs. For an instant the water pressed me to the rock with crushing force. Then it freed me and I was tossed about.

I was back on the surface again, but the air, which I felt pouring into my lungs, was the only familiar thing in this foamy world. The water had lost its orderliness and separated into welts and bumps and ridges, which went roaring and hissing about in mad confusion, as though a vast array of animals had been caught in the darkness, beneath a rubber sheet, and were making a desperate, senseless effort to exterminate one another. I was close to the cliff now, almost under it, and it was beginning to move upstream and to sway back and forth with a crazy earthquake rhythm. A huge funnel appeared from nowhere, and I was lying on its lip. Then I began to slip down its revolving surface, traveling with it upstream against the force from above.

I felt my lungs filling up with air. As I reached the bottom of the cone, my body crouched like one expecting a blow. Then I was spinning. The world grew from black to bright, as though the water fairy were throwing showers of sparks into my eyes. A new roar sounded in my ears. It was the roar of increasing pressure, a roar that was more pain than sound, yet louder than any sound I had ever heard. Then there were voices, whole snatches of conversation, like people talking.

Suddenly the pressure diminished, and I felt as though powerful hands were tearing at me. Then I was swimming. With a cunning insight, my hands and feet opposed the tumult in the water, pushing me toward the surface with a feeling of exaltation.

Again and again I was tossed about on the writhing, foamy waves, locked in the embrace of those hissing cones, and then released to find my way back to the air. My mind grew numb. I was swimming in a black void which was growing light. Then the darkness was gone and my body bounded into the air, which I was again gulping gratefully.

I was naked now, swimming in the soft brown water which rose about me like a well. Somewhere along the canyon my breeches had been torn away. The rapids and gorge were behind me and the sky was above. Across a flat stretch of water lay the fringe of the jungle and the peaceful Bokai valley. The water was making amends. It had repented of sucking me down and now was glad to push me into the air. Second by second my head cleared until the blackness through which I had been swimming began to fade from my memory like the tail of a snake disappearing down a hole. The low jungle fringe turned into a wall of trees. The water was running faster now, and soon I would be at the road where the villagers ferried the river in dry season. I would have to land before the river reached another canyon.

The calm world of green and blue above me was suddenly disturbed by a woman's voice and then by a clatter of voices. For an instant I was uncertain that I was really out of the whirlpool, and expected to see the court of the water fairy. Instead I saw a familiar and reassuring sight. The women of a near-by village were washing their clothes on the big rocks at the water's edge. They had been as surprised to see me emerge from the fountain as I had been to hear their voices. I looked up at them and smiled. They stood there, waving their arms and chattering like monkeys.

The water was getting shallow now. My knees grated against a rock. Just as I was about to stand up and wade from the river, I remembered that I no longer had my trousers. I sank back into the water and decided to swim on so I could land without embarrassing the women. But by this time they had decided that I was not a water fairy. They ran chattering along the shore, pointing to the canyon below and beckoning wildly.

Plague it all! Why must they be so helpful? What was a gentleman to do?

I was swimming closer to the bank now. A banana plant had caved into the water, and as my fingers touched its long ribbonlike leaves, I realized that I had found a solution. I wrapped a leaf about my middle and stood up, trying to look as though I had never worn anything but leaves for clothing.

"Bokai," I said, pointing up the trail.

"Bokai," they murmured in a chorus. They gaped at me as though they were surveying a water fairy after all.

In spite of my leaf I felt naked and embarrassed as I climbed from the river, and helpless as an infant. The avenging angel who banished Adam from the Garden of Eden, with his fiery sword, could not have been more terrible than the cloud face of my mother.

Now my mind did not go with me along the trail, but turned back to that face and to the memory of my condemned feeling, my conviction that I had been found utterly bad and had been justly banished from the garden of human life. Even the recollection of it filled me with astonishment. Surely I had done some mischief, some wickedness, some blasphemy, to accumulate inside me the malignant, crushing, freezing sense of guilt I had felt in the rapids.

Maybe it was wrong to study people and their gods, to observe and record their dreams, their magic, and their ceremonies. Perhaps observing the head-hunters had made me guilty of all the murders they had committed. Perhaps the Negrito god, Tolandian, whose secrets I had learned, was holding me responsible for all the incest and the blood feuds which had gone unavenged since the beginning of time. Or perhaps I had already sinned before that fateful evening, a year earlier, when I visited the Hartendorps and my expedition had its inception. Perhaps Mrs. Hartendorp had realized that I was already lost. Perhaps she had been looking through my skin at some diabolical state of inner stagnation or damnation when she insisted on learning what I was running away from.

# TWO

# The Egg in My Past

My expedition had begun, really, with my arrival at the Hartendorps' home. I remember that I approached the house with excitement, hope, and misgiving. Mrs. Hartendorp met me on the porch of her bungalow in suburban Manila and welcomed me with the gracious warmth of an old friend. My arms were filled with equipment for mental tests, and I still felt more the sailor than the psychologist—having landed that morning from the ship on which I had worked my way from Honolulu—but she looked at me as if I were an ideal dinner guest, helped me set down my gadgets, and steered me to a comfortable chair.

"My husband has been telling me about you," she said. She was slender, and the light-green gown she wore made her seem cool and poised. "He takes psychology and science and the future of the world very seriously. I don't."

She left me with that, but came back in a moment and gave me a glass filled with bourbon and soda.

"I am more interested in what people are running away from," she said. "Lots of wanderers pass through here, and most of them are running away from something. They don't know it, of course, but they are. What are you running away from?"

I was glad I had the drink. I gulped some of it, kept the glass to my lips to cover my shock, and arranged a few stalling phrases in my mind. "I don't know," I said, lowering the glass. "I am going toward something, and therefore I must be leaving something, but whether I am running away from it, or being drawn from it to something else, I don't know."

She gave me the suspicious look which women reserve for a statement that sounds logical and therefore dangerous. At this point, to my relief, her husband came out on the porch with a large, dark-haired man, whom he introduced as Dr. Gilbert Perez, of the Bureau of Education.

"Dr. Perez is interested in the psychology of the non-Christian tribes of the Philippines," Hartendorp said. "He has more knowledge of the islands than anyone else I know. I want you to tell him about your project. He can help you with it, I'm sure."

Hartendorp was editor of the magazine *Philippine*. I had met him that morning, when a reporter steered me to him as the person most apt to know something of the available printed material on the Negritos, the primitive pygmy peoples of the Philippine mountain areas. I had told him of my idea, admitted I was broke, and helped him talk himself into the notion of financing my trip with an advance against some articles about it. He had not committed himself, but had asked me to dinner, after which I was to demonstrate on some neighborhood children the psychological tests I planned to use on the Negritos. With them I hoped to explore my favorite psychological theory—that all men develop from a single mental pattern, and that this pattern can be discovered by a psychological study of successive levels of humans, ranging from the primitive to the sophisticate. This single pattern I regarded as the central mind which builds the physical body of every man from the elements of his environment, and establishes and maintains the vital rhythms and normal states of that body. At the same time, this central mind builds up a personality from the patterns or elements of the social environment.

The Negritos—pygmies who lived by hunting and gathering fruits and nuts, and who did not settle anywhere, even to sow crops —were the most primitive people still available for such study.

Tribes of them were scattered in various parts of the world, in Africa and in New Guinea, the Philippines, and other parts of Malaysia.

I began to explain to Dr. Perez that the first point in my plan was to find the Negritos, when Mrs. Hartendorp interrupted. "He is under obligation," she said, "to tell me what he is running away from."

I could see that I was going to earn any commission I got from her husband, and I was going to earn it by her standards. I decided I would have to be casual, brief, and self-deprecatory. It would be almost impossible to tell it all anyway. What would she make of the fact that I was born a Mormon? To some people that in itself was reason for running away. I thought of my family, old in the religion, moved by their dreams and visions to follow Joseph Smith when the prophet led them west from New York, and to follow Brigham Young on the long trek across the desert to Salt Lake. I myself, like many other young Mormons, had gone off as a missionary at eighteen. I had spent three years in Quebec and Nova Scotia, asking everyone I met to doubt all his previous knowledge and convictions and authorities, and to attempt to learn from his dreams and visions if the message of the Mormon prophet was right or wrong.

I couldn't tell Mrs. Hartendorp more than the fact that when I had finished being a missionary I decided to be a doctor. I had never tried to dig back and codify all the influences and desires that had brought me to that decision. It did not matter much, in any case, since after entering college and starting on a premedical course I had got only as far as the egg.

Mrs. Hartendorp was polite. "The egg?" she said.

I love the egg story. It thrills me even now after so many tellings. After all, it describes my discovery of what, to me, is the mystery of life. It is the key to my understanding of man's evolution, man's health, man's happiness.

It had been a frog's egg, examined in biology class. Dr. Child, the great biologist, had discovered that at the moment of fertilization, a sort of electric whirlwind is established inside the egg. This whirlwind—the axle gradient, he called it—maintained a positive head area at the point where the sperm made contact with the egg, and a negative area across from it, to balance it off. This fascinated me. It had the appearance of a trinity in unity, with its positive, negative, and central area. I had always heard that the God of the universe was such a trinity.

Mrs. Hartendorp showed signs of amusement and I realized I was going to sound like a missionary. I hurried on. I was afraid she would not let me finish.

With our microscope and our electronic equipment, we watched these mysterious inner forces building the body of the frog. It occurred to me that I had forces of this same sort in myself, that, at one time, even I was a mere egg.

"So you looked into the egg and there was yourself. Have you been running ever since?" asked Mrs. Hartendorp.

Had I? It had been frightening to me because my hero, the scientist, turned out to be a villain. When, in the laboratory, he directed a beam of light into the egg, the inner center that was directing its growth lost control, and a second head was seen to form where the light was focused, resulting in a monster.

"A villain in the egg romance," said Mrs. Hartendorp. "Did you stay loyal to your first love, the simple egg child of nature, or was your heart drawn to the monster of the biologists?"

Looking back, it seemed to me that I never did forget my first love, but from then on, I felt more at home with the monster, as though it had joined the brotherhood of human beings. The scientist had introduced into a growing thing an artificial energy pattern which was strong enough to change its natural inner arrangement. All human beings are subject to recurrent artificial patterns, such as words, numbers, machines, and ceremonies. I explained that, like the frog's egg, we are all changed by these patterns—into super-animals or into sickly monsters.

Once man has learned to use language, he never stops growing. He remains forever like an egg, constantly evolving. He goes on endlessly building up separate patterns or centers inside himself. He can see these patterns as the reflection of things at which he is looking in the outside world. Later, in his memory, or in his dreams and visions, he can see what a pattern did to him, how it changed him. He can see the image and feel the impulse or emotion which it aroused. Thus, in the characters, objects, and forces of his thoughts, dreams and visions, he can sense, and can therefore struggle against or co-operate with, the centers he is building up inside his skin. His dream-visions are the most important, because in them, fate gives him a second chance to adjust to, or digest, those patterns which he could not assimilate properly while he was awake. Moreover, they give him a better chance than he can ever have while he is awake because during sleep he is resisting new patterns from without.

My own dreams had convinced me that the photographlike images I built up in my mind in the daytime could dominate my dreams at night as though I were still a helpless infant in them, as helpless as an egg. These images could make me hot or cold like malaria germs, could affect my pulse and breath like a leaking heart, and make my stomach feel as though it were full of rubber.

"Did these dream giants stay ashore when you sailed from Hawaii?" asked Mrs. Hartendorp. "Will they be afraid of losing their heads if they go with you up to the Negritos?"

Yes. The inner giants had bothered me less when, as a child and later as an observer, I spent some time with the Ute and Navaho Indians, and I had grown to like nonliterate peoples. The spirit of co-operation among them was soothing. There was more freedom and less anxiety about order and cleanliness. If I was running away from something, perhaps more work with primitive people would help me to find out what it was.

Mrs. Hartendorp seemed to be in a daydream, which she did not abandon when she got up from her chair. "I think dinner is ready," she said.

At table I explained that I had arrived in the early morning from Honolulu on the S.S. *President Pierce*, on its round-the-world tour, with a camera and five large steel suitcases full of equipment I had assembled for a portable psychological laboratory. In one bag there was a small silk tent and a tarpaulin, a couple of camp chairs, a mosquito net, and some standard books on such subjects as racial psychology, mental testing, and anthropology. The other suitcases contained mental tests of every description, picked up in Europe and America, from which I had, for a number of years, been attempting to select a few which could be given to preliterate peoples of various cultures and races. I had also brought clothing and personal effects.

Attached to me, but not visible, were a family in Utah, a Master of Arts degree in psychology from the University of Utah, four years of research in the fields of psychotherapy, mental testing, and anthropology, and a collection of frustrations which had culminated in Honolulu on the beach at Waikiki, where my field work

—as I pontifically called it—had gotten me into trouble with duly constituted authority, as it had in the State Training School in Utah, and as it had with the Mormon priesthood.

It had all started (and I always remembered this in times of trouble) when I found myself regarding dreams and visions as a key to man's psychological unity. It began specifically when I became interested in the frog's egg. When I was a Mormon missionary, and especially when the mission was completed, I found, to my surprise and chagrin, that the religious authorities were not as interested in the current dreams and visions of man, as they were in the dreams and visions of the leaders of the past.

My attitude on dreams was much too complicated to explain to Mrs. Hartendorp. Anyway, it had such a mystical flavor that it would do no good with the scientific-minded people before me. But it was important. My earliest memory about religion was of hearing that Joseph Smith, a fourteen-year-old farmer boy, had read in the Bible: "If any of you lack wisdom, let him ask of God, that giveth to all men liberally, and upbraideth not." He prayed, and in a vision he was freed from all the authorities of the past and was given authority to start a church. Dreams and visions made it possible to maintain a community where no adult had spiritual authority over anyone else, since each could communicate with the supreme authority in his dreams and visions. At least, I felt that I was a member of such a community.

The idea that God ruled the world of sleep for every man had become an obsession with me. All the major religions agreed on this point. Starting here, they might iron out their differences. Science and religion also seemed to me to reach unity in this area when I became aware of the scientific discovery of the infinitely wise force or mind inside the egg, building up and organizing the millions of cells which would make a frog. If man's central mind, which controlled and was made up of his heartbeat and other vital rhythms, was one with God, as the mystics claimed, then God could better help man to struggle with the disruptive patterns from the outside world while he was asleep. At this time, the work of God inside the self would not be interrupted by the arrival of more patterns from the world of man. For me, this view justified religious faith in dreams and visions, whether, in fact, they came from God, or only from the wisdom of the body.

In the study of medicine the central mind appeared again as the wisdom of the body, which maintained the constant states, such as temperature and the neutral acidity of the blood stream, and the vital rhythms of the body, such as breathing and heartbeat. The positive-negative poles which completed the trinity appeared as the areas of man's body and personality which enabled him to absorb and be receptive, and to be the opposite—afraid, outgiving, and aggressive.

Medical science was investigating the way chemicals and microbes and emotions influenced the power of the central mind to maintain the constant states and normal rhythms on which man's health depended. This scientific medicine had, in a few short years, gone far toward ridding the world of epidemic diseases and dietary deficiencies which, in large parts of the world's population, the central wisdom previously could not deal with. But the social patterns which also got inside of man, like microbes and chemicals penetrating his skin, and like the scientist's beam of light penetrating the frog's egg, could also affect man's emotions, and through them influence the constant states and vital rhythms on which his life depended. These social patterns too could also make him unhappy and antisocial.

Psychology was developing mental tests which indicated how man's mind worked, how the photographlike images were tied to the emotions and through them to the vital rhythms. The testing which had been done in the first quarter of the twentieth century indicated that the central mind was the same in all races. Man performed well or poorly on intelligence tests because the environment had furnished him with good or bad tools for thinking, and had attached them well or poorly to his emotions. For the same reasons, he had a healthy body or a sickly body, a healthy, socially cooperative personality or an antisocial personality. If the central mind, which built up both the physical body and the personality, was the same in all races, there was good reason to believe that the psychologists and social scientists could end the chronic illnesses, neuroses, and war, as the medical scientists had been able to control epidemic illnesses, food poisoning, and poisoning from the chemicals with which man came into contact in various occupations.

If the mentality, emotions, and central mind of the children of all races were the same, it would be possible, by collecting their dreams, to find at what point they encountered the social patterns or policies which stopped their mental growth or made them grow in different directions than we did in the West. Perhaps eventually we might find the patterns which made our own growth stop short of a healthy, crimeless, warless society.

Two years before I had assembled a battery of tests which I felt would further indicate whether or not there was a universal man, with an equal potential for physical, mental, and emotional development, and for social and spiritual co-operation. On a research fellowship I was able to give these tests to the least mentally developed group I could find in our society, the feeble-minded children at the State Training School in Utah. I had no trouble with the mental tests since they were widely used and well known even to the layman, but the authorities looked with suspicion at the Emotional Response Test I had devised, and at the test for suggestibility, and at my collection of the worst and best dreams and daydreams the children could report.

I was obliged to move on and succeeded in getting a research fellowship at the Psychology Clinic of the University of Hawaii. Here I gave the Porteus Maze Test, the Goodenough Draw-A-Man Test, and the Binet Test to a few hundred children of the different racial groups who lived there. English-speaking people, Hawaiians, Chinese, Japanese, Filipinos, and Portuguese were included in the project. During my lunch hour, unofficially, I was able to get some data for the Metal Maze, Emotional Response, and Progressive Fantasy tests (which I had devised the year before and used at the Training School). Teachers of the various schools in Hawaii also co-operated in collecting dreams and daydreams, or fantasies, for me, as exercises in English, from some of the students I tested. On my own, in the evenings at my cottage in Waikiki Beach I collected data on suggestibility and hypnosis. Discreetly, I let it be known that I would use suggestion to work on any problem that people brought around, if they would take my Emotional Response Test and allow me to check the results as part of the trance procedure.

"Were you able to find many subjects?" Perez asked.

"Yes," I said. "I shared the house with a very sociable fellow named Al, who had nothing to do but swim and talk. By supplying a little food and drink at our unofficial clinic, we soon had all the subjects we could handle—stowaways, soldiers, seamen, and tourists soon found their way to our door. But apparently there was too much talk about hypnosis. The officials of the University heard it, and they were afraid such research might not please the conservative taxpayers of the islands. They felt that I should find my subjects farther afield. If I pursued my research on my own somewhere else, I would leave the door open for further financial support from Honolulu later on, when it could be arranged. They were very polite.

"So they fired me out of Honolulu and I came to the Far East, hoping I might find access to some primitive tribes, and scare up the means of visiting them."

"How old are you?" Hartendorp suddenly asked.

"Thirty," I answered. He nodded to Perez.

"He'd better get it over with before he's thirty-five," he said. "After that he won't have the ignorance and the energy to go looking for Negritos without money."

I felt that I *must* start with the Negritos, since they are the most primitive type of society known to science, and are, therefore, living at the most infantile state of social development which is available for study. Then I hoped to study other societies, progressively more highly developed.

"If that's what you are looking for, you certainly came to the right place," Dr. Perez said. "We have not only the Negritos, the most simple type of hunting and gathering society, but also the Ilongots and the Ifugao, who have made the next great steps in human progress. With these peoples you can both test your basic psychological theory that there is a universal man, and look for the dream giants which point up the obstacles standing in the way of their social progress or development."

"A trip to the Negritos would be dangerous, wouldn't it?" Mrs. Hartendorp asked. "Wouldn't they be apt to kill him?"

"Very possible," Hartendorp said.

"Who would kill me?" I asked.

"Any of the groups I just mentioned," Perez said.

He explained why with great care. The Negritos are an incredibly simple people. They live an isolated life in the equatorial rain forests, where millennia slip away with so little change from the outside that they have not been impelled to change within. They are probably living the way our own ancestors did some hundred thousand years ago, thousands of years before the formation of the first Egyptian dynasties, before the domestication of food animals and the origin of agriculture. The lack of these practices makes them apparently even more primitive than Adam's family, since the famous quarrel of Cain and Abel occurred because God accepted the sacrifice of Abel's domesticated animal in preference to Cain's agricultural products.

The anthropologist Dr. Radcliffe Brown had written of the Negritos in the Andaman Islands near Singapore. A British anthropologist named Evans, and Father Schebesta, a priest, had worked among the Negritos of Malaya. There were also books and papers on travels among the African pygmies, but very little had been written about the Negritos of the Philippines. Nowhere were the Negritos known to have agriculture or to use domesticated animals for food.

To the Negrito one was not a human being unless he was a member of the local horde. The Andaman Negritos killed off everyone who landed on their island over such a long period of time that they were thought to be cannibalistic, but neither they nor the Filipino Negritos were now believed to eat their victims. If they feared someone, if he displeased them, or if he had anything they wanted, they would kill him as readily as they would a monkey or a bird.

The Ilongots—neighbors to the Negritos—were also hunting and gathering peoples, but they had a shifting dry-land agriculture as well. This first great step in human progress began the liberation of man from the constant pressure of the food quest. If the hunting and gathering stages are regarded as the racial infancy of human culture, then this first type of shifting, dry-land agriculture, where there is no irrigation and fertilization of the soil, might be regarded as its childhood.

However, the Ilongots had not yet learned to domesticate animals for food. They had a worse reputation for head-hunting than any people in this part of the world, and like the mountain Negritos, they had not yet been reached by American or Filipino law. There were also other groups, such as the Bontocs and the Ifugao, who had taken a third great step in human civilization. They had developed both agriculture and animal husbandry, such industries as pottery and weaving, and some regard for territorial as well as kinship political associations; but they were also head-hunters with only a veneer of respect for American law against their old practice.

"We have described the Negrito tools, methods, and extended family social organization, which takes no account of women's rights, as racial infancy," Perez concluded. "We have described the Ilongot shifting, dry-land agriculture as the childhood of human culture. Therefore, we could describe as racial adolescence the culture of these other groups, who have improved tools and methods of agriculture, introduced animal husbandry, and believe a man has rights because he lives in a place, as well as because of the blood that runs in his veins. If you want to start at the beginning and go to the top of the three great developmental stages of the nonliterate tribes in the Philippines, you should include at least these three types of peoples in your study, but any of them might very well kill you, either for your belongings or your head."

"Yes, any of them might oblige," Hartendorp agreed. "But if, knowing this, you still want to stick your neck out, I would advise a trip somewhat like this. Start with the Negritos in the Bataan peninsula, go north up along the Zambales Mountains, then cross over to the Ilongot territory, and work north and east up through Ifugao. In such a journey you would also have some contact with the Kalingas, the Kankanai, and the Bontocs, who are all quite similar to the Ifugao. The Kankanai do not take heads, and the Bontocs are quite friendly to the Americans, so you can relax while you're in their territory. Such a journey should bring you back to Manila with the answers you want," he said, "if you come back at all."

In total, my purpose was to determine as best I could what kind of native intelligence the people of these nonliterate societies had in the beginning, and then to find out what kind of mind was built up on that basic intelligence by the group processes in which they found themselves involved, especially as revealed by their dreams, visions, and ceremonial procedures.

My emphasis on ceremonies aroused considerable interest and I explained as best I could. While investigating the vision quest and dream life of the Plains Indians, I had found that some of the dreams and visions of the American Indians, and their traditional ceremonial interpretations, led the dreamer into his life's work, while the traditional interpretation of other dreams led to sex perversions, murder, and cannibalism.

It has been observed that ceremonies are the most difficult parts of human culture to change and that therefore they often represent its most ancient elements. The dream, on the other hand, is the freest, most spontaneous and therefore newest type of activity of which a human being is capable. The coming together of the dream and the ceremonial interpretation is, therefore, like the meeting of the positive and negative clouds in the sky which gives rise to the lightning. The lightning itself can turn dynamos of human progress, or can blast the individual and, through him, his society. I wanted to examine with the scientific instruments of the twentieth century those societies which had obviously been stunted or blasted somewhere along the path of social development.

Dreams can apparently give rise to good social practices and healing ceremonies, or to black magic, head-hunting, cannibalism, and witchcraft. I wanted to investigate the social policies which determined in which of these directions man's dreams, visions, and daydreams would guide him.

With the help of experience, and the things a man has acquired from his ancestors, he struggles to make his inner images work for him and for society. Modern research has already proved that one type of help or interpretation of the dream, vision, or reflective thought makes man into a saint; another social policy makes him into a cannibal or a head-hunter. I wanted to find out how this came about, so the dangerous images man built up in his mind could be made to stop working against him.

Hartendorp formulated it for me. "He wants to give a scientific description of the basic man, who is the same as all other men in the sight of God and of the law. And he's brought his tests along to show us what kind of instruments he has for portraying this universal man and for measuring the nonliterate groups to determine if they come up to the scientific specifications of the average man and to determine what the various cultures do to this universal individual, or to whatever types of individuals he finds."

"But why is it so important to find out if such people as the Negritos are ordinary folks like ourselves?" said Mrs. Hartendorp. "There are only a few thousand of them left, and their culture seems to fade away like the mist of their jungle homes when they're brought into contact with more civilized peoples. If you do find that they have the same natural endowment as other races, and learn what kind of mind they build up as they live in their simple society, what then? There's nothing much you can do for them that isn't already being done."

"Stewart wishes not to teach but to learn from them," said Perez, "to learn how man dealt with the images he acquired before he had astronomy, mathematics, religion, and philosophy, as we know it. He's probably excited about them because when they fade away like the jungle mist some hundred thousand years of the history of human thought will be lost with them, unless this most primitive example of the beginning of human thinking still available for study can be made a part of the body of Western scientific thought."

After dinner, I demonstrated my battery of tests on some neighborhood children, and explained how the Maze or labyrinth test measured their ability to solve problems. I explained how the Draw-A-Man Test revealed the comparative ability of the various children to analyze a human figure into its parts, and to fit them together again in the proper position and proportion, and how the test of indirect suggestibility showed the degree to which without knowing it they were influenced by the moods and actions of others. I explained how their drawings and accounts of the worst and best things that could happen to them, their daydreams, and the memories of the painful and pleasurable emotional incidents which the questions of the Emotional Response Test brought to mind demonstrated how mental patterns were attached to their emotions. I explained how their dreams demonstrated the way these emotionally charged images attacked and interfered with the vital rhythms and constant states being maintained in sleep, making it necessary for the sleep-mind to do a double job. It had to both carry on the physical processes and conduct the dream, or carry on the processes and protect itself from the disturbing pattern by tying it up with tension, or splitting it off.

I explained that the scores I would obtain from the various primitive groups would furnish evidence which would affirm or deny the idea of the universal man, and would help us to know if the average individual in these groups was the same as the average individual in the groups I had tested in Hawaii, and if we were justified in crediting them with intelligence and feelings like our own.

Both Hartendorp and Perez seemed convinced, but Mrs. Hartendorp remained skeptical. "I'd like you to answer those test questions yourself," she said. "What you are running away from is more interesting to me than the problem of the universal man. But maybe your answers on the test will be more revealing when you return to us."

Was she then in favor of her husband's advancing me the money? I looked inquiringly at Hartendorp. "I've already made out the check for you," he said smiling.

Instinctively I wiped my brow. It was over. I had won. In a single day I had talked my way from incipient indigence to the status of a gentleman—an experimental psychologist on a field mission to the most primitive peoples in the world. I accepted Mrs. Hartendorp's offer of another drink.

# THREE

# Juan of Bataan

A WEEK later, as I sat in a bar near the ferry landing at Mariveles, on the Bataan peninsula across the Bay from Manila, I had the feeling that my expedition was at last under way. Dr. Beyer, for many years the anthropologist at the University of the Philippines and director of the Filipino Census, had assured me that the five-hundred-peso advance Hartendorp had given me would last me for some time among the Negritos if I was careful with it. He said I would never get to see many of the Negrito hordes if I took more than one person with me as guide and interpreter. There was a risk in going among the Negritos with such a small expedition, but it was a necessary risk, if I ever wanted to find the nomadic bands who had had no contact with the Lowlanders.

Now I was waiting for Juan, the young man whom Beyer had recommended as my assistant. Juan was part Negrito and spoke good English, for he had attended the Negrito farm school on the Bataan peninsula for a number of years, and had even had a stab or two at high school. Beyer knew him well since he had worked for some time as an assistant to various census takers in the Zambales district.

The Negrito hordes in the Zambales Mountains to the north of the peninsula would be the most unpredictable of the groups we would visit, since many of them had had no contact with white people or even with the Lowland Filipinos. Long ago the slave traders had learned that these isolated nomads were so closely attached to their land that they would sicken and die if they were taken away from it, and therefore were of little use as slaves. Beyer thought that perhaps my tests would show why they are so dependent on their land and on each other, and why they adapt so poorly to new situations.

The survey parties that had been through the mountains were so large that the Negritos had given them a wide berth. Many of the Negrito groups were so wily that even the census takers could not find them. Therefore, Beyer's estimate that there were 9,000 of them in the Zambales Mountains and in the Bataan peninsula, which anchored the mountains to the south, was to be considered rough. The census report included a short description of the Negrito's nomadic way of life, his hunting and food-gathering habits, his animistic religion, and his language, which he seemed to have in common with the ancient Lowland Filipinos of the various districts in which he lived.

Unfortunately, this was about all that was known of the mountain Negritos. All of them had a bad reputation for killing strangers, but Beyer thought I would have a good chance of getting through if I employed Juan as an assistant and worked for awhile in the Bataan peninsula with the Negritos whose children had been to the farm school and who had had some contact with Filipino traders. This would give me a feeling for the Negrito mentality and way of life, and I could then decide if it was safe to go among the more northerly groups.

Ernest Jenks had written a book about the Bontocs for the Bureau of Ethnology, and a number of papers had been written about the other groups I wished to visit, but I could return to Manila and study them when I had finished with the Negritos. I had expected Juan at noon, but the bartender assured me that the Negrito sense of time was so dim that I should not be disappointed if he was anywhere up to a week late. I spent the afternoon listening to stories about Negrito raids on Lowlanders, their skill as hunters, the viciousness of their half-wild dogs, and their unreliability as traders.

At about ten o'clock Juan appeared. Beyer had told me he was in his early twenties, but he looked younger. He was chocolate-brown in color, with a flattish nose and wide, flaring nostrils. His forehead was high and slightly bulging, beneath a neat, short crop of frizzy, black hair. His mouth was wide, with heavy lips above a slightly receding chin which seemed a little small for his forehead, giving his face a sort of noble expression. He stood somewhat under five feet, but his body was well proportioned and looked lithe and wiry in spite of his heavy muscles. He stepped quickly, lifting his feet high, as though the smooth floor were covered with litter. Even when his body was still, his large eyes darted from detail to detail of my face, or from object to object round about, with a monkeylike alertness. As I talked to him, he seemed to grow larger, perhaps because of his animated way of moving and speaking. Crumpled by the heat myself, I felt there was a heroic quality to his gestures and postures.

I told Juan that I wanted to visit all the Negritos I could find, to collect their dreams, to give them mental tests, and to observe their healing ceremonies. I asked him what he would charge to accompany me as my assistant and interpreter. He was frightened at the idea of visiting the bands who ranged in the northern territory of the Zambales Mountains, as he knew well only the southern tribes, but the offer of fifteen pesos (seven dollars and fifty cents) a month and his keep outweighed the danger of losing his life.

He explained that the project would have been impossible a few years earlier, but that now, as a result of his attendance at the farm school, he would probably know people who knew people in nearly all the groups. By hiring a few of these lads to go with us from group to group, we would be able to visit most of the hordes. He was tired of working on plantations and was excited at the idea of getting back into the mountains with his mother's people. If I employed him for six months, he would be able to save enough to obtain as wife one of the more beautiful girls in the Negrito country. Also, he would have a chance to examine the entire field for prospects before making up his mind.

We spent the next day collecting supplies and visiting the district health officer, who gave me a cholera injection, antimalaria drugs, and snake-bite serum, some medicine for dengue fever and dysentery, instructions about the symptoms of various tropical diseases I might acquire, and a supply of medicines—especially for skin fungi and scabies—to distribute among the Negritos. I had received antityphoid and smallpox vaccinations on the boat.

Early the next morning we set out for Juan's mother's group, located about halfway up the peninsula on the eastern slope. By nine o'clock we had left the bus and had hired an oxcart from Roberto, an old Filipino farmer who carried on a rattan trade with Juan's people. For one peso he agreed to take us to the jungle trail on which he had seen the men of Juan's group only a few days before. We set off in a bullock cart pulled by a water buffalo, who almost ran his big horn through me when I stepped too near his head while getting into the cart. Roberto explained that the buffalo had nothing against me personally except the way I stank, and that one must never go near a buffalo's head until the buffalo is accustomed to one's odor. I did not feel complimented by his assurance that the buffalo could get used to my odor and might even grow to like me if I were around him long enough.

"We might have brought along an escort of constabulary soldiers," Juan explained to Roberto as we moved along, wishing to impress him with the fact that I was an important person. But Roberto said, agreeing with the advice I had received, that an expedition of more than two people would probably fail to reach most of the groups. In his opinion we were quite safe if we let the Negrito women alone and carried no firearms.

"Guns and women are the things the Negritos are most likely to kill you for," Juan explained to me. "To get hold of a gun and some ammunition, they would risk their lives any time and kill anyone outside their local group. If a man falls in love with your woman, even a man of your own group, one of your blood kin, he may commit adultery with her. If you find out about it, you have got to kill him even if you don't want to, because Tolandian, the Negrito high god who lives inside the earth, doesn't like adultery. If he gets mad, he may destroy everybody. The earthworms are his messengers. That is why you must never sneer at them, and why you must always thank them for allowing you to put them on your hook when you fish with them. If Tolandian gets angry, he turns the earth over so the trees are upside down."

We talked about Tolandian as the wheels of the oxcart squeaked and the buffalo dug his hooves into the steep, narrow road, winding along between banks of cogon grass growing so high that it almost formed a tunnel over our heads.

"Do the earthworms always tell Tolandian if the Negritos commit adultery?" I inquired.

"No, not always," he answered. "Sometimes the monkeys tell things to Tolandian, but they know enough not to talk to anyone else. When the Negritos are hungry they eat the monkeys. So you can never tell when the monkeys are going to tattle everything they know to Tolandian. The Lowlanders stay in one place and the officials make them pay taxes and go to school. The Negritos are not that stupid. They travel around so the officials can't find them very often, but the monkeys are very wise. Monkeys don't talk to the officials at all, so they're free to go and come and steal wives as much as they like. You'd better not make fun of the monkeys if you want to keep in well with Tolandian."

"But you are planning on finding the most beautiful wife in the mountains, Juan. Aren't you afraid she'll get you into trouble?"

"With your own group your friends won't tell you if your wife commits adultery," Juan answered. "Or I can stay with her group, where none of the men want her. You can never marry a woman of your own group because she is your blood kin. Tolandian would strike you dead with lightning if you made love with a woman of your own band. That is what the Filipinos call incest. Or I could bring my wife down to the Lowlands, where the white man's god rules. You don't have to kill people because of the blood feud if they commit adultery with your wife in the Lowlands."

"Why not?" I inquired.

"I don't know. Maybe they tell the saints, but the saints keep it to themselves, because they're dead and don't get angry with you like the monkeys and the earthworms."

"Doesn't Tolandian get mad when you kill a man for committing adultery?" I inquired.

"No, Tolandian doesn't mind if you kill people," said Juan. "He only gets mad if you don't kill them to fulfill the blood feud. If you killed someone in my group, that would not make Tolandian angry at you, but he would be very mad if one of us did not kill you in return to avenge the death. Letting you live would be a violation of the blood feud. I will not get a wife and take her with me into the strange groups we are going to visit in the north, because anyone might kill me and take her, and they would be safe from the blood feud if my group never heard about it. They would also be safe from Tolandian's anger about adultery, since my wife would no longer have a husband. You, as a white man, wouldn't have to worry in the southern groups if you took a wife, because all the Negrito bands down this way were told by Lucas who worked for the United States Army, that all white men are Christians. Becoming a Christian makes you a blood brother with everybody else who is a Christian. Therefore, all of them would have to avenge your death. That would make the blood feud apply to all white men and Filipino Christians if you were killed; so all the southern groups know it isn't safe to kill a white man."

"Would they kill me for a gun if they wouldn't for a wife?" I asked.

"If you had a gun they could take from you, that would make them equal to the white men who pursued them, so they would not be afraid to kill you."

"But will I be safe traveling among the northern groups? Will they know that all Christians are brothers?" I inquired.

"I will tell them about it," Juan reassured me.

"But suppose they spear us before you have a chance to tell them," I asked.

"They aren't likely to do that," he said, "because they will think we are just the advance guard of a party. It would be dangerous to kill us before they knew how many more people they would have to fight, especially since they have to protect their wives and children. They all know that no two people would be foolish enough to travel alone in a foreign territory, and that a raiding party out of its own territory has no wives and children to protect."

The interminable cogon grass at last came to an abrupt end in a wall-like forest of mountain jungle. Juan folded up his store clothes, which he had bought with the three years' savings he had accumulated since graduating from the farm school: a pair of yellow shoes, a cheap plaid suit, an undershirt, and a thin shirt which looked like mosquito netting. He wrapped them in a large piece of paper and turned them over to Roberto. "I'll pick them up next year when I have a wife," he called to him, as the old Filipino drove his cart back into the cogon grass.

The only evidence of civilization Juan kept was a sleeveless, short canvas jacket which, he explained, made the straps of the pack rest easier on his back and shoulders—and a twenty-foot strip of canvas which he wound about his middle and tucked up between his legs, so one end hung down in the front and the other in the back to just above his knees. He said the canvas was a little softer and more durable than the bark cloth used by the Negritos. The pack he had made up for himself was heavy for one so small: a machete, ten pounds of coarse salt, twenty pounds of compressed shredded tobacco, five pounds of cloth, small mirrors and other trinkets, ten pounds of medical supplies which the district health officer had given us to distribute among the Negritos.

My pack was somewhat lighter: a small waterproof silk Japanese tent and a tarpaulin which could serve as a raincoat (brought from Hawaii), a blanket, underclothing and a spare khaki shirt, test papers and equipment, a medicine kit and a flask of alcohol, and a bag of rice. In all, my pack weighed about forty pounds, but I wore a pair of short elkhide boots, whipcord riding breeches, and a canvas jumper, and carried a machete, which added another ten pounds to my burden.

It was cooler in the twilight shade of the jungle trees as we marched up the trail. The gnarled roots, twisting vines, and curtains of moss seemed to be bursting with a sinister power, hiding dangerous animals or insects which now threw out a wall of sound almost as dense as the jungle itself.

Before we had traveled a quarter of a mile Juan laid down his pack. "You must be more careful of the leeches, sir. Your boots are covered with them," he said, pointing to my feet. They looked like tiny strands of harmless moss to me. He scraped them off with his knife. "A white man can easily die from a leech bite," he said. "It pierces the skin and you have a sore that takes weeks to heal. Four or five of these sores and you can't travel. A dozen of them and you have fever and blood poisoning. Up higher in the mountains they aren't so bad, but down here you must watch them every minute."

The very thought of watching every minute was exhausting.

"Where are the leeches?" I asked. "I don't see them anywhere."

Juan picked up a stick and struck the earth. Hundreds of little threads appeared like blades of grass on the trail. "They don't stand up until your foot thumps on the earth," he explained. "Then those that are not under your foot fasten on to the edges of it." I shuddered. I had expected to find snakes in the jungle. Each twisted vine looked like one to me, but these tiny "leech snakes" that grew along the trail like hairs were particularly disgusting.

"You can't rest long or you'll get stiff," said Juan, picking up the pack. Again we trudged up the slippery trail. From the corner of his eye Juan saw me absent-mindedly pluck a leaf and nibble at it. "No, Mister!" There was fury in his voice. "You must not eat the leaves or even take hold of them. Often they are poison. They will make you sick and they have wood ticks on them. If the ticks bite you, it is as bad as the leeches, or worse—they give you jungle fever. There are also spiny caterpillars and tiny tree snakes hiding in the leaves. If you are the first one on the trail, you must decide where to put your hand, what bushes must be cut, and where to put your foot. If you are second on the trail, you know from watching the leader where to put your foot and where to put your hand." He spat and continued up the trail.

It was difficult to follow him. Already my shoulders ached under the pack, and sweat ran down from every pore.

When we had pulled our packs off the oxcart, they had not seemed heavy, but now that we had carried them a mile or so mine felt like a ton. Although Juan was only half my size and his pack was heavier than mine, he neither complained about its weight nor showed signs of fatigue.

The trail we were following crossed and recrossed a small river. I could see why anything more than a loincloth would have been a burden to Juan. I discarded my shirt, jumper, and riding breeches, but Juan picked them up, saying that higher in the mountains it would be cold at night. Each time we crossed the stream I had to take off the boots and empty out the water, but the leeches had already convinced me that the boots were a good idea in spite of their weight.

At about four o'clock we saw smoke in a nearby gully. Leaving his pack with me, Juan went on to investigate. He returned a few minutes later grinning excitedly. The Negrito men of his mother's band were just over the hill robbing a bee tree, and their camp was not far distant. Juan assured me that the Negrito lads would carry our packs to the camp, so I left my pack with his and we started out for the bee hunt.

Ten minutes later we broke in on a very odd sight. The honey was high up in a tree which had been covered by a growth of parasitic vines so thick they had killed their host. Already the tree was beginning to rot. The bees had built their combs in a crack half vay up its massive fluted trunk. Surrounding this crack, and just below it, were a half-dozen Negritos. From a distance I thought they were monkeys whose tails had been set alight by the natives, creating a smudge and causing them to scramble about. As we came nearer, the smoking tails proved to be long bundles of dried grass, bound up in green leaves and hanging from the loincloths of the Negritos. In spite of this, a few of the bees had found their way to the Negritos' bodies, which explained their jerky, monkey-like movements and their yelps of pain. Comb after comb of the honey was handed down along the trunk to the natives below, who like those above, had long bundles of leaves on their loincloths belching out smoke to protect them from the angry bees.

When the combs had all been lifted out, the Negritos scrambled down the tree and gathered about us. Nearly all of them had received a few stings. Naked except for their loincloths, they were a comical-looking crew, with swollen lips and eyes, and ears puffed out from their heads. The pain of the bee stings did not dampen their cordiality. Juan explained to them that the white man's greeting was to shake hands, and each man stepped forward to be introduced. Most of them were a little shorter and darker than Juan, ranging from a deep chocolate brown to black, with the same well-proportioned, heavily muscled bodies. They looked like a small edition of American Negroes I had met, with the same tendency to be cheerful and jolly. At least half of them had patches of scaly ringworm on their smooth, dark skin, and some were covered with it from head to foot, as though they were encased in the skin of a lizard.

The lads smiled shyly and looked at the ground, but the old men greeted me with dignity. Juan pulled out a handful of our finely shredded tobacco, and cigarettes were rolled from leaves which the Negritos produced from their lumpy loincloths. Soon we were smoking happily, but I was astonished to find that all the Negritos smoked their cigarettes with the lighted end in the mouth. Juan explained that this left no glow to be seen at night by an enemy. "Once you get used to smoking that way, you can't taste the tobacco if you smoke from the other end," he said. He told me that I would have to smoke in that fashion myself, or I would be a target for any possible enemies lurking in the shadows. I took a few puffs. The Negritos rolled upon the ground with laughter as

I coughed and spat out the ashes. At once we were the best of friends.

When the boys arrived with our packs, we set out together for their clearing. The boy carrying my pack was less than three feet high, and looked like an ant carrying a grasshopper. I glanced questioningly at Juan.

"It's not nearly as heavy as a deer," he answered. "In order to live, we must be strong. He would take great offense if you insisted on carrying it, or said it was too heavy for him."

The Negrito idea of a short distance was not the same as mine. Before we had traveled an hour, darkness filled the jungle trail like a great blot of ink, and the old men lighted torches made from bundles of long dry grass. As we entered the clearing, the women and the old men at the camp scurried off into the jungle. Amid shouting and laughter, they were persuaded to come back while Juan put up my tent and hung my mosquito net.

Twenty little shacks were set in a rough circle around the edge of a small jungle clearing, not more than thirty paces across. The floors of these shacks were made of split bamboo poles rolled out flat upon crosspieces raised about two feet from the ground. The backs and sides consisted of giant ferns lashed to the uprights with vines. Wild banana leaves, overlapping like long shingles, made the roofs. The inner side of each shack was open to the fire in the center of the clearing. The Negritos put the same kind of bamboo frame and light bamboo flooring beneath my tarpaulin, explaining that centipedes and snakes would crawl up into the tent, seeking the warmth of my body, unless the floor was off the ground. Everybody pitched in and the ingeniously fashioned framework was completed in a few minutes.

Juan gave each family a handful of salt in exchange for honeycomb. Combs which contain larvae are an even greater delicacy than honey. I was handed one of these, not knowing what it was. Juan saw my disgusted look as I bit into it and whispered to me that I must eat all of it, or the Negritos would think I was not one of them and might even suspect me of poisoning their food with magic. For this they would kill me.

I chewed the comb and tried to smile as the larvae wriggled in my mouth.

# FOUR

# Spirit Cave on Pinatoba

THE supplies the district health officer had given us included sulphur and lard, salicylic acid, quinine, and other drugs. We had gladly volunteered to distribute these medicines among the Negritos.

Juan had agreed with the health officer that his people would be pleased if I could cure the skin diseases which plagued most of them from childhood to old age, and if I could relieve, even temporarily, their other aches and pains. Since we wanted them to take our tests, we had to do something for them; the easiest way was to give them free medicine.

Both Perez and Beyer had warned me that I must make no move among these people which looked like black magic. In giving me the medicines, the health officer had cautioned me against treating anyone who was seriously ill. "If someone is about to die when you treat him, and your medicine doesn't save him, the Negritos will blame you for his death and won't let you do anything for anyone else," he said. "It's happened before. That's one reason they still have scabies, ringworm, and the other infections—they won't let us take care of them."

Since I intended to give them suggestibility tests, he felt that, with hypnosis, I might be able to persuade the most suggestible to take the medicines, where all their methods had failed. If I used it wrong, of course, they'd mourn my loss. But no one else would get into trouble, since I was not asking for police protection and was going into the territory at my own risk. In the mountains, the ancient Negrito law of the blood feud still prevailed, and the Negritos would be obliged to kill me if anyone happened to die just after I treated him and they thought I was responsible for the death.

It would take a few days at best for Western chemicals to improve the condition of the Negrito skin, I decided, even if, through hypnotic suggestion, I could assuage or eliminate the burning pain of applying the salicylic acid.

I studied the group by the firelight, while they ate honeycomb, tubers, and jungle fruit for their evening meal. An aspirin and a mild sedative might work immediately to relieve headache or rheumatic pain, and the cure might be permanent if I could reinforce the medicine with suggestion. From working with Indians I suspected that the first few cases I chose would determine my prestige with this group, and with any groups I met through them.

As we ate, Juan explained to them that I was a medicine man, and inquired if any of them were suffering from pains in the head or joints. Several of the older men admitted that they had pains, but they looked so scrawny that I was seized with the conviction that any of them might drop dead at any minute.

I chose as first subject a stocky, middle-aged Negrito named Pana, who complained of a headache which had bothered him, off and on, since childhood. His skin was free of the scaly ringworm. His eyes were clear and his hair not yet white.

I gave him aspirin and a mild sedative. Juan persuaded him to lie down on the bamboo floor of his hut. I knew the drug would make him sleepy within a half hour and that I should be able to produce a hypnotic state if I went on giving him suggestions of relaxation and drowsiness in a monotonous voice and Juan translated in the same sort of voice.

"Tell him that this medicine I have given him is very strong, so strong that it will make him drowsy. It can only do its best work if he allows himself to go to sleep. Tell him to look at one spot on the ceiling."

Juan translated, succeeding very well in reproducing my monotonous tones. I snapped the dial on my stop watch and we began. Pana looked scared and nervous and his eyes very wide-awake as they came to rest on the spot above him.

In a minute and a half his eyelids were beginning to tremble and droop. In three minutes they were shut. I knew the drug had had no time to take effect. The indirect suggestion that the strong medicine would make him sleepy and the direct suggestion that his eyes were closing had produced this effect. In order to prove scientifically this was hypnosis, I would have to demonstrate that he could not open his eyes when challenged to do so.

"Tell him that his eyelids are locked shut, that he cannot open them even if he tries."

Immediately I knew I had made a mistake. A murmur ran through the crowd of spectators. Pana tugged at his eyelids, and when he found they held fast, he went on struggling harder and harder to open them.

"He thinks he's in your power now so that you can work black magic on him, and he won't stop struggling to open his eyes," said Juan in a scared voice.

"Tell him that he can open them now," I answered, noticing frowns of disapproval on all the faces about me.

Pana's eyes came open, but I had had no chance to suggest that his headache was getting better. I had succeeded in creating the one impression about black magic that Beyer, Perez, and the health officer had warned me against.

Juan was disturbed, and I fancied I could see suspicion and mistrust in all the other faces. This was calamity. They would probably not take the medicines if I did not use suggestion, and without suggestion, the Emotional Response Test, which I considered the heart of my whole program, could not be checked in a trance state. Somehow I must correct the impression that I wished to get these people in my power, where they would be subject to black magic. Immediately I must try again, using the agreement trance which had worked so well with the children in Utah.

I had found in Utah that a drowsy, half-sleep trance state could be produced by asking, rather than commanding, the children to relax and re-experience and describe the emotionally charged incidents my test questions brought to mind. This trance state was brought about through agreement, rather than submission. Therefore, I described it as the agreement, rather than the hypnotic, trance. It worked much easier than hypnosis, especially on people who leaned backward when I told them they were leaning forward as a part of the suggestibility test. This negative response to command suggestion occurred with all of the Utah children and with people who were afraid. I would have to try again, using persuasion with Pana instead of hypnotic command. Whatever I did I could not make things worse than they stood now.

"Now explain to Pana that he has seen the power of the medicine to create sleep, and has learned that he need not be afraid of this sleep, since he can come out of it at any time," I said to Juan. "Tell him to let his eyes go to sleep again so we can help him discover and remove the cause of his headache." As Pana's eyes became heavy and flickered shut, I said, "Now you can go deeper into the sleep world and into the past, and discover the color of your headache."

Both in Utah and in Hawaii I had found that looking at an imaginary color or image had somewhat the same effect in deepening the agreement trance as looking at a whirling disc had in inducing hypnosis.

"He says it's this color," answered Juan, picking out a purple skein from my color samples. "There is no Negrito word for it, but there are blossoms and berries of this color which he has mentioned."

Pana began to shiver and whimper.

"He has malaria," said Juan. "All of us have it as children, but we get over it at the age of five or six, about the time we put on our loincloths. It must be the spirit of malaria which is causing him the headache."

This was exciting. It looked as though the fever pattern of malaria had gone on causing Pana headaches long after the germs which had originally caused them had been killed off inside his body. Juan was referring to this pattern as the malaria spirit. Perhaps Pana had headaches caused by emotional conflicts which had tied up with and perpetuated the fever pattern.

"Now I want you to go way way back, Pana, to find when the pain spirit entered you, when you first met the headache spirit. Will you go back?"

Pana said he would, and gradually curled up. "I am not born yet when the pain spirit first visits me," he said, groaning and writhing.

"Ask him if he wants to come back, Juan," I said, with a feeling that calamity had overtaken me and that Pana was perhaps breathing his last.

"Oh no, that would not be right," answered Juan. "He has met the pain spirit and now he must conquer it. Then it will stop hurting him and be his helper. He will become a shaman. He is in the spirit world now, in the cave on Pinatoba in which he lived before he was born. It is a high mountain to the north and looks like a cone. If he cannot best the pain spirit himself, the spirits of the other shamans will help him, but no Negrito would want to come out of the spirit cave before he had conquered the spirit which made him ill, and before receiving a song from him. He is talking to the spirit now."

The violence of the seizure had run its course, and the deep lines of pain had disappeared from Pana's face. The gasping, groaning, guttural sound, which seemed an octave below ordinary speech, was giving way to falsetto gibberish. It sounded like the speaking with tongues I had heard occasionally in religious meetings, when people were said to be possessed by the Holy Ghost. Would Pana bring us a message back from Tolandian?

"What's he saying?" I inquired of Juan at last.

"He hears tapping and voices," Juan answered. "His father and mother are quarreling. She must not bury the tubers until the child is born. She must dig up the ones she has buried already or he will not be able to come out. Now there is tapping again. It hurts his ears."

Now an old man had come forward and was talking to the entranced Pana. "The old shaman is telling him that the tapping spirit wants to give him a drum rhythm," said Juan.

Pana's body quivered spasmodically as though in time with the rhythm he was hearing. Another old shaman joined the first and spoke encouragingly to the subject, clapping in rhythm with Pana's twitching muscles.

"Pana is saying the word 'thunder,'" said Juan. "The thunder spirit is giving him the rhythm. Now he is getting the words of his song. 'It is enough, oh thunder; it is enough; it is enough. I admit my guilt. It is enough.'"

"Ask Pana what kind of voice the thunder spirit has," I directed.

"It sounds like his father's father's older brother's voice," said Juan. "He is hearing it inside the cave. The next time the thunder spirit comes, it will give him a dance. But he is too tired now, he wants to come back from the cave. You must invite him to come back now."

"By all means," I answered.

The old men slapped Pana's cheeks, saying he should not forget the words of the song or the drum rhythm as he came up from the spirit cave. Pana writhed again for a few minutes and opened his eyes, apparently none the worse for the experience.

"For my record I must also have his dreams," I said to Juan. "Ask him what is the worst dream he can remember."

"A black cloud chasing me," he answered. "I've had it many times. Sometimes I was alone, sometimes with the group. The black cloud growled and muttered with the voice of thunder. Always I woke up expecting the lightning to strike me." Pana remembered other dreams or nightmares of black things pursuing him.

His best dream was of a man. The body looked like his father, but he had the head of a horse, light in color, with the mane hanging down in front of his face. He had seen the Filipinos riding horses along the borders of the Negrito territory. This dream character, which he called a "dwindi," had picked him up in his dream and soared through the air with him, showing him strange places where game could be found. Later it had visited him when he was awake, and he had gone off with it alone into the jungle on some very successful hunts. His wife had seen the dwindi one night when it called for him. To break the spell, she had rubbed her naked buttocks all over her husband's body. After that the dwindi had come no more. Pana had beaten his wife for using this magic to scare it away, but his spirit friend had never returned.

"I remember what Pana was like when I was a child," said Juan. "He used to beat his wife and his children. The Negritos think this is very bad. They say a father should never beat his children. Sometimes he would get mad at everyone and challenge other men to duels. This is a great trouble among the Negritos because both men must always die if a duel begins. That's why nobody would fight with him. They called him Thunder Voice when he got mad."

I wondered if the Negritos saw a difference between the dream thunder which had attacked Pana, and the thunder which all of them could hear while awake. Juan had told me that the thunder was the angry voice of Tolandian.

"When Pana was dreaming of the thundercloud chasing him and the group, was Tolandian angry at him and the other Negritos?" I inquired.

"Oh yes," answered Juan. "Someone had probably done something to make Tolandian angry."

"But how could Pana and all the rest of them be running from Tolandian's rage at the same time that they were all sleeping?" I asked.

Juan was a little puzzled about this and inquired of the old men. "They say that your spirit can run away from the thunder even when you are asleep," Juan answered. "But often you can't remember what your spirit does at night."

They didn't make a clear distinction, then, between themselves and their images—the images of them which ran around in Pana's mind—or between Tolandian's voice, which rang out from the heavens, and the voice which issued from Pana's dream giant. If Pana had dreamed that a neighboring group was attacking them through magic, they might have made war with the group, and this aggressive nightmare spirit—this dream giant—of Pana's would have been the cause of the war. This failure to differentiate the object from the image was a serious flaw in the Negrito thinking which might at any time disrupt social harmony within the group or between the Negritos and other groups.

My past experience in collecting dreams was beginning to pay dividends, but the ministrations of the shamans, which helped Pana to go on through the painful experience and to bring back a drum rhythm and a song, were psychotherapy of a type I had not encountered before. I, as operator, had put Pana into a trance before the group. This was to them an acceptable method of therapy, obviously not out of line with their own tradition. Then the other shamans had felt at liberty to offer their assistance to the entranced subject, which resulted in group psychotherapy in a new sense—a group of therapists working on one patient. Whatever was said by the therapist or by the patient was heard by all the other Negritos, which would build up an expectancy in them that their own headaches, or other physical symptoms, could be cured in a similar manner.

This type of procedure would educate the whole group in the ideas and methods of psychotherapy. I had expected to see more mumbo-jumbo, more suggestion, and less meaningful social cooperation. The results achieved in the trance state which I had induced were much like those obtained by the then new psychotherapy being employed in Paris and in Vienna. The Negrito therapists were helping the patient to contact patterns and incidents from a long-forgotten past, painful incidents buried deep in the early time layers of the accumulated experience which made up the personality. Without surprise, they accepted—at face value —the patient's statement that the thunder and the painful quarrel had occurred before he was born.

In modern therapy there was a corresponding practice of contacting and becoming conscious of painful forgotten experiences while in the trance state. The chief difference here was in the amount of pressure put upon the patient to go through these painful events. Some of the children I knew in the Training School in Utah had told of similar experiences. When I had helped them, in the drowsy trance state, to go back to earlier and earlier incidents, by asking, "What was the worst thing that happened before this incident you have just related?" they had found such painful and fearful incidents that I had been afraid to encourage them to go on through them as the Negrito shamans had just done. I had no precedent from Western therapy to urge them on into what looked like an epileptic fit, whereas controlling and utilizing these painful seizures was routine procedure for these preliterate people.

But there was a second feature of the Negrito healing, which was entirely new to me and which was even more exciting than the idea that the patient must go on through the painful event once he had contacted it. The Negrito shaman directed the patient to bring back from the trance state a creative product in the form of music, rhythm, posture, and words. He was asked to stay in the painful event until some indwelling force, which the shamans called a spirit, supplied music for the words he heard from the spirit cave, put the words into some sort of meter like a poem, and attached this music and meter to a series of motor sets, muscular actions, and postures, which we call a dance.

In the West the theory had been adopted that neurosis blocked off man's creativeness. This Negrito healing ceremony seemed a direct support of that theory, and these Negrito healers were not leaving things to chance. They were requesting that the area of the personality which had formerly expressed itself as conflict, rage, and migraine headache change itself into music, poetry, and dancing—on the spot, as it were. In the healing ceremony itself they were requesting that the subject transform the pain into that which was socially significant and beautiful. The astonishing thing was that the patient obligingly complied with their requests. Since he would reproduce the music, words, and dance on future occasions, whenever he asked the help of this newly acquired force or spirit, there was no danger that this new area of the personality, which he had conquered with the help of the ceremony, would slip back into the limbo of the subconscious and change itself again into pain after the ceremony was completed.

In the West, investigators were experimenting with automatic writing done in a trance state, and were aware of the fact that certain men, Beethoven, for instance, awoke from sleep with musical or mathematical ideas already written out in their minds. But nowhere in the civilized world was this creativeness in sleep and in the half-sleep trance encouraged and guided through social co-operation to the same extent as among these preliterate Negritos. Here it was an accepted idea that every member of the group should see and understand the practice of psychotherapy from infancy, and that every member of the group was eligible to become a psychotherapist without any specialized training, except what he received himself through psychotherapy. The very forces that made him sick should become a will, an urge, a drive to heal others. Here healing was regarded not as a guild or priestcraft or secret knowledge, but as the social heritage of all who had suffered illness and received treatment.

Since the Negritos were not surprised when Pana announced on awakening that his headache was well, it seemed obvious that such cures were not unusual. I was now established as a medicine man and given credit for the cure, even though I had not known enough to tell Pana to go on through the harrowing, fearful incident of the thunder. Apparently, this incident had terrified him so much at some time in his past life that it had disassociated or broken off a fragment of his mind, or a layer of his experience, making this inner pattern his enemy and the enemy of the group. Certainly I would have to learn more of this native type of psychotherapy, which the shamans had assumed I already knew. Now I could breathe freely. I had allayed their suspicion of black magic and could apply the medicines which, in a few days' time, would produce results on skin and eye infections which none of their psychotherapists could accomplish.

"Is there any other way of becoming a shaman except through this type of spirit possession?" I asked Juan.

"I know of no other way," he answered. "Not all people who go into trances become practicing shamans. But if their treatments last for any length of time, they usually do."

I felt excited. These trance states were not just a part of a recurrent religious ceremonial. Here was a true psychology of healing which was not fifty thousand years behind Western civilization. In some respects it seemed ahead. "How many shamans are there in the group?" I inquired.

Juan spoke with the old men. Out of the twenty-odd adults, there were four men and a woman who were shamans, and two others who had had treatments over a period of time which might eventually make them healers. This was astonishing. Twenty per cent of the adults had been successfully treated by this trance method. Apparently the shaman was most successful with chronic ailments, with which Western medicine had done so badly, rather than with epidemic illnesses. If I should see nothing more among the Negritos, I had already seen enough to make it worth whatever price I would have to pay.

As the night wore on, the moon came up, making the clearing take on the proportions of a coliseum. Then, as the moonlight faded and the small trees around the clearing were lost in blackness, it became a deep well with a patch of cold, glittering stars at the top, and the warm little fire at the bottom. As I sat there, the fire seemed friendly and more human than the Negritos. I felt myself leaning toward it as a known element in this deep well of the unknown.

But there was also something familiar about the emerging pattern of Pana's dreams and visions. If I thought hard enough and fast enough about them, the bad storm giant and the good dwindi seemed to help the fire bring more light into the blackness of the well. This horse-faced dwindi had made Pana a famous hunter, a leader in his horde. It had given him some sort of second sight, made him a prophet who could lead the group to food, as Moses had led the children of Israel out of Egypt and Joseph Smith had led the Mormons to the west. But Pana's white dream giant, which had apparently made him wander around at night in a state of trance, could not withstand an attack from the social world. His wife's body, her words and gestures, had destroyed the dream giant, or at least had locked it out from his consciousness. He could no longer become aware of it. Neither could his black dream giant withstand the attack of the shamans, once he had introduced it to them in the trance state. With infinite cunning, they had teased, threatened, and cajoled the mysterious inner force into co-operating with them. They had made it express itself in words, in muscular rhythms, in groans and sobs. They had told it that their friendly spirits would wage a relentless, never-ending war with it in the dream life of the patient until it was destroyed, if it did not give up hurting him and become a healing spirit. When Pana awakened, the headache was gone. The presence of the shamans, all of whom had themselves been healed, showed that these cures could be made permanent, that once a black giant had been tamed or harnessed, it would go on working henceforward for the patient and the group, as the white dwindi had worked for him and the other Negritos from the beginning.

From the point of vantage of another culture, I could look at the Negrito as he had never looked at himself. I could see that Pana's supernormal gift had been stanched by his wife's possessive jealousy. He had never before been cured of the baleful effect of his black giant by the shamans because he would not seek treatment. This black force had made him not only ill but at the same time antisocial, to such an extent that he had refused to ask for help. This inner world of the Negrito mind was beginning to seem much less frightening than the darkness of sleep.

It grew later and later. I continued applying my home remedies, accompanied by suggestion, leaving out the challenge of which the Negritos did not approve and which they did not employ in their own shamanistic trances. The subjects went rapidly into trance, told me of the colors of their pain, and answered the questions of my tests. Repeatedly I suggested in trance that the fiery acids and iodine would feel good when applied to their tender, cracked skin. Consistently, they awoke saying that the inflamed areas I had painted felt good and comfortable. I could hardly believe them myself, knowing how painful the treatment was while awake.

Shivers played up and down my spine, as one after another of these little black men told of worlds unfolding before their tightly shut eyes. Some of them were being chased by heads without bodies. Arms without bodies grasped at others. Trees walked and talked to them and fell upon them. In their minds women with the heads of birds and the arms of crabs crawled from under the logs of the jungle. Wild pigs brought them magic plants rooted up from secret forest recesses.

One old shaman found himself on the back of a huge hornbill, flying joyfully over unknown mountains covered with cold white stuff. His description of the snow and ice, which he had never seen and perhaps never heard of before, filled me with an uncanny feeling that he was somehow picking my brain and talking about my own experience.

As the night progressed, I got the impression that the mind of the Negrito was not simple, as I had supposed, but formed a mosaic of complications, and that in some way modern civilization might make man's personality more simple and unified than it was among the Negritos. Perhaps this would have something to do with Beyer's question of why the Negrito could not exist away from his land, or adapt to new situations.

The women were much more reticent than the men on that first night. When they saw that the medicines were strong enough to induce sleep, all but one of them stayed in the background. Un, a woman about thirty years old, the wife of a leader of the horde, stepped forward to be treated for ringworm on the left side of her neck. She was heavier and larger than most of the other women, and extremely talkative. One minute she was shouting with anger, the next, roaring with laughter. Her bulk and her bellow made her the natural center of any cluster of people.

When Juan told her that she was going to sleep, she writhed as though in the throes of an epileptic fit. He assured me that she was a shamaness, and was experiencing a routine call from one of her familiar spirits. Soon the struggles ceased, and sitting cross-legged on the bamboo floor of the hut, she made queer gestures with her hands. The Negritos kept shouting in response to these gestures, which to me had not the slightest meaning, and Juan explained that she was possessed by a spirit which could not talk. It communicated to the group, through her, by means of a deaf-and-dumb language which Un had built up over a period of years, during frequent possessions.

"What is she saying to the Negritos?" I inquired.

"The spirit has asked the people why it has been called here, who you are, and what you want of it," answered Juan. "They have replied that you are a great shaman from across the ocean, that you are my friend, that you are very rich, and that you have come to the Negritos to teach them how to play American games, and to give them tobacco to smoke, salt to eat, and white man's medicine."

Juan told her the medicine would feel warm and comfortable on the ringworm, and painted it. The shamaness gave no evidence that she felt the operation at all. Then Juan told me that her spirit also wanted to know if I was ill and if it could serve me as a physician. He said that this Negrito woman was one of the greatest healing shamans on the Bataan peninsula.

For a number of years I had had a little cyst under the skin of my right forearm. I told Juan that it was a very painful lump, and that I should like to know what caused it and how to get rid of it. He conveyed the message to Un, the entranced woman. For the next half hour the Negrito clearing resembled a circus. She was very resourceful, but she was talking about a subject quite outside the ordinary routine which these deaf-and-dumb gestures had to portray. Each time she made a gesture, the observers shouted the meaning they gleaned from it. At times, there were three or four different interpretations.

At last Juan said that the lump on my arm was caused by the spirit of a woman—my mother—and that my umbilical cord had not been cut with the correct ceremonial procedure. The magic of the midwife had not been strong enough to sever the spiritual cord, and instead of separating from me at birth, the cord had pulled one of my mother's spirits out of her into my own body. To make it worse, it was on my right, the masculine side, instead of on my left, where all feminine spirits should reside after puberty. She would cut the cord with her magic so the spirit could get out, but perhaps it had grown so used to its present home that it would now refuse to leave even after the cord was severed. In that event it would have to be driven from my body by further treatment, perhaps by a long series of treatments.

If I would bind sweet-smelling herbs on my left arm and put some sort of local stinkweed over the bump on the right, I might persuade the spirit to go to the left side, where it would do me no damage. If the stinkweed did not work, I might bind over the lump a mixture of burnt hair and the droppings of wild chicken, which had an intolerable odor.

As she communicated in this wild deaf-and-dumb fashion, I kept getting the uncanny feeling that Un was talking not about a spirit, but about an image—that her mind was reverberating with and sensing something inside me. Mrs. Hartendorp had felt the same thing through her intuition. I had lied when I said there was pain in the cyst, but in any event Un's gestures did not locate the pain there. Whenever she spoke of my pain, she clutched her big round naked breast on the left side, over her heart. Each time she did, I felt like a rejected infant, with a lump in my throat and tears burning their way through my eyelids. Each time her supple hands drew a picture of the spirit which was eating up my heart, they produced the image of a young woman, dressed in old-fashioned clothing. It was as though I caught a glimpse of something in me which was frozen stiff, and had been for a long long time.

Now this strange doctor was thawing me out somehow, and filling me with a vague, painful longing. Now the young woman's face had serenely closed eyes which made her appear like the death mask of the Buddha. Now it was a sculptured image of the pure essence of pain, now of sorrow, now compassion. But in each there was a haunting suggestion of my mother. Some Western curse of false pride was demanding that I must not feel too much, that I must not let go, that I must not express my feelings and let myself writhe and moan and cry as the Negritos did.

The treatment had at least succeeded in pulling a feminine image from my side and planting it squarely in the middle of me, where it was beginning to obscure completely the face of the shamaness, or to remold it into some ancient face that I had known before. With an effort I turned to Juan.

"Tell the spirit that the pain is gone, that the treatment has succeeded, and I have entirely recovered, and that now I would like to obtain the spirit guide's autobiography." My voice broke the tension of the trance as a foot goes through a spider's web woven across a trail. As I turned back to look at her, the figure sitting cross-legged on the platform had lost its luminous quality and shrunk to the size of a Negrito, with a dirty, tear-stained face and frizzy hair. She was shaking her head sadly and making signs which meant I was mistaken. I was not yet well. In vain the group tried to persuade me to go on with the treatment until the spirit guide released me, but I was adamant. Only my intellect had life. She shrugged her shoulders, making signs which her audience had the delicacy of feeling not to interpret.

Indeed, those gestures needed no interpretation since they convinced me with cold certainty that I was a fool. Then Un made a sign which the others said meant that the spirit was willing to tell me what I wished to know about itself. Through her weird, quaint gestures, she conveyed the data that I asked for. When Un saw it entering or leaving her, it looked like a newborn baby, like her younger brother, who was born when she was three. Yet it was as big as a man. It had entered Un when her younger brother was born, but lay sleeping inside her until about the time of her first menstrual period. At menstruation it had started biting her stomach, making it burn and ache, until five or six years later, when she had begun to cough up blood. Then a shaman had treated her. There had been great difficulty because the baby spirit had not learned to talk before it left the spirit world. It was willing to stop biting and to help its mistress become a shaman, but it had difficulty in telling her and the other Negritos so because it could not talk.

If Un did not find work for it to do, the spirit marched restlessly about inside her, but it had not bitten her since it had started talking the deaf-and-dumb language. When Un was born, it also had come out of the spirit cave, but it had just played around as a baby until her younger brother was born. Un had cried a lot at that time because her mother was tending her baby brother. Her crying had attracted the spirit. She had held her mouth open so wide when she cried that it was able to get inside. It had thought the wide-open mouth was the spirit cave from which it had strayed.

Now it was tired and asked permission to leave. Un opened her eyes with a dazed expression, rubbed them a little, and turned sheepishly to another woman to inquire about the behavior of her guide in the presence of the white man. Apparently she never knew anything of what happened in her trance state except as it was recounted to her after she was awakened. I felt that this baby guide was a most obliging fellow, and wondered how accurately the group had interpreted the lightning gestures by which it had recounted its autobiography and explained my spiritual ailment.

Now everyone sat with his mouth open, looking from her to

me. Suddenly it dawned on them that even this powerful healing spirit had come and gone at my bidding.

"They are speaking about the friendly attitude the spirit guide had toward you," said Juan. "Now all of them know what a great medicine man you are."

Despite my mistake of telling Pana he could not open his eyes, Western science had vindicated itself, and my reputation as a great shaman was established.

Already it was past midnight, but the fire was replenished. No one, not even the children, showed any signs of being ready to go to sleep. I soon learned that every day was Sunday for the Negritos, if they wished to make it so, and that the night was for them a time of sociability and group expression. Often they went hungry, neglecting food for the body as they searched themselves and one another for this creative nutriment of the soul.

Now a young man came for medicine whose trance expression largely determined my fate for weeks to come. His father had died the year before, and as was the custom with the Negritos, had been buried in a nearby jungle spot which all the group took great pains to avoid. They explained to me that they even tried to forget where they had buried their dead, and were relieved when the teeming jungle plants had obliterated all evidence of the grave. They did not like to think or talk about ghosts.

However, they never expected the ghost to cease visiting the group until a banquet had been given in his honor. For people who were not important, a small banquet would suffice. In the case of Ogong, the young Negrito before me, the father had been a very important man, and he would therefore require a large feast.

The funeral feast is never held until the ghost has returned a number of times in dreams or visions. The ghost gives instructions to the living person responsible for the feast and comes to an agreement with him. Then the ghost requests that the feast be held. Ogong had had a number of dreams of his father. The last two had terrified him, making him feel ashamed that he had not collected more food for the funeral feast. Now he was afraid to go to sleep.

From his general state of tension I should have known there was trouble ahead. When he struggled to keep his eyes from closing, I suspected that he would see something violent and disturbing, and I considered discontinuing. But one subject who did not go into the trance state at my bidding might lead to many more. I would have to run the risk of controlling whatever forces I unleashed, or lose prestige. At last Ogong's eyes snapped shut, and he saw purple lights that hurt him. From past experience, I knew this would lead to a physical pain or a violent conflict, but I was too curious to act prudently and wake him up.

The skin on his face quivered, and I could see that the muscles beneath were slowly transforming his expression. A murmur ran through the assembled Negritos. Then all were silent as Ogong began to talk. The whole group looked as though it were ready to take off to the jungle. Perspiration glistened on Juan's forehead, and his voice trembled as he explained to me that it was not Ogong speaking, but the ghost of his dead father. All the people recognized the voice and were terrified.

"Jesus, Mary, and Joseph," Juan gasped. "They are all saying that Ogong's face has become his father's mask."

"Tell me what the ghost is saying," I asked with vexation, annoyed by Juan's violent trembling and the chattering of his teeth. His own appearance, more dead than alive, would, I knew, induce no confidence in the Negritos. "We must talk to him and ask him what he wants," I said to Juan, trying to appear calm. "Don't be afraid. The ghost can't hurt you, but it may cause us much trouble if you don't keep it under control. Speak up and ask him what he wants." Despite my show of assurance, I felt shivers going up and down my spine at the transformation in Ogong's voice and face.

"The ghost is telling all the Negritos that Ogong must have a big feast for him very soon or calamity will befall them," Juan said, stammering with fear. "He is very angry with his son because his son has been lazy since his death. Ogong did not follow the advice his father gave him in dreams, and did not get enough food for the funeral feast, so the father could be at-one with his son."

"Ask him where he has been living since his death," I said. All my life I had wanted to talk to a "ghost," and this was my first opportunity.

After stuttering a bit, the ghost answered, "I have been living in the spirit world, but I am still bound to my grave. I have been watching over the Negritos. My son has been very stubborn and slow to come to at-oneness with my spirit and to prepare the feast which will release me from the earth. I have been waiting for the feast that will release me, so I can live happily beneath the mountain with the other spirits."

An idea occurred to me. If I could help out a bit with the funeral feast, I might persuade this group to invite all the Negritos in the Bataan district to the festival, and I might give them my tests then. I could do much more work in one place than traveling about.

"Ask the ghost if he would like me to help his son with the funeral feast and to take part in it with him," I said to Juan.

The idea was very agreeable to the spirit and to all the assembled Negritos. They had not been pleased by this trance-induced visit of the ghost into their camp, but if I were to take charge and help with the feast—which would release Ogong's father from his earthly vigil—everything might turn out for the best. I wanted to ask the ghost many more questions, but after the matter of the feast was disposed of, Juan told me that the spirit was impatient and did not wish to stay any longer.

The change which Ogong's face had undergone gave him the appearance of a haggard old man. Deep lines and innumerable small wrinkles appeared in his skin. When Juan gave the ghost permission to leave, Ogong's face again relaxed and he assumed his normal expression. We assured him that he would feel warm inside and very happy after he awoke. Juan blew on his eyelids. As Ogong sat up, the camp was full of excitement.

Already dawn was beginning to disperse the jungle blackness to the east. I rolled up in my blanket. As I fell asleep, I could still hear the Negritos talking excitedly about the spirit possession.

Some of the old men had seen or heard of such things before, but it was a notable and rare event when a spirit of the dead possessed the body and molded the face and voice of the living.

Juan was deeply shaken at coming to such close grips with the "supernatural." I tried to explain to him that the outside world was reflected in the mind of every person. Ogong had a living, talking, breathing photograph of his father in his brain. This picture could affect his expressive muscles. When awake, he could remember his father and imitate him a little. The father part of himself could appear to him and speak in dreams. In the dreams he could get a clear image of his father. In the trance state he could express that image accurately in his voice and features because he was neglecting the outside world.

I did not have much success with this explanation, but Juan felt that I could control the ghost and that I was not afraid of it. That gave him confidence and seemed to make him feel safe while he was near me. I noticed that from then on he took even greater care to look out for my personal safety. If he was to play around with ghosts, he was taking no chances on losing his ally.

As I went to sleep, I thought about Ogong's personality. Certainly his image of his father had become obsolete with his father's death. This inner image could no longer help him to adapt to his father in the physical world, since his physical father was gone from the world. The facet of his personality which had been molded into the image of his father was now attacking him in his dreams, and had expressed itself in the trance through his vocal and facial muscles. But all the people of his tribe and, therefore, their images in his mind, were willing to help him neutralize the force of this dream father and somehow unify it with their images in the at-onement feast.

The tribe had exercised somewhat the same type of power over the images of his mother and his female relatives when his growth had changed him from a submissive child to a responsible man. The group had done this by the puberty ceremony of scarification and circumcision. All the men had scar designs on their arms and chests which Juan had explained were acquired during adolescence. These designs were caused by making little cuts in the skin and rubbing ashes into them. The scarification meant, according to Juan, that the boy was being cut away from his dependence on the women of the group. Part of this cutting process the boy had to perform himself by going out alone, at a certain point in the ceremonial, and thrusting the end of his hunting knife beneath his foreskin and giving it a sharp blow with a piece of wood. After that the mother no longer asked her son to carry water or do other household tasks. After that he was a man of authority in the group.

Not only, therefore, did he have fewer social images to complicate his feeling of self-consciousness than a Westerner, but with the help of these inherited formal ceremonies, he had the benefit of social action to neutralize the images as they became nonadaptive or obsolete through growth, change, and death. He also had the help of a group healing ceremony when accident and shock chanced to make visual or sound patterns from the social world into enemy dream giants.

This made Dr. Beyer's problem all the more vexing. Why should the Negrito become homesick and physically ill when he was removed from his little group and his land? Why was he so unable to change either his environment or himself? Why should the whole inner show of the Negrito stop working when he left his customary environment?

I seemed to be getting further away from, rather than nearer to, a solution to this problem. Did the Negrito inherit a less unified, less adaptable psyche than that of Western man? Or did the Negrito fail to adapt to new situations because of the way he used his words and numbers—because he lacked some of the unifying ideals and concepts built up by the civilized world? Perhaps my tests and dream collections would throw some light on this field, and enable me to determine if the lack of adaptability was in the Negrito's nature, or could be explained on the basis of nurture.

# FIVE

# Hunting-and-Gathering Magic

WHEN I awoke a few hours later the Negritos had not been to sleep at all. Juan and I discussed the feast with them, and I contributed a few pesos toward a bag of rice and a keg of wine. Preparations moved rapidly. It was to be the biggest affair of its kind in years. Young men were dispatched in every direction to invite neighboring groups to participate. Accumulated rattan and beeswax were taken down to the Lowlands to be traded for rice, fish, wine, and other delicacies. Large-scale hunts for wild pig and deer were organized to build up the meat supply.

One woman in the group, who was a cousin of the Negrito King Alfonso, sent her boy off to invite His Negrito Highness to participate in the funeral feast. The title of "King" had been given to Lucas, Alfonso's father, a few years before, when he was asked by the Army authorities at Fort Statesenburg to call a council of the Negrito chieftains, the lineage heads of the various hordes ranging in the mountains above the Fort. Lucas persuaded so many of the different groups to send representatives to the council that the Army men dubbed him King.

The Negritos had never known any type of social organization which brought unity among the small nomadic hordes. The title meant to them that Lucas was a representative of the United States Army. But the Filipinos were so impressed by it that they kept on calling him King Lucas, and when he died Alfonso inherited both his title and his function of maintaining contact between the Negritos and the United States Army. His coming to the ceremony would give the little group prestige. At the same time, his official visit would bring with it a liberal supply of food, which the Army was only too glad to distribute through him.

My first task was to have Juan take all the tests and decide on the Negrito words to be used for the instructions in each one, and then to learn those words myself, so I could be sure he was not deviating from them.

The Negritos often played games, and Juan rapidly got the idea of testing. His next task was to devise a way to locate the five-year-old children of the group. There had been a flood some five and a half years before, and we included in the five-year group all the children whose mothers had been pregnant with them at the time of the flood. I was astonished and exasperated at the Negrito disregard for time, and the way the years seemed to slip away from their mind without leaving impressions which they could locate, but the taboos of pregnancy and the terrific rains leading up to the floods, which had made the food quest difficult for them, were two facts which tied themselves together indelibly in their minds.

We found seven children in the five-year group. After a week of training and preparation with Juan, the first child was seated at a table before us. We had gone out of our way to play with the children an hour each day, and to show them the stop watch and the toys, so they would not be too shy when the testing program was started. I sat beside Juan, pretending to look at a book, and watched him administer the tests. Not once did I have to break into the procedure. All of the children made normal or above-normal scores.

The five-year-old could remember almost as many dreams as the Negrito adults, and about the same number as the average American child of that age, and as the children of the other racial groups I had tested in Hawaii. The same emotions, and about the same number of dream characters, and the same types of dream situations, were reported. The results in the Emotional Response Test, the Progressive Fantasy Test, and the Sympathy Test were also like those obtained with other groups.

Two weeks after my arrival, King Alfonso appeared, riding on a castoff Army mule which was to be killed and roasted as part of the feast.

The preparations for the ceremony turned out far better for my testing program than I had hoped. Every day new Negritos arrived, and since I was contributing to the festival, they all felt obliged to play my games, draw pictures for me, tell me their dreams, and demonstrate their shamanistic healing powers.

As we found more subjects, the evidence from the first group of seven was reaffirmed. On all the tests, the children of four, five, and six made scores which did not differentiate them at all from the American children, or from the children of the other five language groups I had tested in Hawaii. These children also reported simple terror dreams and pleasure dreams identical with those of the other groups. Dreams of falling, of being pursued by dogs, pigs, snakes, smoke, fire, and monsters of one sort or another, and dreams of eating, of finding fruit trees, flowers, and pets, and of winning out in contests at the festival, were the most common.

Because of the poor Negrito memories, perhaps, or because of their poor mathematics, or their unwillingness to think about the matter, it was very difficult to obtain the ages of the children over seven, so I despaired of getting any data on any of the tests which would be comparable with the year-to-year age norms of the other groups.

The Emotional Response Test of the adolescents showed the same sort of trends, in the main, that I had found in Hawaii in the age group from six to thirteen or fourteen. In both the Porteus Maze Test and the Goodenough Draw-A-Man Test, the adolescents began to fall behind the American norms, because they began to draw stick men, which represented the traditional Negrito way of depicting a man, and because they insisted on telling me how a real rat would act if he were set down on the test blank, rather than how my imaginary rat should act to get out of the imaginary maze trap. On the Metal Maze their scores showed no falling off, and their dreams, like those of the Hawaiian and American groups, grew more complex in structure, including more characters and more of the complicated emotions such as shame, pride, jealousy, and hatred, which were absent in the dreams of the younger children.

The test responses of the very young children soon convinced me that the original endowment of the Negritos was not measurably different from that of other racial groups. By all my yardsticks, the children came up to the specifications which would entitle them to be considered equal to other children in the sight of God and the law.

The adult scores on the Goodenough Test were lower than the adolescent scores. This drop reflected the fact that their culture educated them against drawing the kind of man image which would make a good score on the test. Their scores on the Metal Maze went on climbing, and showed no inferiority to the adult scores I had obtained in my clinic at Waikiki Beach. In this test the Negritos did not have to remember instructions or act as though the paper world were the real three-dimensional world. In the Metal Maze they only had to remember where they had been and to keep trying new trails until they found their way out.

The adults could do this better than the children or the adolescents, which indicated that their mental capacity to deal with concrete things did not stop growing, and that the poor scores on the other tests were the result of experience or education which locked up, rather than developed, their capacity to do abstract, reflective thinking.

A few days before the feast I participated in a deer hunt. The assembled group went with their dogs into a near-by canyon, formed a wide circle, and then gradually closed in on its center, beating the jungle with sticks as they progressed. The men kept up an incessant shouting, reinforced by the barking of their half-starved dogs. A Filipino sergeant who had accompanied King Alfonso had brought with him an Army rifle. He loaned it to me for the hunt, and I got a lucky running shot into a wily buck which had escaped the arrows and spears of the Negritos posted at the mouth of the canyon. This large buck gave me prestige as a hunter as well as a shaman, and since the Negritos also bagged two deer, the hunt was very successful.

I didn't do as well on the pig hunts. The Negritos had located a number of runs where the pigs came down to water, and had watched these runs for days. They then surrounded the area, which was used by the various sows with their half-grown litters, and started up a din, knowing that most of the pigs would retreat along the runs, as was their custom. But the country was so steep and the jungle so dense that the pigs went by me before I could aim. The few shots I did make scared the remaining pigs off the runs into the jungle. The Negritos lay very still on the downwind side of the narrow run, bracing the butts of their spears against saplings, and lifting the sharp ends up into the pigs as they came along, depending on the pig's own force to drive a spear through him. If this didn't work, the Negrito hunter threw another spear as the pig went by, and then ran down the trail a little, grabbing spears which he had planted in readiness at various points. When he reached an area covered by another hunter, he stopped. The Negritos could run along the little trails they had made for themselves beside the pig run almost as fast as the pig himself.

I shot at one boar and missed him. The Filipino sergeant told me not to shoot at any more full-grown boars. He cautioned that a boar wounded in such close country is very likely to attack the hunter, who had better then take to the trees.

A Negrito ceremony of some sort was connected with the gathering and preparation of almost every type of food. Before and after the pig hunt, the men did a pig dance. The night before the women went out to look for shellfish, they performed a dance which was half apology to the fish and half a charm to insure the catch. Similarly, the men held a bee dance before and after the expeditions for honey. It was all right to eat the honey, or even the larvae of the bee, but in order to maintain the balance of the inner universe, the bee image in the mind of the Negrito had to give its permission to be eaten, and had to be given thanks through a ceremony after the event. Evidently the Negrito did not own the bee image, even though the image was part of his mind. The bee image had privileges and obligations similar to those of the Negritos. The rhythm associated with the image of the bee had to be allowed expression in the dance. The thoughts associated with the bee had to be expressed as a song, with the bee's voice and human words.

One old shaman went into trance, and the grandfather of all bees spoke through him, with a song which Juan said he had received in a dream. The bee said proudly that he was a great doctor, that he cured more than hunger—he had cured the shaman's cuts and burns with his honey, he had cured the sores and cuts of others through the shaman, and he had cured the shaman's swollen, aching joints with the venom from his stings. By permitting this expression of the bee's attitudes and by thanking the bee in the ceremony, the Negrito apparently took care of the image of the bee so it would not molest him in his dreams or oppress his conscience.

Moreover, the songs in which the bee expressed pride as a doctor, a disinfector of wounds, a healer of aching joints, and a technician who could waterproof a piece of bark cloth with his wax—these songs denoted an inner process similar to reflective thought. They showed the mind of the Negrito going from cause to effect. "I, the spirit of the bee, can cure your wounds with my honey and waterproof your bark cloth with my wax"—these word patterns had appeared in a dream; the central force which organized the physical rhythms of the Negrito as he slept was also working on the patterns associated with the bee, producing a dream which expressed a relationship of cause and effect. The repeated expression of that dream in a song and a dance would hold this newly organized pattern stable in the dreamer's mind and impose it on the group.

While he was awake, modern man might see the connection between putting honey on his wounds and facilitating the process of healing. Apparently it was easier for the Negrito to make this kind of logical connection in his sleep. Perhaps man's first reflective thinking appeared in his dreams.

Each day, with the arrival of new visitors, the circle of little houses grew. Each night the gypsylike choruses increased in volume, as more hunters participated in the wild, half-prayerful, half-magical dances, expressing thanksgiving to the animals which had allowed themselves to be found and killed for food, expressing the skill and valor of the hunter who had made the kill, expressing the speed and grace and gait and rhythm of the pig, or deer, or bird which had been slain. These were victorious dances, in which the Negritos demonstrated how grateful they were to the slain members of the animal world.

To me the dances also expressed a message from the Negrito to the animals—that this food was being transformed into song and dance and rhythm, into human joy, good fellowship, and good will, as though he said, "Be happy, my slain friends, that you have died to contribute to the higher forms of expression and joy which human beings have attained, and which you cannot attain except as you are incorporated into the nerve, sinew, blood, and emotion of human beings."

Toward morning there were also dances held in honor of the projected hunt of the morrow, dances which were both plans or rehearsals for the coming hunt and magical spells or messages to gain the permission and co-operation of the animals which were to be hunted and of the elements of nature.

These dances showed that the images of things, as well as the images of people, that went to make up the Negrito personality received constant attention through the co-operative action of the Negritos. Apparently there was in the mind of each Negrito an image of the animal kingdom which he used for food. If the Negrito planned to obtain honey, pork, or venison, a bee, a pig, or a deer came alive in his mind and demanded expression. Killing a member of the species in the hunt evidently made this representative image again become active. So the Negrito expressed its tensions or pressure through his dance and song, and then was able to dismiss it until new plans to hunt the creature activated its image once more.

However, the images of members of the social group and of animals were not the only ones which had to remain balanced in the mind of the Negrito. The trees which gave up their poison for his arrows, their fruit for his diet, and their bark for his clothing required similar ceremonies; so did the rivers which furnished him fish, the rocks which held him up as he walked, or which blocked his way, and the earth, which furnished him with roots, grubs, and tubers. Even the shrubs and tiny insects which were disturbed as the Negritos spat upon the ground or urinated were warned of the coming disturbance in their universe, and given an expression of appreciation for accepting what had become a burden to the Negrito.

Tolandian did not like trouble, and the Negritos judged by their own feelings what would trouble other orders of beings and therefore make them complain to Tolandian.

The Negritos behaved toward things and people according to this sense of total inner balance. Although they had no idols, I had the feeling that they were constantly worshipping idols inside themselves through their continual round of ceremonies. They were idolators with a vengeance. They did not have to make graven images to worship. Nature had given them a plentiful supply. Nature had carved the image of the sun, the moon, the star, the mountain, the river, the plant, in the Negrito's mind, and he credited each with his own feelings and with supernatural power.

This was clearly demonstrated in a dream which one of the Negritos had a few nights after they began to assemble for the ceremony. The old men had decided to increase the size of the clearing. Each horde which was represented chose an area to work on, and began cutting off the brush and carrying out the dead logs, which they broke up for grubs and then left for firewood. After the first day's work, Zog—one of the leaders—dreamed that the earth spirit in his area resented the clearing. His whole group stopped work the next morning and moved to another location, with a total loss of the first day's activity. The earth demon also demanded tobacco and betel from the head man, toward which all had to contribute.

This terrifying dream character had successfully attacked the dreamer, all of the members of the dreamer's group who were cooperating with him, and the other Negritos who had helped to plan the project. If this fearful dream image had not been able to affect the behavior of Zog and his group, it might have made him ill. Then it would have been attacked in the healing ceremony by the Negrito shamans. As it was, it received the respect and obedience of the Negritos as though it were, for the moment at least, the supreme god of the universe.

The incident terrified me. I asked Zog how big the earth demon was and he said it was a regular giant, as big as myself. With an inner quake, I inquired about the color of the dream giant. If it was white and as big as I, the Negritos might suspect that it was my spirit. Fortunately, it was yellow, the color of the earth in the vicinity. They did not connect it with me in their mind, but I was ill at ease and could not keep from thinking of the incident.

Preparations for the festival were even further complicated by the taboos on pregnant women. The earth, the rifle barrel, the medicine kit, all seemed to fall into the same category as the womb of the pregnant mother. She could not be present when the Negritos dug up the tubers which had been stored to ferment away the poisons in them. She could not be present when the bullets were taken out of the rifle barrel, and the medicines had too much force in them to be regarded as ordinary things. They were full of energy, like people, and might make the child want to come out of his mother's womb before its time, or might make her womb want to get rid of it. Also, the expectant mother had to refrain from eating twin bananas, or any type of fruit which had an unusual shape. Eating these might cause the baby to split in half or to change his shape. I despaired of testing or even of obtaining dreams from any of those with child, because of the endless taboos surrounding them. As the days passed, I was seized more and more with the conviction that I differed from the Negritos mainly in the matter of inner simplicity.

Since childhood I had not felt such breathless excitement as all the Negritos were able to maintain day after day as they looked forward to the approaching feast. Every minute not occupied by organized hunts for food was filled up with the children's spearing matches, foot races, and tree- and vine-climbing contests. Wrestling matches and dog fights were always in progress, and the outcome of each seemed a matter of life and death to everyone.

The habit of regarding the image as though it were an object in the outside world and the outside object as though it were a vital, living part of the self made everything that happened around him seem as important to the mature Negrito as it would to a child. It was as though the categories of the mind would not absorb energy from each other, or would not yield at all under pressure, making it necessary for the central mind to absorb the wear and tear of each event that happened, and keeping the adults in a state of constant excitement such as I remembered only from childhood, when each thing that happened was happening for the first time.

As the sun set, the drums and sticks and bamboo flutes were brought out and the hunting-gathering dances began, each led by those who were organizing the hunt or those who had been especially successful in it, each describing in a short-versed song, which the group echoed in chorus after each verse, the plan for the project or the story of it. After these more formal dances, there were sometimes others, accompanied by songs which the spirit guides had given to the leaders of the dance or to their ancestors —dances which dramatized and described the moods and sounds and philosophy of the wind spirit, the spirit of the moon, the tree spirit, the bounding spirit of the rolling rocks, even the hard, jagged, fearful spirit of the lightning, the floating spirit of the clouds, and the soft spirit of the rain, each with its peculiar flavor of rhythm, of intonation, of minor and major notes, each very similar to the others, yet with a subtle, haunting originality. Each dance began with complicated and disciplined movement patterns, each grew to an orgiastic explosion of wild abandon at the end. Each expressed skill and stamina and inspiration, every dancer struggling to outdo his fellows.

Everything about this strange Negrito world was whipping my mind and my senses into a constant frenzy of feverish activity. Some things were beginning to make sense, but they only made the others more disturbing. It was one thing for the student to watch a frog's egg being attacked by beams of light. There was no danger that one of the beams of light might make the egg turn around and kill him. Here I myself was the external irritant—and the Negritos might react by killing me at any moment.

Ever since the night the earth giant had appeared and ordered the Negritos to stop clearing the land, I had been watching closely how they interpreted the various nightmares the children reported. Usually the elders told the children to say a prayer or make a sacrifice to the terrifying dream character, and if it spoke to them, to do what they were bidden on awakening. The presence of this pattern of response supplied the explanation of some characteristics of Negrito behavior.

Zog, the lineage head, an authority because he was the oldest son of an oldest son, had apparently moved off the soil with his group because since childhood he had been doing what his terrifying dream giants told him to do. Here the Negrito culture had obviously taken a false step which partly explained why the Negrito did not grow up mentally and learn to think in abstractions, why he could not change his environment or his social order.

I knew that the earth demon was only a nonmaterial image, an abstraction, since the old man had seen it when his eyes were closed in sleep. He was afraid of it. He had to do what it told him. It was his master, rather than his servant. He was obliged to allow this fragment of himself to use him. He could not change the outside earth because it would then no longer correspond to the inside pattern, which was the dominion of the dream giant. This view fitted into the egg theory. The central mind or force could not change the dream pattern because it was supported by outside authorities. Thus, the Negrito acquired two heads, two controlling centers, his central mind and the dream giant.

On further inquiry, I found that if the dream giants told the subject of a nightmare to do things which were taboo they met opposition from the old men. The old men refused to support, and even attacked, dream characters which impelled the children to do antisocial or violent things toward the members of their own group (it was not taboo or antisocial to kill a stranger). If the adults did nothing about these nightmares because the child failed to report them, or because the adults were too busy, they often showed up as neurotic symptoms or illness in adolescence or adulthood, as had the giant baby of the shamaness and the thunder spirit of Pana.

Apparently the central mind of the Negrito could successfully oppose and conquer the dream image only when the authorities told him to do so. If they sided with the dream image, or neglected it, the central wisdom had to adapt itself to this image instead of making use of it. Obviously the central mind of each Negrito had to keep his inner universe balanced as he built and maintained his personality, just as the egg had to keep a balance as it built and maintained the physical body. The authorities, the elders, were like the scientists who controlled the light beam. When the child awakened from sleep and reported a struggle of the central mind with an image, the authorities could tell him to break down and control the image, so it could not build up a second head. In doing so they turned off the beam of light from the outside while it was still a stimulus and before it had given rise to a monster. If the authorities did nothing about the nightmare image, it might later make the child sick mentally or physically, and if they sided with the nightmare image, they robbed the child of the power to do abstract thinking, or to change his environment, or himself—to control his own destiny.

Why didn't the fools tell the children to break up and control all the dream giants as they appeared? This I could not answer, and what was worse, I could not escape the clearer and clearer realization that I was in no way protected by their taboos. The more I understood the Negrito mentality, the more frightened I became, but I was powerless to leave. If they liked me, their dream giants wouldn't tell them to kill me. I tried to be pleasant and useful, and told Juan not to forget to instruct them about the blood brotherhood of all Christians, so they would be at least as afraid of killing me as they were of their dream giants.

# SIX

# Olan

Un, the mistress of the infant spirit guide, who had treated me the night of my arrival, had each day kept in touch with Juan. Apparently she was convinced that I was being eaten away by the spirit that had been drawn from my mother and lodged in my right side, and she was determined to do something about it. One day she told Juan of a dream she had had about me, in which she had seen me turned into the stone house of the invading ghost. Later, her spirit guide informed her that I must get married, or else the ghost would make me sicken and die. With the arrival of each new group she inquired the bride price of the marriageable girls, and suggested to Juan those she thought would be suitable for me.

I was not sure of Juan's motives in telling me of the virtues of the various wives available. He was as interested in Un's information for himself as he was for me, and as the days passed it occurred to me that he had an ulterior motive, perhaps hoping that I might buy a wife he could not afford and bequeath her to him when I left the Negrito territory. Each time he returned from talking to the shamaness he had a dreamy look in his eyes, as though she had spun a fantasy in his mind more powerful than any he could concoct himself. I could have sworn he was in love.

Cut off from the girls in his own group by the incest taboo, which made even his second or third cousin in his father's group as forbidden to him as his mother or sister, and cut off from all other girls by the bride price, the Negrito boy had but to hear of a girl to build a fantasy about her, to deify her, and so to fall in love.

One night Lango, a visiting boy, commenced the twelve-day courtship dance around the lean-to of one of the local girls, on whose bride price the fathers had been able to agree.

This dance was full of frustration, anguish, and longing. Its purpose, Juan explained, was to express his undying love and devotion for his bride-to-be. I could understand the frustration. As part of the bride price Lango was to work for her father for a year, during which he would see her constantly but not be able to enjoy her. In the song which accompanied the dance, Lango told of his own virtues, his strength, his wisdom, his bravery, his grace in the dance, his favor in the world of spirits, his honesty and integrity. Twelve days of those songs, composed as the spirits moved him in the dance, would certainly make his betrothed feel that being the love object of such a hero left nothing to be desired.

"Why doesn't he say something about the girl in his song?" I inquired of Juan.

"She knows how wonderful she is," he answered. "In the courtship song you tell a girl about yourself. Anyway, he doesn't know her yet, since he's hardly met her."

I could see no flaw in Juan's logic. The melancholy of Lango's song was contagious, and moved Juan so deeply that at last he had to speak. He glanced nervously in the direction of the shamaness, swallowed hard, and announced that Olan, the most famous girl in Bataan, was arriving from across the mountain on the morrow. She was seventeen, old to be unmarried, but she was so beautiful that no one had been able to raise the bride price which her father asked. Un's infant guide had predicted that I would be unable to resist her, and that she would save me from the spirit which Un had seen eating away my life.

"But how would we take her into the northern territory if I did marry her?" I inquired.

"Her family will guard her for you until you come back," he answered evasively.

"But suppose I never come back?"

"Then you could give her to me when you left," he suggested.

"But Juan, it would be adultery if you took my wife before you knew I was dead. You'd have to murder me to escape the adultery taboo."

"Oh no," said Juan, with a shocked expression. "I could become a Christian."

Now it was plain why Juan had been so interested in Un's therapeutic marriage project. Doubtless he himself had fallen in love with Olan. He had known that the bride price would include a carabao or two, and other things which would be beyond his reach even with all the salary he could accumulate in my employ. Of course, the whole idea was ridiculous, but I did not have the heart to dash his splendid plans.

"We can see about it when she arrives," I assured him.

The love song of the Negrito lad had suddenly lost some of its melancholy. The idea that one could think of these women as having beauty had not occurred to me before. I would have to look at them again.

I did not think of the marriage project or of Olan again until, in the late afternoon, I looked up from the picture of a dream a young Negrito boy was drawing for me and saw Un standing in front of me with a Negrito girl by her side. Apparently they had been there for some time, watching me. The Negritos always moved about so quietly that I could never shake off the impression that they materialized out of thin air.

This time it was a shocking impression, since the wisplike girl who stood beside the sturdy shamaness was, at once, more a dream than a reality. She was tall for a Negrito, towering at least three inches above the shamaness, who was over average height. Yet, for one so slender, she did not seem tall. As I stared, unable to extricate my mind from the dream the lad was drawing, I hardly comprehended that she was a person at all. Instead she seemed to break up into circular areas of intense darkness, as though space had received a blow that knocked some fragments from it. There was something about the brilliance of the scene which gave the figure the mechanical, unreal appearance of a hallucination or a memory, made it as unhuman there in the sunlight as an abstract painting. Her greater height made her short bark-cloth skirt appear even shorter. In fact, it was molded so neatly to the curving line of her hips and thighs that it was not a skirt at all, but only one of the circles. She was black as ebony, but standing there in the shaft of sunlight, which bounded from her smooth skin like metal, she seemed lighter than the green of the foliage. I blinked as though the light hurt my eyes, and fancied I could see my reflection imprisoned in each of the round drops of shadow which marked the place where space had been a moment before.

Stupidly telling myself that it must be the heat, I looked away from the girl into the good-natured countenance of the shamaness. Un's face seemed luminous and large again, as it had in the trance, and I half-expected her to break into her deaf-and-dumb language.

"Olan," she said with a sly twinkle, making a gesture toward the other. I looked around for Juan. He sat with his mouth open, obviously more affected by the shining spirals of jet revolving there in the shaft of sunlight than he had been by the ghost visit of Ogong's father.

"Juan," I said gently. He did not stir. "Would you ask Un if her spirit guide has given her any more dreams lately?"

"Juan," I repeated, a bit louder. "Perhaps you could give Olan a test if you spoke to her."

"Oh yes," he responded, without looking away. But when he tried to convey my message, he could only stammer, opening and shutting his mouth without words. Un was bursting with amusement. Would she offer to loan her guide to Juan so he could communicate in the deaf-and-dumb language until his voice returned? Having sponsored the girl's journey to the festival, Un was enjoying the force of Olan's impact upon the men, with no less pleasure than she would have if her own beauty were striking the fatal blow.

I was convinced that she had a healing interest in everyone, but apparently she was woman enough to take some satisfaction in the undoing of masculine pride. Only in shamanism and through feminine beauty had the Negrito woman an opportunity to escape the rigid domination of masculine authority. Here, obviously, was a debacle of masculinity. Her mischievous eyes were suggesting to me that I could no more withstand her protégé than did Juan.

I looked again in Olan's direction. This time I was able to attend to her face, but that feeling of getting tangled up in circles still persisted, even now. The spirals of her hair were not so small as the peppercorn ringlets of most of the Negritos. Perhaps way back she had some Polynesian or black Hindu ancestry.

The vine with which her hair was tied was as black as the hair itself. It was some variety of creeper, and its tendrils went swirling into space like the stray wisps of hair on her own head. Her lids were dropped against the glare of the sun, so that no white showed beneath her lashes, and her lips rested immobile, their perfect symmetry unspoiled. It was as though she had been made according to a plan that had been drawn with a compass.

At last Juan found his voice and his feet, and drew up a stool for Olan by the table. When I looked back toward the shamaness, it became obvious from her smug expression that she did not realize the mathematical nature of my absorption in this wisp of the night she had produced. If I had seen Un's spirit guide, who was as big as a man and looked like an infant, he would have aroused about the same degree of curiosity as this girl before me. During Un's trance he had had for me about the same amount of substance as this thin-waisted, full-breasted aggregation of gleaming circles, with a suggestion of human life only in the small, flat disc formed by her abdomen, which bounded in and out as she breathed.

She did amazingly well on the test and had an abundance of dreams to relate. In no time at all she was using the pencil and paper to depict her dream characters, as though she had grown up drawing them. Actually, like all Negrito girls, she had scratched designs on her bamboo combs, so that the art of drawing was not completely unknown to her.

From the autobiography Juan collected, we learned that Olan had been ill at the beginning of her menstrual cycle four years before, and had been successfully treated by Un. She had been in the trance state a number of times during the treatment and under Un's guidance expected one day to become a shamaness. As she spoke, I wondered if she had absorbed and was sharing the infant spirit guide of the older shamaness. The wealth of expression and gestures she employed made her torrent of words scarcely necessary. It was fantastic how anyone as immobile as she had been there in the sunlight could so rapidly appear to have no form at all, to be made entirely of force and movement.

It was late afternoon. The cool air was moving down from the higher mountains, lifting the oppressing heat. The break in the trees above the clearing was filled with rosy light reflected from the clouds.

The sky around the glowing clouds was almost as green as the leaves of the lofty trees. Juan had apparently said something funny, and for the first time I heard Olan's laughter. It was high and penetrating and had a tinkling quality, like the strips of glass which the Japanese hang up for the wind to play with. Looking down, I saw her for the first time in profile. Leaning back slightly, she had turned away from the table and faced Juan. Every part of her was throbbing with laughter. In profile she was a different being from the one I had seen standing in the sunlight.

The roundness which invited one on and on into the space through and behind her had been transformed into smooth, straight lines and gently dipping curves which met with other lines and curves in a wicked series of penetrating angles. Unlike the straight or slightly bulging forehead of most Negritos, hers sloped gently back at a perfect angle from her incredibly straight nose. Her lips were full and protruding, but the profile line sweeping down from her nose and up from her chin was graceful; her teeth were blood-red from betel chewing; and her breasts, no longer round from this angle, but long and sharp, thrust themselves up into space. As she threw back her arms in the laughing gesture, the straight tips of her breasts curved skyward like the obscenely aggressive horns of a rhinoceros.

The next minute she was sitting erect and still again. A strange thing happened. The sun had come out from behind a cloud low on the horizon and shot its rays almost directly into my eyes. As I narrowed them to shut out the glare, the straight-backed profile figure before me turned a shining ghostly white, like marble in the moonlight. As I looked, I could feel the goose pimples puckering up my skin from head to foot.

Un had joined us. Olan was rising to her feet. Juan was speaking to me. Yes, that was what she looked like. A Babylonian or an Egyptian, not a Hindu—and certainly a princess. Probably I had seen a picture or a statue in some book or museum, when I was a child so young I couldn't read the inscriptions, and had been profoundly moved or shocked at the time. Probably I had slipped back again into that experience, and was hearing the voice of someone tell me what the statue was. Ever since that first evening with the Negritos, when I had seen the transformation of Ogong's face and voice, and the deaf-and-dumb gestures of Un's infant guide, I had often felt like a child in the presence of something beyond my power to touch or comprehend. Juan was speaking to me again, and the broad grin of the shamaness made it evident that she had noticed my dazed expression and confusion. She probably thought her love magic or her infant guide was affecting me.

As we put our testing things away, Juan told me that the evening was to be devoted to a special ceremony. Just before noon I had led a girl over to the testing table and, unknowingly, had sat her down next to her father-in-law. She had been so frightened of me that she was powerless to protest. I had pushed her into one of the greatest sins which a Negrito can commit—ceremonial incest. I knew about the taboos which forbade the father's speaking to his son's wife, marching next to her on the trail, or sitting beside her. It was as though the Negrito god, Tolandian, looking up from the center of the earth, could not tell clearly what the father and his daughter-in-law were up to if they communicated with each other. He would think that they were sleeping together, or that their proximity would make the son jealous of his father and disturb the unity and good will of the closely knit extended family. Or, it was as though the god had decided that trouble with in-laws could be avoided if they kept away from each other and like his messengers, the monkeys, refrained from communicating with each other through words. Whatever the explanation, I had broken a Negrito taboo and pushed the young lady and her father-in-law into a ghastly offense against Tolandian, for which they were not responsible, and yet for which they could not hold me responsible since I hadn't known of their relationship.

Half the night was spent in apologies to Tolandian and in cleansing rituals. As for the offended feminine dignity, it took a plug of tobacco to earn pardon for me.

As far as I could now see, the world of the Negrito mind was organized with Tolandian at the center, with the angleworms and monkeys bringing information to him as though they were the inner and outer skin of the human body, and the thunder and lightning bringing authority and anger out from the center as though they were glands and muscles. The rest of the living photographs in the Negrito mind, whether of people, trees, or other things, behaved in the same routine fashion as they did out in space, or else they got tangled up in conflicts which aroused the anger of Tolandian and required ceremonial action by the Negrito social group.

I had been running into a good many of these Negrito taboos of late, and was glad to hear Juan on frequent occasions promoting the doctrine of the blood brotherhood of all Christians, so no one would feel free to take Tolandian's justice into his own hands without having to settle with my Christian family. A week earlier I had eaten a piece of fish along with a morsel of the flesh of a hornbill, which had been presented to me from the communal hunt. This was inviting a major catastrophe. To eat fish at the same meal with fowl was like committing blasphemy; it was an insult to the demigods of both the sky and the water. It made most of the Negritos vomit. All night long they burned feathers and muttered their charms. A day or two later I ate some blue-colored berries along with a handful of what looked like red thimbleberries. I had seen the Negritos eat both these types of fruit and was unaware that mixing them was taboo.

With the Negritos, nothing came off according to schedule. The frequent infringements of taboo on my part delayed everything much more than usual. Juan kept attempting to cheer me up by saying it was good for me to learn these taboos before we reached the northern territory, where the Negritos might spear me first if I got them into trouble with Tolandian, and think of their possible difficulties with my Christian brotherhood later. It was scant comfort, since the things one might do to anger Tolandian without knowing it seemed endless.

Tonight, as they performed the ceremonial of apology for my infringement of the incest taboo, I noticed Juan deep in conversation with Un, and later I saw the two of them having a conference with Glin, the father of Olan. He was a stolid old fellow, with something of the Egyptian appearance of his daughter. Of course, they would not be able to arrange a marriage for me. The whole idea was ridiculous, but I had to admit to myself that it did not seem so utterly fantastic as it had the day before. Certainly I would learn more about the Negrito if I went through their marriage ceremony, and although I could not quite consider Olan a human being, or think of her as more than an animated ebony statue, I felt a little more than amusement later when Juan came back to help me record the words of the apology ceremony and more verses of Lango's love song.

At last I asked Juan the question which I knew he was bursting to answer: "How much bride price does the old man want for his daughter?"

"He asks five hundred pesos," Juan answered, with a sad look in his eyes. "He thinks all foreigners are very rich."

"It seems you have gone out of your way to exaggerate my wealth to all the Negritos," I answered, with an amused feeling that Juan was getting just what he deserved. He knew that such a figure was entirely out of reach, even for me; it was my entire working capital.

"Glin says he was offered three hundred pesos by an old Filipino who runs a little trading post on the other side of the mountain. I do not think he will settle for any less. Olan did not like the old Filipino and said she would run away, so she is not yet married because of this. Since some of the Negrito children have gone to school and heard about American ways, they are not so obedient to their parents as they used to be. Glin thinks he may collect from the old man when he and Olan go home. But Olan told him she will run away and go down to the city if she has to marry him, and then her father will have to return the bride price."

"Even three hundred pesos is far beyond any bride price I could afford," I said. I wondered at the very idea that I could be speaking thus about a subject which had appeared so completely outside the limits of reality the day before. Juan agreed without conviction that three hundred pesos was too much.

When Lango had completed his dance, Juan did a dance before the lean-to of Olan. He had not explained the nature of his dance to me, but from the phrases of his song—those I could understand —it was evident that it concerned me. Several times he spoke of gold and pearls, of power, of credit, and of the "American Way." Apparently he was not willing to give up his matrimonial quest on my behalf so easily.

I had a cheap gold-plated fountain pen and pencil set from Japan, a fourteen-carat-gold watch and chain, a fraternity pin with some seed pearls in it, a pearl-handled pocketknife, and a graduation ring set with a synthetic ruby. Juan had seen these on several occasions and had displayed great interest in them. After his dance, he asked if he might show them to Glin. "Altogether those things only cost about two hundred pesos," I said to him as I handed them over, "and one probably could not sell them for over fifty pesos even in Manila."

"I just want him to see how much gold you have," he said. "It will do no harm."

As I went to sleep, I could see Juan and Un talking at Glin's lean-to. They were still talking when I woke up next morning, and when Juan returned he seemed hopeful again, and excited. He may have impressed the old man, or he may have been excited only because this was the great day of the *wakai*, the funeral feast for Ogong's father.

King Alfonso had attended a number of large gatherings, since the Army used the feasts as a way of getting in touch with the various Negrito groups. Everyone looked to him for leadership, and he obliged.

At daybreak Juan went with some of the other young men, who could travel fast, for more wine and some last-minute supplies. He asked if I would give five pesos toward the wine, and I suspected that he was contributing a month's salary of his own, and that his request involved Glin in some way. I had left fifty pesos with the Filipino trader at the end of the oxcart road, to be changed into ten-centavo pieces. Most of the Negritos had seen these silver coins and valued them as trinkets, even if they did not know that they could be spent at the trading posts.

Paper money was not valued by the mountain folk, so I carried it without fear of being robbed, but I needed silver to pay the lads who would escort us to the north. Juan had arranged for three of them to go along, at ten centavos a day. He now suggested that I convert another ten pesos into silver, saying that some of the Negritos had not seen silver pesos and that the large coins would be of interest to them. I suspected that the wine and the silver, like the gold, were being marshaled for their effect on Glin.

I had a pint silver flask and a gold-plated cigarette case. The flask was full of alcohol which I had brought along for medicinal purposes. Juan produced an aluminum Army-issue canteen for which he had been bargaining with the Filipino sergeant, and suggested that I pour the alcohol from the pocket flask into it. On his trip down he planned to fill up the flask with some especially potent sugar-cane brandy, which Roberto kept on hand.

"Should we arrange a betrothal," said Juan, "it would be good to give Glin a drink from the silver flask." He also asked for my cigarette case, saying that he would fill it up with special, black, molasses-coated cigarettes. The Negritos valued these highly, but could seldom afford them. I wondered if these were only stage props, or if I was going to be asked to sacrifice the case and the flask, along with my other possessions, on the altar of love.

As the morning wore on, I wandered leisurely about the camp, observing the preparations for the feast. By the middle of the afternoon they were moving along smoothly. None of the natives had ever seen such a large group of people. Never before, according to the old men, had such a stack of food been assembled on Bataan. Ogong's dead father would have occasion to be very proud of his at-onement feast. He would undoubtedly invite some of the other ghosts to take part in the *wakai*.

The idea that ghosts were to be present at the feast made the Negritos nervous. All of them had heard how I had called up and controlled a ghost, and all of them, even Glin, seemed more friendly than usual. All looked forward to the arrival of the wine, which they knew would be plentiful.

# SEVEN

# Funeral Feast and Betrothal

Toward sunset the sound of whooping down the trail announced the approach of the young men with the wine kegs. Soon the first keg was opened and everyone was fortifying himself against the presence of the ghost who was being honored, and of any friends the ghost might bring along.

After the mule, the deer, the wild pigs, the porcupines, and the bamboo rats had been placed on the fire, and the other food had been arranged, the men settled down to drink and exchange their never-ending stories. All were brimming over with cordiality and good will. When the animals were roasted, some of their parts would be burned and some would be raw, but the Negritos would not mind. The carcasses were cooked whole because meat was now so scarce in the territory that the natives seldom got all they wanted. They had none of the white man's prejudice against the insides of an animal, and they liked the flavor of the digestive juices. The bittersweet of bile-impregnated liver, combined with honeycomb, the sour taste of the hydrochloric acid from the stomach, and the limburgerlike flavor from the intestines were all welcome to the Negrito gourmets. After a Negrito feast, nothing was left but bones, and even these were cracked open for the marrow.

The women took care of the rest of the feast, cooking the rice, tubers, and vegetables in large lengths of green bamboo. Even the children were put to work, gathering banana leaves for the combination tablecloths and plates and keeping the dogs out of the enclosure. This was really the greatest problem of the entire feast. Everyone had brought his dog, and the pack fought constantly just outside the clearing. When the fight went badly for their own dogs, the children intervened with clubs and loud shouts. Every few seconds some dog which had tried to enter the clearing to snatch a bit of food would go off yelping in a pitch so high that it rang out shrill and clear above the babble.

The older women, and those not busy with the food, formed a circle on a low bamboo platform which had been constructed at the eastern border of the clearing. There they murmured their prayers for the deceased. In the afternoon, only a few of the women chanted, their quavering voices scarcely audible above the yelping of the dogs and the laughter of the men. But as evening approached, the chorus became steadily louder and the cries more piercing. Now the men occasionally encouraged the singing by giving the women bamboo lengths of wine.

By sunset the chorus had all the fury of a tempest, rising and falling like the howling of wind. Though few of the mourners had ever known the deceased, I was sure there had never been a more convincing expression of unconsoled grief. In the voices there was bitterness, longing, sadness, and heartbroken protest against the cruelty of death.

Leaning far back on their heels, their naked breasts toward the sky and their arms outstretched, the women sobbed with deep, guttural, wheedling sounds, straightening up to a kneeling position as they increased the volume. Then the pitch of the chanting became higher and more demanding. As it ended, the women leaned forward and pounded the bamboo platform with their clenched fists in a paroxysm of high-pitched, angry screaming which had not yet lost the sobbing rhythm. Then they leaned back again, as though drinking in force from the heavens, and then once again went forward and pounded the floor. Gradually the gestures and the song and the rhythm took hold of me with an hypnotic force.

Each time I looked toward Olan, who was talking to Juan and

Un, the whole chorus melted into her. From the front, the inviting planes of her body suggested that receptive leaning back, that imperative submissiveness, which the Negrito women were showing at the beginning of each verse of their song. The screaming, pounding, frantic demand expressed at the end of the verses brought her insistent profile into mind.

These women were different from any I had ever seen before. For all their receptivity, there was a violent aggressiveness about them. The wine was softening a barrier in me, combining with Un's constant repetition of the fact that I, being a man, must have a woman, and with Juan's persistent suggestion that Olan belonged to me but for the exchange of a few trinkets.

The entire atmosphere was permeated with magic, with hypnosis, which made each person act as though his wildest fantasy were already a reality, as though the outside world were no more than his own daydream. Certainly I had no feeling of love for this wisp of black shadow which had boldly pierced the sunlight, as it was now piercing the glow of the fire. But as I watched her there, talking with such smooth animation, I could not deny that she was becoming entangled with my feelings. The stab of hatred I felt for Juan as I watched them, and the rage Un aroused in me for no reason I could think of, were warning enough that a void inside me was filling up with something which might spell disaster. I had first noticed this void when Mrs. Hartendorp had asked me what I was running away from. It had been increased by Un's tantalizing gestures in the trance, which had seemed to me to pantomime the severing of some imaginary umbilical cord.

The next moment the cooks yelled that the food was ready. Sorrow and tears disappeared like magic. The throng of mourners charged upon the food with yells of merriment and ecstasy. The feast began soon after sunset. By that time, all the men were a little unsteady on their feet and uninhibited by even the usual Negrito restraint about food.

Although I was hungry, I could scarcely eat for wondering at the speed with which the food was vanishing. One little old man, hardly three feet high, started on a haunch of deer. I could swear that it disappeared before he had drawn a breath. The whole group ate with the same degree of concentration which had possessed the women in their expression of sorrow. In spite of the rapidity of their eating, however, the feast went on for hours. As it progressed, the Negritos ate more slowly. I was astonished at their capacity. Where in their little bodies did they find a place for such mountains of meat?

Gradually their slim, well-proportioned torsos took on the rotund lines of kewpie dolls. As they finished eating, the women once more took their places on the mourners' platform, and the old chant, half wail, half song, of the afternoon recommenced. As the minutes passed, some of the men joined the chorus.

As bone fragments and bits of burned skin fell upon the ground, the battle with the dogs became more desperate. The poor half-starved creatures were continuously beaten back, and their wailings, as they licked their wounds and looked longingly at the food, remained my most melancholy memory of the Negrito funeral feast.

The wine had released ugly aggressive tendencies in the men. They enjoyed beating off the dogs. I did not, as usual, identify with the sufferers; this time I identified with those who were delivering the savage blows. I wished that the dogs were Glin and Juan and Un, and all who were talking and laughing with Olan as I should have liked to be talking and laughing with Olan, but for age, custom, and the million other barriers which I knew could never be surmounted.

As the feast wore on, my appetite returned, and soon I was tearing at a bloody haunch of the Army mule. The sugar-cane brandy had no strength at all. I enriched it with the medicinal alcohol from the canteen. The meat had no substance, now that a monster inside me had been unleashed upon it. I felt happy as the chunks of gristle and raw fat, which would have gagged me an hour before, stretched my throat, and as blood from the meat trickled down my beard and fell upon my chest. Gradually, the raw, bestial feelings which had threatened to consume me were assuaged. I was beginning to look more like a kewpie doll than any of the others, having more spare fat of my own to help out. And at last I could again watch Olan with only a mild feeling of falling into the net of abstract circles, or of being tossed about by the curved horns of the rhinoceros.

Now Juan detached himself from Glin's group and darted into my little tent. Soon he emerged with one of the salt sacks full of coins which he had brought back from Roberto's. He came to me, his eyes wide and his nostrils dilated. "Come," he said. "Come quickly. Glin will take a bride price of three hundred pesos! You can become engaged to Olan!"

I felt as though the Army mule I had just eaten had kicked me on the head and left me stone sober. Had Juan cashed in all the money I had amassed for my expedition? I was afraid to look at Olan. Something in me was saying that one moment with her would be worth three hundred pesos.

"I can't possibly afford three hundred pesos," I said to Juan.

"Oh," he said confidently, "for the betrothal you'll only pay ten per cent of the bride price. That's only thirty pesos. Then you'll give her your ring for the engagement. I explained to Glin that this is the American Way."

"Oh," I said.

"Yes," he said. "I told Glin that you must kiss her when you give her the ring, and that the marriage will not take place until you can make her love you. I've been teaching her English, so she can talk to you and know your words of love. She is pleased to love you by consent, but she is afraid of you because you are big. She thinks it might kill her to bear your child. But I told her my father was as big as you, and she knows that many Negrito women have married Lowland men. So she has agreed to the engagement and to allow you to court her in the American way."

I took a quick look in Olan's direction, and I heard a voice in my memory saying, "You've got a chance to come out of the mountains alive if you leave the Negrito women alone." Was this warning which I had heard so often in the Lowlands abrogated by a formal engagement?

Juan took me to Olan. She looked dreadfully shy as we approached. I thought I could again see her as a white marble statue, but this time the statue was blushing. As we stopped in front of her, the burning in my own face and throat made me realize the source of the redness in the face of the statue I saw in my mind. In my long thirty years of life I had never seriously considered being engaged. How had I got myself into this situation? Olan was standing on a log, and still she was hardly higher than my shoulder.

Juan handed the sack of coins to Glin and tugged my ring loose from my finger, where I had replaced it when he returned it to me that morning. He was obviously afraid the old man would change his mind and reverse his decision, which had been helped along by the wine and food of the festival.

Olan extended her hand as Juan directed. He slipped the ring over her thumb and told her that she must kiss me. She stood immobile, as she had those first minutes in the sunlight. Her eyes were closed. Mechanically I extended my arms. As my hands touched her back, she whirled, as though she had lost her nerve and wished to flee. It was too late. I could not have released her if I would. The rotation of her body had placed her breast in my hand, and her back was falling against my chest. My right hand was at her chin, turning her head toward me. The softness of her skin and of her slender throat, and the delicate bones of her jaw, which felt even smaller than they had looked, startled me, but not enough to break the continuity of the action which was in progress.

She struggled for a moment and then, as I felt her lips, her body stiffened and pulsated with violence. I released her, and she ran off into the shadows. I felt as though I had shorted an electric circuit. The throbbing of that cone-shaped heart continued in my hand, and the sensation showed no signs of abating. I felt stunned and I dropped my hand to my side with the feeling that it was no longer mine, and that it would go on beating, independently of me, with that shocking, startled rhythm.

I became aware that everyone was looking at me. The broad grin on Un's round face announced that her guide was winning out against the spirit of the lady whom she had seen using my body as her stone house. Juan handed her a betrothal present—from me to Olan. Un unfolded it and held it up for inspection. The gift had not come from among my possessions; it was something I had never owned or purchased—a pair of old-fashioned lace panties. Juan told Un to see that Olan put them on and wore them on this first night of her betrothal.

Juan shook hands with me and told the other Negritos to do the same. Glin stood munching his cud of betel nut and clutching his sack of money. He looked dazed, which convinced me he was hardly more aware of how this betrothal had come about than I was myself. Juan pulled out the gold cigarette case, and passed the coveted sweet, black, molasses cigarettes. He must have seen a wedding or a betrothal party at the plantation at which he had worked; he knew just what to do.

He led us back to the wine and chopped out the head of his special keg, for which he had requested financial assistance while I was still half-asleep in the morning.

"Where did you get those lace panties?" I muttered as we walked along.

"I bought them at a Filipino store before I left," he said. "The Filipino boys always beg a pair of panties from their lovers when they are betrothed. The Negritos do not wear them, so I brought a pair along, in case I wished to obtain a keepsake from my sweetheart."

"But why did you think they were necessary for my American engagement?" I said. "I never heard of such a thing in America."

Juan looked mystified. "It was the boys who go to the American high school who told me of the custom," he said, wrinkling his brow. "They said that when a girl agrees to love a boy, she gives him her panties as a pledge, so he can rest his head on them at night when he longs for her and she is not there."

"Well," I said, "since you're the expert on the American way of courtship, I can't question your procedure, but I'm afraid you've dragged in an old Spanish custom stemming from courtships carried on in the presence of chaperones." I realized that if my courtship was to be conducted according to the old traditions which had come to the Philippines with the Spaniards, there were more surprises ahead. I had no experience in courtship carried on in the presence of a chaperone, but if that was what I had to do to fulfill Juan's idea of an American courtship, I would do it.

# EIGHT

# Courtship the American Way

THE barrelhead of Juan's special keg was splintered, and the bamboo lengths of wine were drunk by all in honor of Glin. The wailing had continued, but now it was interrupted by the men bringing wine to the mourners. The women drank and then immediately resumed the gypsylike cadence of the funeral dirge. The throbbing in my hand grew faint as the endless verses ebbed and flowed. Each verse told the history of all those in a generation who had loved with sorrow and lost with rage—lost to time, death, and fate.

Only the chief mourner, Sari, offered relief from the gloom. She was large for a Negrito, and very fat. She had come along with the King's party from Fort Stotsenburg, where food was plentiful. Before the mourning commenced, she had put on a dirty pink negligee, which she took from an old Army saddlebag. Alfonso told me that the negligee had been given her by the wife of an Army major. Even though Sari wore it only on special occasions, it was now bedraggled, and its ostrich-feather border looked like a long black caterpillar. Periodically the awestricken women ran their grimy hands along it to see what American finery felt like.

Being mourner of honor, Sari had received more wine than the others, and she was now a little drunk. Leading the funeral dirge as though she were singing "Sweet Adeline," she bubbled with good humor, and slapped the women about her if they failed to fit into her alcoholic rhythm. Then, suddenly, she would drop off to sleep, awaking only when the others tickled her across the face with the feather border of her negligee.

The contortions of her lips as she awoke from these frequent lapses were a source of humor to those tribesmen not engaged in argument or sleep. The children, not interested in sorrow, laughed each time she had to be awakened.

Sari was now getting back into action, and I watched and listened as one after another of her mellow notes rocketed into the air. Suddenly, there was a desperate heaving of her fat arms and legs, and her negligee-clad body shot into the air, following her voice. For a moment she seemed to be suspended, a mass of arms and legs and fluttering silk. Her long hair, trained upward, emphasized the terror in her screams. The next instant she was back on the platform, face downward, writhing and roaring with a superhuman voice.

Whenever I think of absolute terror, the frozen faces of the other mourners come back into my mind. As Sari writhed on the platform, knocking her colleagues about, I saw something bobbing around on her back, under the negligee. Then I noticed a black thread extending from her neck into space.

The other mourners sat petrified, while Sari writhed and screamed, kicking those who were near her. The waving thread stiffened, and the bobbing hump moved steadily upward and broke into view above the ostrich plumes. It was a small black monkey. As it went upward, it fastened its feet in Sari's hair and clung so tenaciously that her head strained violently backward.

The mourners screamed. Then almost instantly, the suspense was broken by shouts from the children. Down to the clearing dropped an impish little boy, convulsed with laughter. He had been perched on a large limb which extended over the platform. While the other children created a momentary diversion, he had lowered his pet monkey, attached to a strong black fiber, down her neck. The monkey, not in on the joke, had scratched and bitten Sari's back. If the lad on the limb had not lost his perch from laughter, the monkey might have been successfully drawn out of sight and gone down in Negrito history as a ghostly visitor.

As the Negritos began to understand what had happened, their terror turned to mirth. The boy who had promoted the trick became a hero, and his fame throughout the mountains was assured.

At sunrise, all of the camp was aroused for one last burst of conventional weeping. Then the feast had officially ended. Everyone felt it had been a most successful occasion.

The next few days were filled with feverish work for me, as I gave mental tests to the last few people who had straggled in, recorded dreams, and prepared for the journey north. A careful check showed that whenever someone died, his children dreamed of him repeatedly until the funeral feast. In groups where people were not taught that their parents would visit them after death (in America and Hawaii for instance) a large percentage of those I interviewed did not remember dreams of their dead parents. When they did, they usually described the dreams as terrifying or depressing. Among the Negritos, the dream of the parent was expected, and did not, therefore, arouse fear or depression. Providing the children were willing to do what the image of the deceased parent requested, this type of dream aroused no sense of guilt.

Perhaps I had discovered a law: to help people to make a healthy adjustment to the shock of death, teach them to expect dream visitations from their dead loved ones. The idea was exciting. If man's power to balance his nervous system and to grow in sleep, through dreams, was dependent on the attitude of his group toward dreams and on what he heard about dreams as he grew up, then the expression and interpretation of dreams might become a vital part of our own educative process. Perhaps the neglect of the dream in Western education was one of those blind spots I was looking for, which made us stop short of a crimeless, warless civilization.

Before the two-hundred-odd Negritos who had assembled left the festival, I was anxious to get short series of dreams from all who had become shamans. I had already found that most of the shamans asked their patients about their dreams, and that the dreams of the shamans and of the people undergoing treatment were more complicated than those of other people and consistently included two features missing in ordinary dreams. One was the appearance of the spirit guide and other powerful dream characters who communicated with and helped the dreamer. The other was the co-operation of the dream characters on the dreamer's behalf. Also, the spirit which talked through the patient or was seen by him in trance often appeared in his dreams, doing what it had been asked or told to do by the shaman while the subject was in trance.

This was even more exciting than the dream visitations of dead parents. It confirmed the law I had formulated, showing that man would have dreams and remember them if he were encouraged to do so, and it also showed that the special type of social contact occurring in the agreement trance helped the individual develop powerful dream characters which would assist him in the reorganization of his personality while he was asleep as well as during the period of the trance.

In the afternoon Olan came shyly to the tent and talked with Juan. Toward sunset, when work was put away, Juan told me that she was ready to go for a walk with me, with Un as chaperone. We went along the trail to a small river, half a mile from the encampment, where I usually went swimming in the late afternoon. An inch or two below her short bark-cloth skirt, I could see the white ruffles of the betrothal present. It was astonishing what an undressed appearance those two inches of lace gave to my bride-to-be. As I climbed from the pool to rest on the little sandy beach, Un pushed Olan down beside me, and resolutely turning her back on us, went down the stream, pulling up small rocks in search of prawns and shellfish. I did not know whether Juan had instructed her about the proper functions of a chaperone, or whether turning her back on us and wandering down the stream out of sight was her own idea, or whether she was following the command of her infant guide.

Whatever the source of her inspiration, it was appreciated. The splash of her receding footsteps was lost in the gurgle of the stream, as it swerved around the huge rock below which the deep swimming hole formed. The swirling water trapped the sunset colors in a series of tiny whirlpools. A green lizard, scurrying across the white sand toward the shelter of the rock, paused to cock its head and look at me. A massive hornbill, disturbed by Un downstream, swished by, beating the air with its wings.

I was at a loss to know how Juan's "American Way" courting

should proceed. Instinctively I took Olan's hand, as she settled down beside me. For a few minutes we practiced the English vocabulary which Juan was teaching her, but the white lace ruffles against the ebony skin above her knees were too horribly distracting to permit communication in such awkward, halting language symbols.

Plucking at the ruffles, I asked her in my best Negrito, "Please give to me." Apparently Juan had not failed to give the proper instructions. Obligingly she pulled out the tucked-in end of the strip of bark cloth which served her for a skirt, and unwound it. It was surprisingly long and piled up around her like the coils of a snake. At last she stood up, and turning her back to me, loosened and slipped out of the betrothal panties, neatly folded them, and looking back over her shoulder, handed them to me. Then, stooping, she reached for the end of the bark-cloth skirt, which had fallen close to my shoulder. The fear that I was being watched by men from her group carrying poisoned spears, or that she would dart away at my slightest gesture, never to appear again, was swallowed up in the impulse to grasp that shining arm.

In a moment she was beside me, struggling, but now each of her lithe movements caressed me, even as she attempted to push away. No sound issued from her lips, and there was no anger in her wide eyes, only fear, fear so deep that I could see it extending back to infinity in the blackness of her dilated pupils, and feel it pounding into me from the rhythm in her breast. With it, through her entire body, spread the stiffness I had felt the night before, giving her muscles the consistency of marble beneath the softness of her skin. It robbed me of desire. I let her go.

Gradually I again became aware of the red in the sunset, the green in the trees, the curtains of moss above, and a spray of orchids which the slanting sunlight had discovered. Olan relaxed and pushed away from me, as though waking from sleep. I felt a tenderness toward her, the feeling I had had in childhood when I had imagined myself a knight in King Arthur's court. Her eyes opened.

"Un!" I shouted. "Come." I wondered if she would now see the stone house, which was my body, divided into two apartments—and in each a ghostly feminine occupant not on speaking terms with the other.

Un came splashing back up the river, a coil of her skirt filled with shellfish. She was grinning, and I felt sure she thought of me as a puppet whose strings were pulled by her spirit guide. She led us back to the encampment.

The songs and dances going on were a welcome relief from the afternoon. I went to bed early and slept well. Next morning Juan greeted me with his excited look, a look which I now knew announced some great step in the progress of the marriage project. "Glin has agreed to accept the silver flask and the cigarette case, the pearlhandled knife, and the pin with pearls, and the gold pen, for two hundred pesos of the bride price, and to come along with us until we leave the southern territory," he said triumphantly. "And Un has also agreed to come along with us as chaperone. We will only have to give her five of the silver pesos."

I had noticed that Un was already in possession of most of our bolt of cloth, and I wondered with some anxiety if both of us would end up as bloody sacrifices on the altar of Olan's beauty.

Still, the thought of having Glin's group pull out within the hour, taking Olan with them, was somehow intolerable. The price of keeping them with us was a matter of trinkets, and I handed them to Glin without hesitation.

A few days later Roberto, the old trader, appeared in the camp. There was a long conference between him, Glin, and Juan. When I inquired about it, Juan admitted that it had to do with the bride price. "After all," Juan explained, "I have been to school and lived in the Lowlands. I have guaranteed the rest of Olan's bride price in case you do not return. And Roberto, since my possessions are at his house—he has known me long—has guaranteed to pay the rest of the bride price if I do not return with the money or work it out in servitude."

I had to admit that Juan was a man of some importance. He was a thousand times more important among the Negritos than I was in my own native city. I could have nothing more to fear from Glin, since in his mind the bride price was now paid in full. So far as Juan was concerned, whether or not the marriage was consummated would now depend on the caprice of Olan, my success in courtship, the disposition of the strange Negrito groups through which we traveled, and the magic of the love songs and dances which Juan was now performing each night in my behalf around Olan's lean-to. She had agreed to marry Juan when he returned to the territory in order to complete the payment of the bride price—that I would default was evidently already an accepted fact. Apparently she had also agreed to allow herself to love me if I could win her love.

"Suppose Olan *does* decide to marry me?" I said, looking at Juan very straight. "How will you feel about it?"

"Even so, you will not return," he answered. "And when I went down to get Roberto, I was baptized a Christian, so now I can hold no ill will against you for the love you feel for Olan, or for the love she feels for you, my brother."

"But suppose there were a child," I said. I wanted to plumb him to the bottom, half from a desire to remain alive in the mountains, and half from curiosity about his ideas of Christian love.

"That would not matter to a Christian," he said with conviction. "When I told the old Filipino foreman who was my friend at one of the mills where I worked that some men were bragging about their affairs with his beautiful young wife—and I said I would shoot them with poisoned arrows for him—he said: 'My boy, the flowers grow in my lovely garden. I care not who plants the seed.'"

"Do you think that is better than the Negrito way?" I said.

Again he answered with conviction. "The murders and duels and blood feuds which love makes among the Negritos do not please me at all. That is why I wish to go to the god of love."

I had the feeling that Juan would find Christians who would disappoint him in this doctrine of loving one's enemies. But he would learn these limitations of Christian love soon enough, so I let the matter drop.

We spent the next month on the trail and in the camps of Negrito groups where those of our group had connections. Olan was a constant source of delight. On the march, Juan arranged that her place should be in front of mine. Putting my foot down precisely where my leader's foot had been was now not a burden, since each shift of Olan's weight and each change of posture resulted in a picture of such sheer beauty, balance, and rhythm that I wanted to save it forever.

When we worked now, she helped Juan with the testing, or watched us as she and Un prepared the food, or as she fed the campfire, or pounded out the cloth from the inner bark of saplings. In the evening she danced with the other women, and sang a song she had composed on the day's march. Gradually she became less afraid of me, and co-operated more freely with Un in the exciting game of frustrating the vigilance of her father in order to find out whether I could make her love me. She acted more like a princess than any royal lady my imagination had been able to construct in my childhood fantasies.

Before dawn on the morning we were to take leave of Glin and his party, she stole into my tent and lay with me for an hour under the mistlike folds of my mosquito net. Had Un's guide directed her to say good-by to me thus, or had Juan told her that it was the American Way? I did not know or care. For the first time since I had known her there were tears in her eyes and on her cheeks. I lay still and listened to the poem which she sang into my ear in a voice which was lower than a whisper yet seemed to have the volume of a pipe organ. I could not understand many of the words, and lay there half out of my senses, expecting her Negrito god, Tolandian, whom I had long ago accepted as my rival, to blast open the earth.

For once, her hands were not pushing me away as though they were the slaves of her father. For once, her heart was beating with a rhythm which was not protest. Her movements, in rhythm with her song, brought her body closer to my own. Even her feet and ankles, which I had never felt before except as they bumped or brushed against me in gestures of protest, frustration, or escape, were moving in rhythm, caressing the calf of my leg. I felt the weight of her knee against my waist.

I slipped drowsily into her rhythm. Then, quite suddenly, there was the old shudder, the stiffening in her body, and the wall between us. Things were as before, as they had always been.

I could not see her face as she rose to go, but I knew it was again filled with a dazed, wondering expression, as if she did not know what she was doing or where she was.

# NINE

# Nomads of Zambales

MY mind was almost numb when Juan and I took leave of the group and set off to the north. Although I felt relief, as though I were escaping from some force that had got completely out of my control, my legs were heavy on the soft trail. They seemed determined not to carry me in the direction I was headed. The third time I fell, landing face down on the trail, Juan suggested that I should have spent more evenings receiving treatment from Un and the other shamans.

"When your whole heart does not go with you on the trail, the demon of accidents and sickness finds a home inside you," he said. "Only the shamans can find the demons who pull you back, and tell them to work with one another and with you. You have been falling all morning like a man in the dark, and you are in danger. Do you wish to turn around and follow your feet?"

"Then my head would be going in the wrong direction," I said. "We Westerners are cursed by our plans, as you suffer from lack of them in your search for food. I must go on, even if my foot catches under every root."

The compassion and warmth in Juan's face helped me. Now that he had spoken of it, I did not fall so often.

By noon, however, I was possessed by the thought of going back, feeling that somewhere in the distant past I had seen not an Egyptian statue but Olan herself, and that I had failed her then and was failing her again now. Juan looked at me perplexed, aware that I was troubled. But my conviction that there was a rational explanation for everything soon came to my aid. The words and images I had heard and seen must have come from my childhood, and even if they had not, even if they were an echo from a more distant past, there was no reason why that echo should not recur in the future. I went on more easily than before. We traveled north, stopping for a few days at each encampment along the way.

In the next two months I saw two funerals. The burial is an entirely different affair from the funeral feast, and I changed my opinion about the Negritos' capacity for sorrow. At the feast I had reflected that they were hardly human, but when I saw them actually burying loved ones, I repented my judgment. I realized that the year or two which had elapsed between the death and the funeral feast accounted for the seeming callousness of the guests.

At a funeral the ceremonial weeping continues all night before the burial. The half-sung, half-wept laments are poems about the deceased, expressing sentiments of appreciation and longing with great simplicity. No humorous interludes are injected by the children, and the cumulative effect is overwhelming.

The first one we attended, a week after taking leave of our friends in Bataan, was for a little girl of three. By now I could understand most of the words of the short verses of the dirge. Each verse seemed to voice some sentiment, idea, thought, or protest which had been in the back of my own mind as I stumbled on the trail north from Bataan. Over and over the mourners sang the verses of the song. I joined in.

Each repetition took hold of a deeper layer of my past, until at last I was seeing again, and weeping for, the pets which had died in my childhood. In their work, in their healing, and in their sorrow, these people attained a degree of social unity and co-operation which I had never observed before. As I heard and repeated the words, I was carried along in a river of human action which made individual effort unnecessary and which took me back into the past like a canoe on a gentle stream. From this Negrito funeral, and from the healing trances I observed at the various encampments I was learning that the group can help the individual to feel and express emotions which are not otherwise available to him.

"*I knew I could not have you long.*" Was I hearing the song, or was this my mother crying at my brother's funeral, when I was two? These words were spoken in English. How had they gotten entangled in this Negrito song, and why did they release such pain and terror inside me, making me feel feverish, as though I were strangling under a load of blankets?

"*We did not mind it, little friend, when your crying awoke us in the night.*" The verse of the song brought back the picture of a Negrito father and mother I had seen a week before, walking around the fire, softly crooning to their distressed infant, whose illness they did not understand. They had asked the spirits of plants, the spirits of water, and the high god, to help them sustain the slender thread of life in the frail body, and had rocked it back and forth in the narrow confines of their tiny leaf house, supplying it warmth from their body against the pouring rain and the raw mountain air.

As the verses were endlessly repeated, they aroused echoes in me—voices which I could hear again out of my own forgotten past—releasing shock, pain, fear, and anguish, as though I had myself returned to infancy. I fell into the same trancelike state of oneness and agreement that I had experienced when I watched the moonlike face of Un as she spoke with her queer, dumb gestures of the mother spirit which was plaguing my life.

"*Before you were born, I loved you, little one. I knew you before you were born. Before you saw light, I knew of your gentle nature from your movements inside my womb. Before you were born, I heard your name.*"

It seemed probable that these ceremonies helped prepare the mind and personality of the Negritos for their journeys back to infancy and to the spirit cave, in agreement with the healing shamans.

Every detail of the burial is extremely important. The stick with which the corpse is measured to determine the length of the grave has to be broken and buried with the body. At the bottom of the grave a shelf must be dug out, and under it the body is placed, the head pointed toward the east. While the grave is being filled, the footprints of whoever tamps the earth must be carefully erased with a willow broom, to keep his soul from being imprisoned in the grave with that of the deceased. There are ceremonial washings for all who help to carry the body. Sacrifices of food must be left by the grave. Throughout the whole procedure, the Negritos speak to the departed spirit with advice, instructions, and magical commands, supplications, and prayers to Tolandian.

At the second burial, of the headman of a group, I watched a subtle change in the emotions of the mourners. Love turned to sorrow and sorrow became fear. With the closing of the grave, fear turned to hatred. The father who had loved and protected his family was gone, and a negative, destructive father had taken his place in their minds. He symbolized the fearful unknown, and his survivors would have to step carefully to avoid his wrath. They threw rocks at the grave as they backed away, threatening to harm the ghost if it should come near them. They did not look around, once they had turned their backs on the grave.

As we traveled along the mountain trails in search of Negrito bands not represented at our festival, we kept high enough to avoid the leeches, and yet stayed below the level of the fogs which usually shrouded the mountain peaks. The new bands we met did not like me at first, and I could feel no confidence in them. I read suspicion in their faces when I glanced up and caught them looking at me. The feeling made me miserable.

One day I discovered the trouble. Since leaving Olan, I had fallen into the habit of observing only the scaliness of the Negritos' diseased skin, the dirt on their faces, or their ugly scars and deformities, and I was repelled by the odor of some of them. They were conscious of this attitude. Earlier, I had had a friendly feeling, and they had responded. I realized that I must stop disapproving of these people. In this more northerly territory, if one person in a group was suspicious of me, none of the others would thaw out and co-operate. They were bound together by some mysterious force or sympathy.

I resolved to look for my own good motives, my own friendliness, and my own virtues in every Negrito I met. Stimulated by the fear that they would kill me if I fell short of my resolve, my efforts succeeded admirably. Soon I felt a warmth in their reaction and lost my suspicion of them.

From the Bataan peninsula we worked our way north along the western slopes of the Zambales range of mountains, and by the end of the second month we arrived at the northern border of the district above the farm school at Villiar. So far we had been guided from one encampment to another by friendly Negritos, but from here on north we would have to search for the camps unaided.

The Villiar natives had long been the traditional enemies of the more northerly groups and could not be persuaded to venture farther north. But as Juan did not speak with a Villiar accent he had no special reason to be afraid, and we went on without local guides. Just above Villiar we encountered a group whose members, although no larger in stature than the Negritos, were much less black than those of the other groups and looked like pygmy versions of the Malays. Their dreams and test behavior did not, however, differentiate them from the Negritos in any way that we could see.

On the afternoon of our third day of hiking north of Villiar, we met a young man on the trail. He disappeared as if by magic, but Juan assured me that he must be with a group, and that although the group would keep out of sight, they would watch us constantly until they decided whether to attack us or to let us go on undisturbed through their territory.

"The best thing we can do," he said, "is to make camp as soon as possible and put out some presents for them so they will know we are friendly and willing to pay for traveling through their territory. Then maybe we can get them to camp with us for a few days if they are not too short of food."

The glimpse I had caught of the small but strongly built young man was not reassuring. He had been so close that I had seen the dark, crusted poison on his arrow tips, the sharp points of his blackened teeth, and the long, powerful bow he held. Also, the back of his head had been shaved, so that his hairline was a well-defined arc extending from behind one ear over his skull to the other. As we walked along looking for a flat place in which to camp, I fancied I could see him peering at me from the depth of every shadow. Juan showed no agitation.

"A band is out hunting or a group is on the move," he said. "They always have a guard out front and one behind, so no one can surprise them. But that does not mean they won't be friendly. They have to find out if others are following us down the trail, and they won't show themselves until they have done some investigating and have looked us over carefully."

Before we had gone half a mile we found a clearing on a little spur and put down our packs to make camp. Juan placed some salt on a smooth rock beside the trail, just out of sight of our clearing, and we went ahead with our preparations for the night. In a half hour Juan returned to the rock. Although we had seen nothing of the Negritos and had heard no sound, the salt was gone. Juan put out some more. This time he sat down beside it and chanted a little song to an old Negrito tune he had learned from his mother in early childhood, improvising the verses as he went along. The song expressed the friendly purpose of our visit.

I remained in the clearing, where I could watch Juan. Suddenly, there was a rustle in the leaves. From both sides of the trail, gleaming black figures stole out of the foliage. In an instant Juan was surrounded by a half score of muscular little black men, alert and menacing. An old man with a thin, straggling beard and graying hair talked quietly to Juan for some time, periodically scratching his ribs with his left thumb. Scooping up the salt, Juan put some into the extended hands of the tribesmen. They all ate it greedily. After a few more minutes of talk, most of the Negritos disappeared up the trail, but the gray-haired man, whose name was Jabon, and a couple of his older companions came with Juan to talk to me.

"They will bring their camp up here for a day or two," said Juan. "Then if we wish to travel north, they will go to the end of their territory with us."

He told the old men about me and explained that the natives were supposed to shake hands with me, demonstrating how it was done. Each Negrito in turn extended his hand. The scaly bodies and the black stumped teeth were a strange contrast to the dignified demeanor of the old Negritos. Their expressions were grave but friendly. Juan fished out some tobacco and we all rolled cigarettes. By this time I was becoming quite adept at smoking with the lighted end in my mouth.

As we smoked, Juan jabbered away with them. Every now and then, they would look up at me with expressions of growing wonder. I often asked Juan what he told the Negritos about me, but all I could ever get out of him was: "Oh, just about our work and the blood brotherhood of all Christians." After awhile Jabon produced from his loincloth a pack of betel leaves, some lime made by burning snail shells, and a few betel nuts. Cutting one of the nuts open, he wrapped half of it in a leaf, sprinkled lime on it, added a few shreds of very crumpled, black, sweat-soaked tobacco, and handed it to me to chew. I was getting used to the ceremony by now and was acquiring a taste for the betel. When I first crunched it in my mouth, it was bitter. It had something of a coffee taste which was not particularly agreeable, but I was learning to relax as the numbness spread to my lips, gums, and tongue, and to permit the wave of relaxation to filter down through my entire body.

Jabon and his companions helped Juan to build a floor for my tent and started to construct their own shelters. Just before sunset the rest of the Negrito band arrived. I never ceased being startled by the quietness and rapidity with which these little people moved. One minute we were alone, and the next minute a village had grown up around us.

This band was quite large, as Negrito communities go. There were twelve men with families, five adolescent unmarried men, and eight male children. The females were less numerous—there were only the twelve wives, and four girls between the ages of seven and twelve. A couple of babies completed the group. Even though the sun was very low when the horde arrived, little well-made houses were erected and firewood was gathered before dark. The building of a Negrito camp always seemed miraculous.

To light the fire, one of the old men drove stakes into the ground, slipped a piece of bamboo between them, cut a little niche in the upper edge of the bamboo, fitted another shaft of bamboo into it, and sawed vigorously for a few moments, while dropping cotton-like fuzz into the point of friction. Soon little wisps of smoke issued from the pile of fuzz collecting on the ground. The old man blew on it and it burst into flames. Dexterously, he picked it up, wrapped it in a dry leaf, and blew on it again, tucking it under the woodpile when it started to blaze. Usually one of the old women carried a glowing ember along the trail, but this day, in the excitement of hearing about our arrival, she had lost it somewhere and the fire had to be rekindled.

When the evening meal had been eaten, we sat around in the firelight. The alert, tense expressions on the grimy faces of the Negritos relaxed. Smiles began to twist the corners of their thick lips. The Negritos smile and laugh a lot around the campfire, but I always felt some discomfort at the sharpness of their chipped teeth.

In Bataan I had seen chipped teeth only among the older men. Juan explained that the custom was dying out. It had been the practice to chip the teeth when a boy reached the end of adolescence, after the scarification was completed, and the Negritos of northern Zambales still did so. All the upper front incisors were chipped. A block of wood was held behind the tooth of the initiate, and the point of a jungle knife was held diagonally against a corner of the tooth. It was then struck a sharp blow with a rock. It was a painful process, but the initiate was not allowed to cry out. If he did, he had to wait another year to receive this badge of adulthood. They said no one could be a good leader if he cringed at pain, and one could not be trusted unless he was willing to suffer to become one of the group.

The betel chewing colors the teeth of the young men a shocking blood red. The teeth of the old men, blackened by a longer contact with the betel, are both ludicrous and horrifying.

That first night, as I tried to sleep with my back to the fire, I pictured one of those poisonous arrows burying itself between my shoulders, and wondered, listening to the wind and the jungle sounds, if this crazy image was a premonition or a fear. At last I decided it offered no protection, whichever it was. Sometime in the future, the moment of death would arrive. I could bring that moment down to the present in fantasy, but one could use the imagination to see better things than death.

I went to sleep.

In the vicinity of the camp were some ant colonies. I had never thought of ants as anything but pests. When Juan told me that the Negritos were hunting them, I was mystified. What did the Negritos own that could be harmed by ants? To my surprise, I learned that the ants were not attacking the Negritos or their property. The Negritos were eating the ants.

Old Jabon, the head shaman of the group, sat down by an ant hole and scratched it gently. When the big honey ant looked out, he picked him up by the head and motioned for me to bite off his abdomen. The taste was sweet; it was like eating berries the size of navy beans. Strangely enough, the idea of biting the ants instead of being bitten by them appealed to me.

By the end of the afternoon I felt as satisfied as if I had eaten chocolate. Learning to eat the ants was an interesting game. I became quite expert before we left the camp, but sometimes I failed to watch for those returning to the hole and was nipped from the rear.

That morning one of the young men had reported a dream of seeing me speared by a tree demon. I had paid little attention to the warning, but as the pain from the first ant bite shot up into my leg, I suddenly remembered the tree demon with an overwhelming pang of fear. The Negritos were alarmed by the howl I emitted. Then, seeing what had happened, they were much amused. They are very sensitive to creeping things, and were amazed that an ant could crawl up my leg without my being aware of it.

As food was scarce at our camping place, the old men decided that we would move on early the next morning to a fruit grove, a day's journey further north. Reluctantly, I left the warmth of my bedroll for the raw, cold air. But for the dawn smell of the earth and the imbecile chatter of the monkeys, I would not have believed it was daybreak as we shouldered our packs and were assigned our places among the Negritos.

A thick mountain fog saturated the air, converting the world into a hollow, leaden sphere through which trees and rocks passed silently as we marched along the narrow, slippery trail. Gradually, the sphere grew larger, turned from lead to slate, and then became a sickly gray, while the grim little black people bobbed noiselessly up and down, and the dripping moss-covered wall of the jungle loomed in front of us and disappeared behind. To avoid revealing the presence of the group to possible enemies or frightening away the game, no one in the marching line spoke a word.

The clammy fog condensing on my face was like a death mask. Suddenly, through the fog on the descending side of the trail, I saw a towering black rock. Those ahead had stopped and were facing its gleaming, pitted surface in a semicircle, mumbling in hushed, unnatural voices.

"There is a demon in the rock," said Juan. "He owns the canyon ahead of us, and we must join the others in giving him some tobacco before it will be safe to go over the portion of the trail he guards."

Glancing up, I could see the cliff above, from which the rock giant beside us, and many others like him, had come tumbling down the steep hill, carving swaths through the heavy jungle foliage. Before we had paused three minutes, I was shivering in the raw mountain air. A wind howled down the canyon and now the fog was filled with tiny stinging drops of moisture. How could human beings live in the midst of such desolation!

"We must give some tobacco for the spirit," said Juan.

I nodded my assent, and the line moved on. Again the natives were immersed in a silence more disturbing than the gibberish they had spoken to the rock and the freezing discomfort of the stinging rain.

Since the pause at the rock, all the sympathy I had ever felt for these people had begun turning into resentment. Why had the old graybeard Jabon changed his place to walk next to me, making Juan step back behind him? Why had he been dogging my footsteps since we left the rock?

For awhile we climbed, and as we topped a little ridge and started down, the man ahead of me made a gesture toward a tree to the left of the trail. It was slippery underfoot, and I reached for the tree to steady myself. As I did so, the shadowy figure behind me shouted something almost in my ear. Then I felt his hand in my hair jerking me backward. My feet flew from under me and I sat down with a thud.

I sat there blinking stupidly. My forebodings of evil were groundless. Now Juan was standing by my side, pointing excitedly to a large caterpillar on the tree. The old man scraped it onto his knife blade and showed me some fine black spines concealed by the greenish-yellow hairs which covered its body.

"The tree demon was about to stab you with the caterpillar spines," said Juan. "When they penetrate your flesh, they break off and release a poison. If you had leaned against that tree, you would have lost your hand, if not your life."

Again the whole band assembled on the trail. This time a ceremony was directed toward the tree demon.

"Old Jabon said there was danger ahead for you on the trail," said Juan. "That's why he insisted on walking behind you, but I thought he was afraid of the falling rocks. Now he has admitted that his familiar spirit was warning him of the tree demon."

Jabon then went into a trance to find out in what way I had offended the spirit of the tree, and how I could make restitution. Speaking with a different voice, which all believed to be that of his spirit guide, Jabon told us that I was possessed of an unfriendly witch spirit, white as a cloud, which did not like me to leave my native land. This spirit hated strange people and strange places, and would get me into trouble wherever I went, unless it was either drawn out of me or forced to give up its opposition and work for me. Juan was requested to put a red cloth around my neck, which Jabon, still in his trance, pulled back and forth awhile, so the spirit, who liked red, would take hold of it. Then he let go of one end and snapped it from around my neck to dislodge the spirit. I was also asked to pay Jabon a handful of salt, a few grains of which he deposited on the tree trunk. I wondered if Juan had told the old man about Un's diagnosis, as this one sounded much the same as hers. He denied having discussed it with anyone. I willingly paid the fine.

As we walked on, the silence was no longer oppressive. The fog which had shut me in before now formed a silver web tying together the rocks, the feathery mountains, the Negritos, and the past and the future. Later, as we crossed the prostrate trunk of a great tree which spanned a torrent, my depression of the morning was entirely gone. In its place I had a warm feeling for the lady spirit of the river, whom I fancied I could see in the amber foam below. In the early morning my mood had not been that of giving. I had bought the rock for the shred of tobacco I had laid by its side, rather than presenting the tobacco as a gift, and I had had the feeling that the rock was mine to hate.

The Negritos had left the rock behind as their friend and ally. Their fear had changed to confidence through the sacrificial expression, mine to disgust and hostility. I had been crediting the rock and the Negritos with my ugly mood, rather than with my good motives and good will.

But now the passage along the trail no longer suggested a grim march of prisoners. I was walking with them, stepping carefully, so that no twig would snap to warn away the mouse deer as he drummed proudly for his mate on a hollow log.

In late afternoon the young man who walked ahead of the line bagged a deer. His pride as he sat carelessly beside the carcass waiting for us to approach was mine. His only reward for the kill was a feeling that he had been important to the group, but his expression as he minimized his deed, which was much praised, and later as he watched them eating the meat, refusing the better cuts himself, showed that his reward was great.

In America, I had never felt love for the butcher, the farmer, or the shoemaker because of the services he performed for me. Now, as I longed for a glimpse of Olan, as I opened and shut the hand which I would have lost but for the vigilance of old Jabon, as I tasted the roasted meat which was mine through the skill, patience, and generosity of the frizzy-haired, black young man before me, I repented of the bored, depressed, and shallow feelings I had had so often in my own land.

The next morning, I watched fearfully while the children scrambled high up the durian trees to bring down the odd-smelling yellow fruit. I was astonished at the number of opportunities afforded each member of a Negrito group to feel important. The wisdom of the old men and women, and their knowledge of jungle lore, the strength and courage of the young men, the bubbling activity of the children, all found expression in the daily routine. The children were not scolded for their recklessness, and no one suggested that they would fall and break their necks. Indeed, such a suggestion was considered black magic. Surprisingly, nobody did hurt himself, though hairbreadth escapes were frequent. The sense of rivalry was keen among them, yet their only reward was the knowledge that everyone could eat more because of their personal efforts and bravery.

The dreams I collected on the morning of the second day at the orchard were nearly all of climbing or falling. It was obvious that the fear of the actual situation, which the children resisted while they were in the trees, was expressed in their dreams at night.

And it was not only the children who had these terror dreams of falling. Two of the old men also dreamed that the climbers had fallen.

The fruit diet was not quite as monotonous as the honey-ant diet had been, because we were able to obtain fruit bats. A number of them hung head down in the trees. If they were too high to be reached by a rattan loop at the end of a long pole, the Negritos shot them with their arrows. The fruit bat, after cleaning, is about the size of a small cat, and the meat is delicious. Juan and I always added a handful of rice to the Negrito diet; the greens, fruit, and meat left me hungry no matter how much I ate. After five days at this camp, all the fruit bats had been killed or frightened away, and we moved on.

In the late afternoon of the next day, Igun, the young man who had speared the deer a few days before, had a curious accident. On a level section in the trail, over which even the children traveled without difficulty, he plunged his foot under a protruding root, wrenching his ankle. I was astonished at the incident, since he and all the other Negritos had the tendency, which I had seen in Juan that first afternoon in the saloon, to lift their feet high even when there was nothing to step over. The next morning, when we called at his lean-to to make our daily poll of the dreams of the night before, Igun was talking to a group of young men about a dream which, he said, was removing the pain from his sprained ankle.

The root over which Igun had stumbled the previous afternoon had appeared to him in the dream as a gnarled, bent old man, and announced that he would pursue Igun forever, if he, Igun, did not retrace his steps the following day and leave a tobacco leaf on the root spirit's humped back, which stuck out of the ground.

I went along with Igun and his friends to observe what happened at the root as a result of his dream. He put a few shreds of tobacco on the root, apologized for his clumsiness in kicking it, and invited us all to join in the sacrifice. We left tobacco along with his, and set off on the double to catch up with the group. I felt that the effort of keeping up with them as they hurried back was a small enough price to pay for what I had seen. Here was the birth of a ceremony, an institution, from the creative genius of a human being. To me it was like a seed falling into the soil of the teeming social jungle. As long as Igun lived, each time he chanced to pass that way, he would leave some little token by the root, along with a little prayer of apology and good will. If his son were with him when he left the tobacco leaf, the son would inherit the ceremony, and his son's son. The sociability which the incident occasioned when his friends went back with him to the root gave the spot a special significance for them as well.

As we hurried along the trail to catch up with the group, Igun appeared to be talking to himself. Later I learned that he was making up a song, both words and music, to the spirit of the crooked root. He told Juan that the song had completely taken the pain of the sprained ankle from his mind. He said the spirit of the root was teaching the song to him as he walked. The spirit would be his friend and the friend of his children and his children's children, so long as they sang this song and paid the tribute. The root spirit would help him to walk more skillfully through the jungle, and to avoid offending other roots by kicking them. I had no doubt that the memory of the root, which was now in his mind as an image and a pain, and the creative process which had been set up as a distraction to the pain, would certainly protect him from stubbing his toe in the future.

I found that he had had a number of accidents, all of which had led to songs and dances. Although the Negritos did not have the word for it, he was an artist. Some inner creative demon seemed bent on punishing him, if he did not constantly create something or other. In the West, we would call him "accident prone," but his Negrito culture had helped him to utilize the offending root image in accordance with an inner need for emotional release and expression. His song gave pleasure to the whole group and won for Igun applause and recognition. I had never heard more gripping music than the gypsylike tune which he produced. And the strange conflicting emotions which the grumpy old root character revealed in the dance which Igun performed that night made it as interesting as any I had ever seen.

After this ceremony, I had the feeling that the Negritos forgot with a vengeance, as though they were saying, "My inner self is so complicated that I will keep the outside world simple. Since creation is as necessary to the life of the soul as food is to the life of the body, I will not record my creation and take away the audience from my fellows less gifted than myself, or from myself in the future."

Once I had discovered some reason for the Negrito ceremonies, and seen how they enriched, enlivened, and socialized the long drab hours of the food quest, I found it possible to think of them with pleasure, and I felt myself entering into them more and more as the days went by.

Another two days' march brought us to a little plateau where there were fields of plants which looked like parsnips. These tubers must be treated to remove the poison they contain when fresh. The Negritos dig a pit and store the tubers away to sour for a few months. When they are ready for eating, they taste like a combination of sauerkraut and limburger cheese.

By now we were getting well on toward the northern border of the territory in which this group ranged. We had tested and retested everyone. In both the Porteus Maze and the Goodenough Draw-A-Man tests, the scores ceased improving at the seven-year age level. The only tests that could be used with the adults were the Sympathy Test and the Metal Maze. Like the Bataan Negritos, they did about as well in these as any of the other groups I had tested.

Nor did the children's dreams differentiate them from the other groups. They also drew splendid pictures of animals, trees, and flowers, which showed that the Negritos' ability to analyze and synthesize symbolically in drawing was not inferior to that of other races, although their conventional way of drawing a man prevented them from getting a score of more than seven years on the Draw-A-Man Test.

In the agreement trance state, which I induced when I gave them medicines, these men, who had had little or no contact with Western civilization, were not noticeably different from their fellows on the Bataan peninsula. Neither did the Emotional Response and Progressive Fantasy tests set them apart from the others—until adolescence. At this point the poor memories of the Negritos became evident. The incidents of fear, shame, pain, humor, and the like which were mentioned by those taking the Emotional Response Test were usually chosen from the very recent past. The answers showed no consistent trends to differentiate them from the children or, except for the recency of the incidents, from the racial groups of Hawaii.

In the Progressive Fantasy Test the responses of the older persons did not tend to include larger and larger groups of national and international importance, as they did in Hawaii. This was not surprising. As far as this little band was concerned, there was no human world outside which threatened to influence them or which they desired to influence. They would bargain for wives with the bordering hordes and would die fighting to defend their territory. The best thing that could happen was to live long and find favor with the spirits which could give good luck, health, food, and a child or two who would live and find favor with the spirits. A man might wish to become a great father, a great healer, a great hunter, a great storyteller. The worst things that could happen were illness, hunger, uncontrollable rage, accidents, and a dearth of females in the neighboring groups, which would make it difficult to obtain a wife.

Unlike their waking accounts, the accounts which they gave in the agreement trance of the worst things that had happened, did not consist entirely of recent memories. In the trance state they showed ability to return, in memory, to pain incidents of childhood and infancy, and to the spirit cave, as they did in the healing ceremonies.

During my last evening with this band, I asked old Jabon to cure the cyst on my arm, which Un's infant guide had described as a feminine spirit eating my vitals. I had come to know him as a shaman and respected his wisdom and strength. Again I lied about the cyst, saying that it was painful and distressed me greatly. But I did not fool the Negrito patriarch. When he went into his trance, the spirit of the wild pig with which he was possessed informed me that I should not have the cyst removed, that I did not really wish it removed.

"That cyst is your luck," said the old man. "I will not prescribe any medicine to remove it from your arm. You do not really wish it to be removed. You are not sincere in the request which you have made."

None of the Negritos resented the incident. I could not quite decide if they felt that I was trying to test their medicine, or if they thought that I was mistaken about the cyst. But whatever they thought of me, they accepted the old man's diagnosis and were much amused by it.

That night, just after the ceremony, an airplane flew over the mountains, close enough for us to hear its roar and see its lights. It was going north, perhaps on its way to Hong Kong from Manila. The next morning, as a last request, the old men of the band asked us for rice to put out as a sacrifice to the great birds which of late had been flying over their territory. We gave it to them and performed a little ceremony which, we assured them, would make the bird-men their friends in case any of them ever fell into their territory. They were more grateful for this bit of magic than for anything else we had done for them. When we departed, I felt that I was leaving behind some of the best friends I had in the world.

Two days later we came across another campsite, but the Negritos apparently had seen us coming and had left hurriedly. In spite of the salt and tobacco we put out, none of them returned. The next day we could find no sign of their campfire, and there was nothing to indicate in what direction they had fled.

After hiking another two and a half days, we met a small group on the trail, and for one night we camped with them. One of the

## NOMADS OF ZAMBALES

old men had fought in a war against the Lowlanders years before. Nothing we could do or say had any effect on his unfriendly attitude. They accepted our salt and tobacco and gave us some food in exchange, but we were not welcome to stay more than one night with them. One of the young men went with us for some distance to carry my pack, but Juan felt that he was only interested in keeping track of us until we were out of their territory.

# TEN

# Typhoon

THE next group we found—a week later—was larger, and the old men were friendly. They had had some contact with Filipino traders, and had heard of white men. They were co-operative from the start, both in taking our tests and in telling Juan and myself about their dreams and their ideas on the origin and structure of the universe. Through their ceremonies the Negritos were constantly encouraged to go back to the beginning of life, to the incidents which had accumulated as indigestible fragments of experiences so painful that their images were enemies and strangers when discovered again.

As the shamans became acquainted in their trances with these strangers and enemies, and destroyed them or converted them into allies, the trail of the trances led further and further back, until at last they found Tolandian, the Creator.

During the many hours of each month which the Negrito shaman spent in trance, he searched for answers to the mysterious problems of man's illness; he was always looking deeper and deeper into himself for these answers, until at last he appeared to see back to the beginning of himself, to the moment of creation or conception.

We had collected enough Negrito dreams now to confirm definitely the trend I had noted earlier among the people who had assembled for the funeral feast of Ogong's father. Everywhere the dreams of the shamans and aspiring shamans proved more complicated than those of other people. They had features in them which were not found in the dreams of children and adults who had not received shamanistic treatment. This indicated strongly that a deep personality reorganization took place as the patient worked with the shaman in the agreement trance, and that this type of relationship with the shaman encouraged, strengthened, and directed the natural inner will to health, so that even while the patient was asleep it went on working toward the health of the individual and reorganizing inner patterns.

It did not seem strange that man's mind should work while he was asleep, as well as while he was awake, to cure his illness. It did seem strange, however, that the shamanistic treatment should enable the patient to dream more extensively and more effectively than people who were not receiving such treatment, and that the shaman's image and the characters he worked with in the co-operative trance should go on working for the patient in his dreams.

In this camp we met Gloc, a young adult who was in the process of becoming a medicine man. He had been periodically ill for years, and each time his illness returned the older men worked patiently to help him gain mastery over the spirit of the fountain which attacked him. The shamans agreed that Gloc must have made many bargains with this spirit before he emerged from the spirit cave into the world.

They said that all shamans went through similar periods of struggle with their familiar spirits. These spirits were sometimes masculine, sometimes feminine, and sometimes monsters having both masculine and feminine characteristics. Sometimes the struggle lasted for years. With others it was over quickly. Some spirits were very powerful; others were not much help to the individual or the community, even after they had been mastered. A shaman might become famous in his group and even be sent for by friendly groups, if his advice proved wise and if his medicine made people well. They explained the difficulty in controlling the spirit of the fountain on the basis of the fact that it was feminine and all women are fickle.

As we talked to the old shamans I noticed that everyone was more animated than usual. Even the sky seemed different. The night was clear, yet there were few stars. Those which did appear had a peculiar luster, an amber sheen which I had never seen before. I found myself wondering if Gloc's amber-colored lady of the fountain were responsible. After my experience with Un's infant guide I could believe almost anything.

The air had substance, some strange nutriment which fed the imagination. Before I knew it, the sun was thrusting its glowing rim over the eastern ridge of the canyon. As it swung clear of the treetops, I had the frightening feeling that I had never seen it before: something was masquerading as the sun. It was not shedding its customary light, and seemed only a showpiece, a glowing artificial sun from some stage setting. Everyone noticed the strangeness of this sunrise, and stood around as though waiting for the scene to change. At any moment I expected Gloc's spirit of the amber fountain to step out from behind the sun and sing us her spirit song, or to throw it back down behind the horizon.

The men did not go looking for food, as was their habit in the morning. The women left their digging sticks lying unused beneath the little banana-leaf shelters. The children took no interest in their usual games. Everyone talked in voices which became more and more subdued, until they were whispers. Something was most certainly about to happen.

As the day passed, the wind grew stronger. Shortly after noon, I put away my testing materials. The Negritos were only giving half a mind to the problems. Juan wrapped up our packs in the tarpaulin and stored them in the hollow of a big tree. He said that we were in for wind and much rain. The Negritos strengthened their leaf shelters and brought dry sticks for the fire. The sun looked more and more like a theatrical prop.

The old men formed a dancing circle and began to sing, one following another. We sat down beside them to record the words —part prayer, part song, part lament—which they were singing. The suspense of the morning turned to terror as the wind became a gale, filling the air with leaves and twigs, and our ears with the sound of crashing limbs against a background of hoarse, unearthly groans. The men tore handfuls of hair from their scalps and threw them on a burning log, the only part of the fire which had not been blown away.

One after another, the little leaf shelters were picked up and carried into the air like toy balloons. The Negritos went for refuge to the cleft of a huge rock which stood nearby.

Before twilight the sky resembled an inverted copper bowl, and even in the sheltering cleft of the rock the wind blew the breath from my body. Talking was impossible. There was a blinding flare of lightning, and the Negrito universe exploded. Then came the rain, a merciless torrent of water so thick that it seemed to run about in the air instead of falling. The Negritos congealed into knots of human flesh, and found their voices. The prayers which they had been mumbling in the afternoon were now poured out as screams flowing up from their stomachs and their hearts, convulsing their bodies with violence. With a grim expression, Juan explained to me that a typhoon was approaching and that we were probably in the very center of its path.

"One can never tell what these people will do when they become afraid," he muttered. "If this thunder goes on for long, God knows what will happen to us. The Negritos believe the thunder is the angry voice of Tolandian condemning them. Last night the old men told us many of their secrets and they may blame us for this thunder."

Some forty of us were huddled in that narrow cleft. With the downpour of rain had come blackness as deep as midnight. For the first time since I had been with them, the natives had to face the night without the friendly glow of the blazing fires which formed the nucleus of their camp.

The hoarse mutter of the water, the scream of crashing timbers, and the earsplitting bombardment of thunder gave evidence of danger from every side. If the brook that ran alongside the rock grew full enough, it would wash us from our shelter. If any of the trees being mangled before our eyes fell into the cleft, we would be ground to jelly. One flash from that yellow-tongued lightning, descending from every quarter, might burn us to cinders.

Several members of the group, separated from the others by the taboo of the menstrual period, the incest taboo, or the father-in-law taboo, sat, like lepers, almost entirely outside the protection of the rock. I was trembling. One of the Negritos near me leaped into the air with a scream that penetrated the wall of sound thrown up by the typhoon. In his right hand he clasped his jungle knife, the sharp edge gleaming in the lightning almost directly above me. Small tongues of flame played on its glittering point with a dry, crackling sound. "This is the end," I thought. My body shriveled, as though attempting to shrink out of sight into the tiny crevices of the rough surface on which I was lying.

"It is enough, Old Man," the Negrito roared in a voice which was huge for his small figure. The lightning illuminated the cords and veins on his neck, giving him the distorted perspective of a photographic image. "I admit my guilt. I have blasphemed your name by saying 'Bee' when I was angry. I have insulted your earthworms and laughed at your monkeys. I am sorry for my sins. Please accept my sacrifice."

I could only shrink further into the crevices of the rock and wait for the knife, as though hypnotized by the tiny flames which played on its descending point. But I was not the sacrifice the Negrito had in mind. The knife described an arc above me as he bent over, and found its way to the inner surface of his own thigh, cutting a gash in the skin. He caught the blood in his cupped hands. Some drops spattered upon me as he leaped to the edge of the cleft. The warm drops seemed to burn into my skin like coals. Illuminated there in the flares of lightning, leaning hard against the wind, he threw his hands skyward. The rain washed the blood from his hands and arms, and from the wound in his thigh.

Before the storm subsided, I saw others make the blood sacrifice to the angry god of thunder. Each time a Negrito bounded out into the rain, my own blood bounded to my forehead, neck, and cheeks. Each time I felt a sting of shame that I should be so frightened and horrified by the performance. Toward morning the incessant pounding of the thunder became more and more like the rhythm of a drum.

As the storm abated, I inquired of Juan if he had ever seen the blood sacrifice before, and he said that he had not. We inquired about it of the old men. It had been performed at a previous storm many years before. They said they used it when they could not burn the hair sacrifice because rain had put the fire out. They did not know whether other bands of the Zambales also practiced it, or whether it was an invention of their own group.

The second morning after the typhoon I awoke from fitful sleep to find my body covered with welts. I itched all over. Wherever

I scratched a new welt appeared. Juan looked very grave as he examined them.

"You have sopot-sopot," he said. "You must slap the welts when they itch. If you scratch them, you will die."

I spent the day slapping myself. The sting felt soothing, but at night I often awoke to find I had been scratching in my sleep. Before noon I had so many chafed areas that I was beginning to run a temperature. Juan poured alcohol on me at intervals, and fanned me so the evaporation would lower my temperature. I got some sleep, but our alcohol was exhausted in one night. The slightest skin abrasion is dangerous in the tropics. The warm, moist atmosphere incubates germs and fungi with great rapidity.

Juan insisted we must find medical treatment at once. We were only a few days' journey from the main road, where we could catch a bus to the city of Bangued, capital of the mountain province of Abra. Juan had a friend there who would be able to find a place for us, and we could obtain medicine from the district health officer. We decided to leave the next morning.

Two young Negritos went along with us to carry my pack and show us the trail. Three days of hiking brought us to a Filipino trading station near the barrio of Mangatarem, on the main road, where we caught the evening bus to Bangued.

# ELEVEN

# The Sopot-Sopot Demon

WHEN we arrived, Juan looked up his friend's family. He had agreed to stay with me a month without further salary. In fact, he was so anxious to visit his friend that he suggested paying half the expenses if necessary. Juan's friend was not at home, but his sister volunteered to help us find a lodging, and led us to a two-story house which she said was for rent. I had already spent half my money and explained that I could not possibly rent such a big place, but the girl insisted that we talk to the woman who owned it.

The bottom floor was occupied by some chickens, a water buffalo, a lamb, and a couple of mangy dogs. We threaded our way through the livestock and called out at the foot of the stairway in the center of the house. Three young women, all in their teens, appeared. They were friends of our guide. One of them fetched her mother from a neighbor's house. We explained that I had sopot-sopot but not much money.

The father of the family had died a year or two before and the widowed mother was in desperate circumstances. She wanted thirty-five pesos a month for her house, but if we could not pay more, she was prepared to rent us the top half for fifteen. Sopot-sopot was a dangerous disease and she would not allow me to leave and go back into the mountains. I felt very embarrassed at accepting the rental of the house for so small a sum, and suggested that I could live in the bottom half quite well, but that was not agreeable.

We were installed in the house. The landlady, Mrs. Salvador, with her three daughters, Conscientious, Conception, and Candid, moved down to the ground floor. She asked us, please, not to mention how much we were paying for the house, and explained that people would not accept us socially if they knew of my financial difficulties.

The next day Juan and I went down to the high school with the three girls. The student body was composed of a great variety of the groups. A few of the students had Negrito blood. There were a good number of Igorots, together with a few Bontocs and some members of other groups from higher up in the mountains. The teachers were quite willing to excuse their pupils from class so they could take the mental tests and were glad to co-operate in my collection of dreams. Before the day was over, the testing program was well under way.

Three days later the doctor arrived in town, and he shook his head gravely at the condition of my skin. He had known people to die from erysipelas or other skin infections resulting from sopot-sopot, and was not nearly so confident as Juan had been that his medicines would cure the condition. I must be tied, spread-eagle fashion, in bed at night, he said, so I would not further irritate my skin by scratching in my sleep. He left ointments of various sorts with which I was to be rubbed from head to foot. He prepared various drugs which he hoped might restore my chemical balance. Leaving me a supply of medicine, he promised to return in two weeks to see how I was progressing.

In the daytime we went on with the testing, and I followed the prescribed course of treatment. The chafed areas cleared up, but each day I grew weaker and more nervous, and my skin became increasingly sensitive. Sleep was almost impossible.

The doctor changed his prescription on his second visit. As he was leaving, he said, "It is hard to tell where nervousness leaves off and chemistry begins. If you have not recovered in two more weeks, I will have to take you to the General Hospital in Manila. Perhaps they can do something for you down there."

On his first visit, he had suggested that the trouble might have arisen from my diet, but since then Juan and Mrs. Salvador and all her friends had been co-operating to supply the diet he had recommended, and it had not helped.

As the days wore on and my condition became steadily worse, it was obvious that something drastic would have to be done. Everyone in the village suggested some kind of medicine, food, or charm. One morning my landlady appeared with a determined look.

"All night long you were moaning and crying out in your sleep," she said. "For three weeks now you have become worse every day. Every night you struggle harder and cry out more often. Every day you become weaker and more pale. Medicine can't help you. We have all suspected that. Food can't help you. You are possessed of a devil, and unless you receive supernatural aid, you will die. We have seen the sopot-sopot devil kill many people. We knew the doctor could not help you, and we have been praying for you in the church. The saints would like to help you, but they have not lived long in the Philippines. We have burned many candles for you before the saints, and they would have helped you before now if they could.

"You are possessed of the sopot-sopot devil and to cure you we must commit the great sin of asking the help of people who have traffic with this devil. My son had sopot-sopot and the saints could not cure him either, but a native woman was able to help him when everything else had failed. I have sent word to the witch doctor who can coax the sopot devil out of your body into her own, but she is very old. She lives in the nearby village of Bokai and is so famous that she will not come unless I go after her and pay her the fee in advance. You must give me ten pesos so I can bring her to treat you. It is your only chance. Already you look like a ghost."

I looked at her in bewilderment. A protest formed in my mind, but I never voiced it. It would be an opportunity to observe some of the ancient magic.

I gave her the fee, and Juan accompanied her to the neighboring village to bring back the magical paraphernalia. He returned late that night laden with a curious assortment of medicines and equipment. I looked at them with misgiving. There were herbs, roots, leaves, brightly colored berries, the barks of various trees, a huge clay pot and a big stone bowl, bones and bits of hide and feathers, and a lot of dried-up odds and ends which I could not identify.

Juan, having been instructed most carefully by the old witch doctor, chopped up the berries, herbs, and roots, and put them in the pot. Two gallons of water were added, filling it to the brim. Juan built a fire and set the concoction on the coals to boil.

Toward morning I contrived to sleep with the aid of pills left by the doctor. When I opened my eyes, I felt as though I were still in a dream. Juan was bending over me, undoing the straps from my arms and legs. In the middle of the floor, under a big hardwood chair, was the stone bowl, full of glowing coals. Leaning over it, wielding a dirty feather fan and muttering incantations, was an incredibly old woman, whose face, under stringy gray hair, was a mass of wrinkles.

The next thing I saw was a long, glittering knife which lay on the floor by the woman's side. The handle was of water-buffalo horn, carved in the shape of a distorted human body. The edge had been freshly whetted to razor sharpness. On the other side of the woman was a pile of folded blankets, and in front of the chair sat the huge pot.

Still half awake, I was escorted to the chair. Hot from the radiation of the jar of coals beneath it, the seat burned me slightly. I protested weakly at the prospect of being broiled alive. But the old woman had instructed all her assistants well, and the family and neighbors obeyed her orders briskly.

Layer after layer of blankets was tightly swathed around me and the brazier of coals under the chair, until only my face was left uncovered. The jar was moved close to the chair and Juan thrust a reed into my gaping mouth. "Drink," he said.

I sucked up a mouthful of the scalding liquid. It tasted like the essence of gall. I coughed, and the greenish fluid trickled over my chin.

"You must drink," said Juan pleadingly. "You must drink all the water from the pot. Until you have done so, the ceremony cannot be completed. The sopot devil hates the taste of those plants above everything else on earth, and he will never leave you until he fears their juices are drowning him." I took another pull at the reed and decided that I fully shared the sopot devil's opinion of the beverage.

As I started to swallow, an old man, whom I had not previously noticed, began to beat out a slow, odd rhythm on a drum made from a hollow log covered with snakeskin. The old woman was now sitting cross-legged beside the pot in front of me, mumbling. She thumbed the edge of a long knife, which she kept showing to me. Suddenly, my stomach rebelled and I struggled to keep it from spewing up the bitter liquid I was drinking. The old woman screamed and leaped into the air, wildly swinging the knife so close that it fanned my face as it passed, chilling me from head to foot. Again she shouted and swung the knife at me, and I felt its breeze on the other cheek. Desperately, I appealed to Juan, but he was deaf to all voices except hers and was watching the knife like one hypnotized.

Once more the reed was thrust into my mouth. Now the danger of being roasted or poisoned was not so immediate as the threat of that glittering bolo. Again I began to drink, and each time nausea gripped my stomach, one glance from the knife to the crazy, determined eyes of the old woman cleared it up like magic. Whenever she screamed at me I felt the perspiration start from every pore. Soon it dripped from my forehead and ran down my legs and arms, feeling like a procession of ants. I noticed a tiny stream of it flowing out from my feet across the floor and through the corner of the doorlike Spanish window.

The old hag began to walk around the chair, mumbling to the rhythm of the drum. Each time she passed in front of me she shook the knife in my face and screamed. I could not tell what she was saying, but the fanatical look in her eyes convinced me that my head would be lopped off if I stopped drinking for an instant. Juan came over and peered into the jug.

"It is going down," he assured me. "She has commanded the sopot demon to stop squeezing your stomach. He won't be able to make you vomit again."

"The woman is mad," I concluded. "She has forgotten me entirely and thinks only of the demon. She would probably think nothing of killing me to release me from it."

I went on gulping. It was a bit easier to swallow now. My sense of taste was deadened and I was learning to drink to the rhythm of the drum.

"Half the liquid is gone," said Juan at last. "You will soon be well."

I was certain that I would soon be dead. I was drinking automatically. The mumbling of the old woman had grown into a song, and that song, combined with the rhythm of the drum, had taken hold of my throat. Each time she passed before me, my eyes fastened on the knife. No longer was she staggering as though she were a hundred years old. Instead, her bare feet were taking hold of the smooth board floor with a youthful step. The rhythm of the drum became faster, and the pitch of the woman's voice gradually rose.

At last the fluid got so low that Juan turned up the pot and stood it on its side, and finally he removed it. All I could do was sit and wait. Either the liquid or the heat was making me feel faint. Suddenly the drumming changed to a furious pounding. The old woman screamed, leaped high in the air, and fell to the floor, her body stiff.

My head cleared. The witch doctor was in a trance, writhing before me like a dying snake. The impulse to scratch my skin had left me and a great burden seemed to have been lifted from me. The blankets were unwrapped, and the old man who had beaten the drums inspected me, scratching here and there. No welt appeared. They led me to the bed.

"You are cured," said the old man. "Now you must sleep." I obeyed. Late the next afternoon, I was awakened by Juan. His eyes were full of tears.

"You have not moved since you went to sleep," he said. "The sopot devil is really gone. Soon we will be able to go back to Zambales."

"Maybe I won't be able to go back with you," I answered. "Last time the doctor was here he said I would have to stay out of the Lowland heat for awhile even after I recovered. He mentioned Baguio and if that climate doesn't agree with me I may have to go back to America. He'll return in a few days, and we can decide then."

For a few days I did little but sleep. I was the center of attraction, and everyone in the neighborhood dropped in to see me. Many different theories to explain the cure were suggested. Juan put most faith in the witch doctor's knife.

"All demons have a great fear of bright, shiny objects, especially sharp knives," he said. "The demon heard the witch doctor saying she was going to slice you up, and was only too glad to leave such a dangerous abode."

I admitted to Juan that I had felt firmly convinced that the old woman was going to cut the spirit up even before it left my body. At first, Juan's explanation seemed a huge joke, but to avoid offending him I agreed that the spirit might have been frightened out of me.

Mrs. Salvador suspected that the sopot devil was on very good terms with the witch doctor, and that it had been sent to live in my body because of her selfish desire to collect a fee from me. To the girls, the bitterness of the fluid assumed major importance. They had the old-fashioned idea that medicine must make one suffer in order to be effective.

I myself believed that the sweating had had a cleansing effect, and that the herb concoction had restored the chemical balance in my body, accomplishing what the doctor had been attempting to do with his medicine. Shortly after the cure, Juan asked me for a few pesos to give to Mrs. Salvador.

"She has bought many candles to burn at the church," he said. "She could not afford to spend the money, but she had to atone for the sin of having the witch doctor in her house, and for the greater sin of recommending this treatment for you."

I gave Juan ten pesos with a feeling that the saints were very reasonable to charge me so little for calling in other experts to help them out. The living saints I had known would not have been so willing to accept the witch doctor as a consultant. When Juan returned from town he told me, with a distressed look, that the district health officer was back and that he had talked with him. "He doesn't believe you are well," said Juan. "He says you can't leave town for a week or two, and even then it won't be safe for you to go to the Lowlands."

"I was afraid of that," I said, "but I think you'd better go on back to Bataan. Glin will be worried about the rest of the bride price, and he's liable to sell Olan to someone else if you don't return. How much more do we owe him?"

"Fifty pesos," said Juan. "I paid him another twenty before we left."

"How much have you got saved up?" I said.

"Forty-five pesos," he said. "I haven't spent anything since we left, and it's been three and a half months."

"By the end of the month I'll owe you sixty pesos," I said, "but if you stay that long you're liable to get homesick and there'll be another doctor's bill, so I'll pay you now. That will give you sixty pesos, which will pay the bride price, buy your busfare back, and leave a little to spare." His eyes filled with tears. I gave him another five pesos so he could buy Olan a few presents, and saw him off on the afternoon bus. Once I had mentioned leaving, he seemed to waste away by the hour with homesickness, and I feared he wouldn't last until he arrived the next morning. He left with the understanding that my betrothal was canceled, and that if I ever returned to Bataan, I would serve as godfather to his first child, which he insisted he would name "Kilton," whether it was a boy or girl.

The wistful eagerness in his face when I mentioned Olan gave me a pang of guilt for the jealousy I had felt toward him on the night of the *wakai*, and on later occasions. When I thought of her now, I felt strangely indifferent about seeing her. That week on the trail, with my feet always turning back as though she were in possession of them, had furnished a moment of pain to weigh against each moment of desire I felt for her, until she had, at last, become impersonal for me again, as she had been that first day, standing in the sunlight and throbbing with laughter beside the table.

As I waved good-by to Juan, I was flooded with a feeling of love and brotherly affection. I was not quite sure if it was Christian love, or if something deep inside was telling me that the fear in Olan would always rise up at the moment when she tried to give, so that she would possess the man she loved with the instinct of a courtesan and make him always love her to distraction without fulfillment.

The witch doctor had chosen the full of the moon for the ceremony. I noticed that all the dogs in the community barked and howled at the moon. I had been much disgusted by the Filipino dogs. All of them had skin diseases. As I saw them scratching and bleeding and squirming, I had been doubly conscious of my own skin.

The next morning, when Conception brought me fruit from the market, as was her habit, I asked why the dogs bayed at the moon.

"They are afraid of it, sir," she answered.

"What does the moon do to you?" I asked.

"It makes me restless and sad," she said. "It fills my mind with daydreams. If its light falls on your face when you are asleep, it will drive you mad. The dogs are very foolish. They sit and stare at the moon, and if you do not tie them up, they will run off on moonlight nights. Our dogs howl and whine when it thunders, too."

I had often been shocked by the yelping of the dogs in the Salvador household.

"If you know that dogs have fear and other feelings like your own," I asked Conception, "how is it that you can be so cruel to them?"

"God punishes *us*," she said. "When the dogs are bad, it is our duty to punish them."

"But if they are bad so often, why do you keep them about?" I protested.

"They are very necessary, sir," she said. Her grave brown eyes grew larger. "They are watchdogs."

This sounded like the height of folly to me, for the Salvador family lived almost as simply as the Negritos. A few pots and pans, a few rolls of bamboo matting, clothing that was always in use, and trinkets which Mrs. Salvador kept under her pillow, were about all the property of which the household could boast.

"What do you have here that anyone could possibly want to steal?"

"If it were not for the watchdogs, the young men would steal into our beds at night," she answered with conviction. "The dogs help us guard our virtue."

I had often seen the sleeping compartments of the Salvador household. Only screens separated the various beds, and they were placed close together.

"Could you not cry out if someone tried to steal into your bed?" I asked her.

"If a girl did not want love more than she wanted to please her mother or the priest," she said, "why would she marry, and what good would she be to her husband if she did marry? Mother says that no woman can resist a man when she falls in love, even if she wants to. My mother is quite willing to protect us until we have husbands. Of course, we could cry out if the young men came to our beds, but we wouldn't."

## THE SOPOT-SOPOT DEMON

The testing at the school progressed rapidly in the next few days. At the end of the month, I paid off my bills, but my fortune had dwindled. The Indonesian mountaineer children I had been testing at the school interested me. They included representatives from some of the groups that Hartendorp and Dr. Perez had mentioned, and had come from the main mountain range of Luzon, on the eastern part of the island, which was higher than the Zambales Mountains. These eastern mountains were older than the western range, according to the geologists, and less precipitous, and they therefore had more high tablelands—which had been cleared from jungle long ago for shifting dry-land agriculture.

The health officer who had unsuccessfully treated me for sopot-sopot strongly recommended that I live for awhile in these eastern highlands, or leave the Philippines for a cooler climate. He had seen sopot-sopot return to people like myself, who had grown up in dry mountainous areas; this eastern range, he thought, might serve my health as well as my research.

The human race had apparently begun the climb from the ancient, simple, nomadic, hunting-and-gathering type of culture to modern industrial civilization by domesticating plants and animals for food and settling down on the land. Having caught a glimpse of the first rung on the ladder of human progress in the Zambales Mountains, I might now find groups in the eastern range which had reached other rungs, groups in which the Negrito type of culture had moved in the direction of modern civilization.

Dr. Beyer had told me that he had found individuals with Negrito characteristics scattered through the population of these eastern mountains, especially across the island from the Zambales Mountains, where the Negritos had been in contact with the Ilongots of the eastern range up to the coming of the Americans at the beginning of the twentieth century. Some Negrito, or part-Negrito, hordes still ranged on the eastern slopes of the Palali range of mountains in the province of Nueva Vizcaya. I could take the bus to Bayombong and then work down the central mountain chain to the vicinity of Manila.

Beyer believed that the Negritos had ranged over the whole island at one time, before they were replaced in the Lowlands by the agricultural peoples. For centuries, they had been mixing with the agricultural groups of the highlands. In this vast mountainous country to the east might be found groups among whom the simple spontaneous ceremonies of the Negritos, originating, as I had seen, in their dreams, fantasies, and accidents, had evolved further and become more permanent. I might find instances where the Negrito type of ceremony had been adapted to agricultural practices, so that men believed the spirits of their magical worlds controlled not only accidents, such as stubbing one's toe on a jungle root, but also the process of growth itself in the animals and plants they raised for food.

At the school there were two or three part-Ilongot children, whose parents had migrated to Abra from the vicinity of Bayombong. The Indonesian Ilongot tribe was believed to have mixed more with the Negritos than any other group. Its members were also thought to be related to the Ainus of northern Japan and the Todas of India, because they had certain Caucasian features of bone structure, and more abundant face and body hair than neighboring groups. Both the Ainus and the Todas were referred to as proto-European and were believed to have migrated from the vicinity of Europe or the Caucasus Mountains in very ancient times, the Todas taking a southern and the Ainus a northern route.

The Ilongots had not yet settled on the land as permanently as most agriculturalists, but they did practice shifting dry-land farming, and they were just beginning, on the border of their territory, to domesticate pigs and fowl to be used for food. They had never been conquered by the Spaniards, and were not yet a part of the Filipino political state, since the American administration had done little more than confine them to their own territory and insist that they take no heads from the Lowlanders. Much of their territory was as yet unexplored.

I had approached Gabriel Juarez, a senior-high-school pupil who was one of the part-Ilongot emigrants from Nueva Vizcaya. As a means of improving his English, he was willing to go along with me to work with the Ilongots for the same fee I had been paying Juan.

I decided to go back to Manila by way of Bayombong and the central mountain range. Then I could study what had been written about the Bontocs and the Ifugao before I went into their territory to complete the program Perez and Hartendorp had recommended. They had told me that almost nothing had been written about the Ilongots. By hiking south along this chain of mountains, which runs the length of Luzon, and testing the groups I encountered

## THE SOPOT-SOPOT DEMON

along the way, I should be able to get back to Manila in three to six months.

The Salvadors arranged a party for me on the afternoon of my departure. All the neighbors came in their picturesque Spanish-style dresses. We drank tea and ate sweet cakes. Some of the people had tears in their eyes when I left, and I too felt like crying. When you are so poor and weak that you must accept people's help at every turn, friendships grow rapidly and very deep.

The Salvadors knew Jesus, the young man who drove the bus, and persuaded him to call for me at the party on his way out of town. He was a handsome lad of Spanish extraction, who thought of his bus as a mustang. The bus was overcrowded with people, to say nothing of the goats, pigs, dogs, and chickens which lay tethered in the aisles or hung from the roof. But Jesus had saved places for us beside him on the front seat.

We departed with a flourish, in the midst of an uproar. The motor snorted, the passengers shouted, and the livestock added to the din. A violent spasm of the engine sent the bus lurching dangerously over the ruts in the road. I caught a final broken glimpse of Conscientious, Conception, and Candid waving handkerchiefs from the roadside. I noticed that Jesus also was watching them instead of the road. Miraculously, we missed a tree and skirted a ditch.

# TWELVE

# The Head-Hunters

THE journey to Bayombong was anything but dull. To many of the people we passed, an automobile was still a miracle. Some of the passengers had never been in a bus before, and they sat tense and excited. Only the chickens and dogs cried out against the atrocious driving. How could a mere machine stand such a beating and escape overturning around the murderous curves on the narrow roads?

As the bus ground out the miles to Bayombong, Gabriel told me about himself. He was a shy lad and so far had not spoken more than two words to me except in answer to my direct questions. Now he was beginning to thaw a little. I suspected that he reacted to the driving of Jesus like a man who, falling from a height, sees his past life parade in front of him.

Some years earlier, the Bureau of Education had attempted to maintain a school on the northern border of the Ilongot territory, in the vicinity of Bayombong. Some of the Ilongot children had been persuaded to attend it. The experiment had never worked satisfactorily, for the students periodically became bored with the discipline of school life and burned the schoolhouse and all the gov rnment equipment. The Bureau of Education finally abandoned the project. Before this happened, however, Gabriel's mother had fallen in love with the schoolmaster and married him, thus becoming one of the few Ilongot girls ever to leave her territory and become Christianized.

Gabriel told me that although his mother had not visited her father's people since her marriage, she had taught him the Ilongot dialect and many of her native songs, and had interested him in the myths and customs of her people. The Lowland students knew that his mother was from Ilongot territory and treated him with reserve.

Until the American conquest of the mountain territory at the time of the Spanish-American War, the Ilongots had waged constant war with the Lowlanders, and even since that war they had taken many Lowland heads. The Christian children could not forget this, and Gabriel could not feel at home among them. He seemed glad of the opportunity to visit his mother's people, but as we approached our destination, he grew steadily more tense. The stories he had heard from his mother were not at all reassuring. During the past few years the Ilongots had not taken any heads from the Ifugao or from the Lowland communities in which he had lived, but they had only discontinued this practice after repeated and severe discipline by the United States Army, and the threat of annihilation if they did not reform.

We left the bus at Bayombong, and bargained for a ride in an automobile to the village of Caliat, a few miles to the south, where we stocked up with silk threads of various colors and fine copper wire, which Gabriel said we could use for currency. These, with white horsehair which Gabriel had been collecting ever since he had first thought of coming with me, would make us rich among the Ilongots. Then we set off on foot up a tributary of the Magat River, coming down from the direction of Mount Palali.

As we trudged up the trail, Gabriel often paused to inspect our supply of silk thread, copper wire, and horsehair. The prospect of being a rich man among the Ilongots for awhile was having a noticeable effect upon him. All his life his family had been poor, and this sack of supplies, he said, was equivalent to a large bank account in the Lowlands. The romantic picture of what his wealth would buy was outweighing the unknown dangers in the lush green mountains ahead. Each time we stopped, he opened the sack and admired the gleaming mass within.

The excitement in his eyes was contagious, as we climbed the steep canyon leading to the south. I thought how the world of my mother's people would have looked to me at seventeen. On each of those green ridges that became purple in the distance were the houses of the Ilongots. In each house was a door which would open at our command and yield up some mysterious treasure.

We spent the night at a farmhouse which was also a trading post. It was run by Manolo de Leon, an old trader who had carried on an uncertain business with the Ilongots for many years, dealing mostly in rattan, for which he bartered colored thread, copper wire, calico, knives, and tobacco. He had a strongly built wooden house surrounded by a wooden fence reinforced with barbed wire. The place was overrun with dogs, which looked like a cross between bull terriers and the native variety. They barked at us savagely even before we reached the compound. Some were so vicious they had to be chained.

Inside the compound, behind his house, were a half-dozen native houses of thatch and some shacks inhabited by Filipino families who worked for him as servants. Gabriel said that the costumes of the natives showed they were Kalingas from the province of Isabela. The houses were well built. Two of them had roofs of large bamboo poles which had been split in half and ingeniously laid over one another like tiles. I was told this construction was characteristic of Kalingan houses. In one corner of the compound, toward the back, a few old spears were stuck into the ground, supporting baskets containing flowers, bamboo joints full of *basi*, the native drink made of fermented sugar-cane juice, and little bowls of rice and scraps of meat—offerings to the ancestor spirits. Old loincloths and bits of skirts and blankets hung from the fence and were draped over the spear ends. Gabriel told me that the people of the compound "made" spirits they called *anitos* here. This choice of a special place for performing rituals was a step up toward the fixed ceremony and the temples of modern man. The Negritos had no such places.

Inside, the storeroom looked like a small arsenal, since it contained a rifle and a number of sawed-off shotguns. The old trader did not trust the Ilongots; he depended for his safety on his dogs, his servants, and his guns.

Outside the compound, inhabiting leaf shacks not unlike those built by the Negritos when they are on the march, were a number of Ilongots who were there for trading. Rattan and baskets were piled up around the palm-leaf shelters, and dogs were tethered to the uprights on rattan leashes. The Ilongots knew that their dogs were no match for Manolo's terriers.

There were fourteen Ilongots at the camp, who, Manolo said, would probably stay around for a day or two, carrying on their trading in a leisurely fashion. Before these left, more would probably drift in. The Ilongots had completed harvesting their dry-land rice, and usually at this time traveled about from rancho to rancho to do their trading.

I told Manolo I would like to test thirty-five to fifty of them. He thought that many would certainly show up in the course of two or three weeks, and agreed to let us unroll our beds in his storeroom and to sell us food. The Ilongots, he said, were curious about everything, and we should have no trouble getting them to play our test games. His opinion proved correct. The next morning his servants built us a bowery lean-to against the house—a bamboo frame laced with branches—and a bamboo table and some chairs. I had had an opportunity to train Gabriel in the testing weeks ago, while working with the students in Bangued. The testing program was commenced.

The Ilongots were a colorful people. Their loincloths differed from those of the Negritos in that the ends did not hang down in front and behind. All of them carried spears ornamented with spiral bands of metal and wound with fiber or horsehair interspersed with bright colored threads. They had long, narrow shields of light wood which might stop arrows or fend off enemy spears.

In their houses, they kept bows and a variety of arrows. The heads of some of the arrows were detachable, tied to the shaft with strong cords designed to catch in the brush and thus stop an animal attempting to flee after being hit.

They wore elaborate arm bands of woven copper wire, horsehair, dyed rattan, and thread. Geometric designs were tattooed on their chests and their hair was long, confined in hair nets of coarse, woven fiber string. Just above their loincloths each had a girdle of small, well-matched cowrie shells. Some girdles consisted of a single strand of shells, others of a greater number, and some of the older men displayed broad bands or ropes of them. Three of the men also wore a band of shells which attached to the girdle at the right hip, went up over the left shoulder, and attached again at the right hip in the back. These cowrie shells were passed from father to son, and the number of shells denoted the wealth of the wearer. Apparently the shells had been accumulated, through centuries of trading, from the Ilongots to the east and the Dumagates, a seafaring tribe inhabiting the east coast. The Dumagates were believed to have come to the Philippines long ago from Melanesia and to be Papuan in origin.

There was an astonishing variety of physical types among the Ilongots. Some had straight, blue-black hair; some, wavy hair which glinted red in the sun; some, kinky hair and distinctly Negrito or Papuan features. Some were brown with a saffron tint, and yellow where the skin was protected by the girdle. Others ranged from chocolate brown to almost black. They were taller than the Negritos, varying in height from four and a half to five and a half feet, and so slender that they looked even taller. Slender as they were, they had well-developed muscles, especially the thighs and buttocks. At least half of them had some show of beard. Two were fairly heavy, and most of them had a European rather than an Oriental look about the upper eyelid. All of them were gay, playful, and friendly. I found it difficult to think of them as treacherous head-hunters. The whole group obligingly stayed on to tell us of their dreams and to take our tests.

The Goodenough Draw-A-Man Test could be scored only up to the fourteen-year level, and all the Ilongots made drawings which exceeded the fourteen-year norm and compared well with the drawings made by normal American adults which I had obtained in Hawaii. I also noticed some other trends in the drawings of the Ilongots, which were confirmed by drawings I collected later. Nearly all of the subjects drew their men in action, rather than standing still. And they drew unusually large feet in proportion to the rest of the body.

Miss Goodenough had noticed that there was a sex difference in the test results obtained in America—that the girls tended to draw larger eyes and smaller feet than the boys. The Ilongot males drew even larger feet and smaller eyes than the males I had tested in Hawaii. This was partly because the Ilongot drawings were more realistic. Perhaps they also drew the feet larger and better because feet to them were more important, since they were accustomed to going barefoot. I found the same trend in the other barefoot mountain groups I tested later. These larger, better-drawn feet might also, I concluded, indicate a high degree of masculinity, individuality, and virility among these people. Everything about them bespoke an independent, democratic attitude and a high regard for their own institutions and culture.

On the Porteus Maze they did not do quite so well, but like the Negritos they had had no experience whatever with pencil and paper, and they usually wasted a blank or two getting used to the fact that the pencil rat could not cross over lines which would cause a real rat no difficulty.

On the Metal Maze the Ilongots did as well as the adults and the high-school students I had tested in Hawaii. The Sympathy Test did not differentiate them at all from the Hawaiian subjects or from the Negritos. On the Emotional Response Test their memories of the various types of incidents covered a much greater part of their past lives than did the memories of the Negritos. Spirits, whom they called *anitos,* played a greater part in the fearful incidents they remembered, and in their dreams, than spirits did among the Negritos.

Their answers to the Progressive Fantasy Test showed a much greater fear of attack from spirits and from other men than the Negritos displayed. None of them mentioned a fear of being attacked by a high god like the Negritos' Tolandian, but all of them were living, as far as I could see, in constant fear of losing their heads, in fear of blood feuds, and in fear of spirits. Nearly all considered the ceremonial feasts the best things that had happened to them. Feasts were also often mentioned as the best thing that could happen, along with gaining favor with the *anitos,* wealth, more wives, more copper wire, more cowrie shells, and more fame throughout the Ilongot territory as rich men and head-hunters.

All of the older men answered that the best thing that could happen would be the withdrawal of the United States Government, which had made it so difficult for them to take the heads of the Lowlanders that they had found it necessary to take more and more heads from other Ilongot groups. Apparently taking heads from their Ilongot neighbors resulted in retaliation worse than they had ever experienced from the Lowlands, and in endless blood feuds. It never occurred to any of them that they might stop taking heads altogether, since they seemed to believe that the spirits would not yield up life-giving food to man unless man gave human lives in return to the *anitos*. After examining the test results I could not agree with Manolo, or with the school authorities to whom I had talked in Bayombong, that the Ilongots were deficient in native intelligence.

We also tested some of Manolo's Kalingan retainers. They had seen photographs, maps, and calendars around Manolo's house, and apparently even this little experience with two-dimensional drawings helped them in doing the Porteus Maze, as they scored a little better than the Ilongots. On all the other tests they did about the same as the Ilongots.

From both the Kalingas and the Ilongots I inquired in vain for any evidence of the shamanistic healing trance which we had observed among the Negritos. When I asked them for the worst things that had happened to them, and attempted to get them into the trance state, they reported dream after dream of encounters with the *anitos*, which indicated that they had no tradition of going back to infancy and the spirit cave to find the origin of their headaches and bellyaches, as the Negritos did.

They tended to have more terror dreams than the other adolescents and adults I had tested. Instead of the usual forty to sixty per cent of bad dreams, about seventy per cent of the Ilongot dreams were bad. In their dreams there were fewer dogs, wild pigs, cats, snakes, and other animals, and more humans and humanlike *anitos* than I had found in the dreams of the Negrito and the Hawaiian subjects.

Most of the dreams were of punishment by the ancestor spirits and of quarrels and fights, which they associated with attacking or being attacked for heads. Two of the Ilongot dreams were directly concerned with head-taking. In one, a young man asked a beautiful girl he met in his dream to marry him, but she refused, saying that since he had not taken a head, he was not a man. An older man dreamed that the *anito* of his victim stepped out of the body as the dreamer hacked off his head, and promised to be the dreamer's servant if he would leave the head by the body and not carry it off to his rancho and have a ceremony over it, as the Igorots did.

I noticed no other trends in the Ilongot dreams which differentiated them from the dreams of adolescent Hawaiian subjects, and found no dreams similar to those of the shamans and the aspiring shamans among the Negritos.

I also inquired of the Kalingas about their methods of treating illness. One old woman in the group specialized in healing, but she was a priestess rather than a shamaness. As far as I could learn, she neither went into trance herself nor put her patients into trance in the healing ceremony. She thought she had been called to the priesthood by Kabunyan, the high god. There were lesser gods, who personified the thunder, the lightning, the clouds, the rainbow, the sun, and the moon. The Kalingas spoke of Damanig, a demon who possessed the moon and made her eat up her husband, the sun. But none of these gods seemed important to the priestess. She said she prayed only to the high god, asking him to protect and save her patients from the lesser gods and from various spirits, especially the hunting spirits and the spirits who lived in big rocks, hot springs, and volcanoes.

The main cause of illness, however, which the priestess countered by her prayers and by sacrifices, was the ancestor spirits. These ancestor spirits also had to be propitiated at rice-planting time. After planting the rice and praying to the ancestor spirits and the high god at the planting ceremony, the head of the family and his wife would take a sacrificial plate of rice, pork, and bananas to their terraces.

An old man described these prayers to us. They were addressed to the ancestors who had built the terraces in the first place and had been buried there when they died. These ancestors were told: "You who built and improved these rice paddies, do not linger on and eat the crops we plant. Please take this food we have prepared for you and depart, to come no more. Have pity on us who inherited your land. Do not harvest any of our crop. We have killed a pig to end your residence here. Do not come back again." Then the prayer was addressed to the high god: "High god, Kabunyan-un Kadaklan, thou art the greatest. Drive these spirits away, so this soil will furnish us a good crop. Keep them away, always, thou who art the greatest and the most supreme above all others."

The old man then pantomimed the placing of the rice, meat, and bananas on the wall of the rice terraces, and again addressed his prayers to the ancestors: "Here, this is the end of you," he said. "Eat and go away."

I was very interested to learn that the old priestess had received her calling to the profession of healer in a series of dreams which had made her ill. She had lost her appetite and grown thin, and at last she had decided that her soul was married to an *anito* and that she could only survive by becoming a priestess (*manga-alising*). Since she had become a healer at the age of thirty-five she had not eaten eel, dog, and certain kinds of fish and beef—all taboo to a priestess. If eating any of these foods made a woman ill, she would be advised to become a priestess.

The high god, Kabunyan, she told us, had ordained her in a dream, and she had had no special training for the priesthood. Since all the children in the group, however, witnessed the healing activities of the priestess from babyhood on, it was obvious that they would need no special training to perform the same rites. Her healing methods seemed definitely inferior to those of the Negritos, since they consisted only of making sacrifices to the ancestor spirits, asking them to go away and stop bothering her patients, bribing them with sacrifices, and asking Kabunyan to keep them away, after assuring him that he was all-powerful and could, therefore, very easily protect her patients if he wished to do so.

This seemed like a method of healing by suppression and splitting up, rather than by insight, self-acceptance, and integration. With this type of healing, the patient had to remain dependent on authority to keep the offending parts of the personality suppressed or split off, since the offending parts or spirits were not attacked directly in the trance state and made to change their ways and work for the patient, as they were among the Negritos.

Perhaps the series of dreams which had brought the woman into the priesthood depicted a reorganization which was going on in her personality at that time. She did not, however, inquire about the dreams of her patients and stimulate a similar reorganization in them. She seemed content to function always as the emotional mother of her subjects.

Insofar as we could learn, there were no old-woman specialists among the Ilongots to correspond to the priestess-healer of the Kalingas.

Among both the Kalingas and the Ilongots the men were chiefly interested in the ceremonies clustering about head-taking and paid little attention to the art of healing. They did not look further and further into themselves for the cause of illness, as the Negritos did, but tried to propitiate a wider and wider circle of spirits through the shedding of blood and the taking of heads.

Although the Ilongots were suspicious of my medicines, as they were of anything foreign to them, one old man who said that he had a headache took an aspirin I gave him and agreed to let me try to put him into a trance. "I see a man," he said, when his eyes went shut. "He looks like an Ilongot, but he is bright red in color. He is an *anito*, and says he is squeezing my head because we have not taken a head to avenge the last death of one of our number, which was caused by a neighboring group." The *anito* said he would keep squeezing the subject's head until the blood feud was fulfilled. When I asked the old man to go back to earlier and earlier occasions when the pain spirit had attacked him, he told of previous times when this red *anito* had squeezed his head because the blood feud had not been satisfied, and of other occasions when a white, moon-like *anito* had attacked him because there had been no heads taken to put the fertility back into the land at harvest time.

I urged him repeatedly to go to earlier and earlier times, and he did get back to experiences of childhood where he had broken taboos. But the red or shining white *anitos* which he kept seeing frightened him, so that at last he announced that he would go no further, and that he wanted to come out of the trance and see no more *anitos*. It was not a successful venture, for in spite of the aspirin, when he opened his eyes he said his headache had grown worse.

Perhaps when I got deeper into the territory I would find subjects who were less frightened and whose minds were not so set by tradition. But already I had learned a great deal about the emotional make-up of the Ilongots. They were less afraid of the spirits of rocks, trees, streams, and mountains than the Negritos, who had a mild fear of, or respect for, the individuality, the living force, in everything about them, but fear had not been eliminated from the mind of the Ilongot. It had been transferred to, or concentrated in, the images of the *anitos*. When these aggressive *anito* images attacked them in their dreams and visions, the old men did not call them up to consciousness in the agreement trance and persuade them to assist the patient to become a healer. Instead, they looked for a scapegoat.

The Ilongots did not animate the images of the outside world with their own motives, desires, and emotions, to the same extent that the Negritos did. They were less animistic. But as they gathered in their fears and hopes from the images of outside things in general, they concentrated these fears and hopes into a class of images which were built up by education through words and ceremonies, and they were learning to think in terms of these man-made images. Certainly this was a step toward abstract thinking. Intellectually it was a step in the right direction—toward thought which was in some ways more efficient. Their memories, for instance, were far superior to those of the Negritos.

Emotionally, however, it was a misstep. It helped to relieve the feelings of aggression of the inner man, but it turned the man and his group against others. This was interesting, but not especially reassuring. The men were so gentle, friendly, and soft-spoken in their treatment of each other, and so charming and co-operative in taking the tests, that I felt perfectly at ease about traveling into their territory. But this deeper side of their nature, which the test revealed, did seem to fit in with the reputation they had for taking the lives of human beings who were not in their lineage groups.

The Kalingas had carried the blood sacrifice further than the Ilongots, but they said the *anitos* loved the blood of pigs and chickens and would accept it as a sacrifice, as well as the blood of human beings. Now that head-hunting was no longer allowed among the Kalingas, some of the men were performing healing ceremonies.

Both male and female Kalingas wore their hair long, but the men cut it off in front, leaving a bang across the forehead. Gabriel told me that the Kalingas had been head-hunters, feared as much by the Lowlanders as the Ilongots, but they had not resisted education and Christianity to the same extent. Apparently Manolo had chosen them as servants because they were even more efficient as warriors than the Ilongots, and more reckless. The Kalingan men had some scant tattooing on the arms and chest, and most of the women had a throat tattoo. They said the tattooing had no special significance, but they thought it was decorative and brought good luck. They looked more Oriental than the Ilongots, with high cheekbones, a broad upper face, and longish eyes. In the main they were a little taller and a little heavier. They carried head axes, which they always kept handy and used for everything but picking their

## THE HEAD-HUNTERS

teeth. They held on to them even when they were not working, as a warning to the Ilongots, who did not have head axes.

By the end of three weeks we had tested thirty-five subjects. One of the Ilongot latecomers, Ijah, who had an especially heavy girdle of cowrie shells, denoting rank, and who lived in a clearing only two days' march from the trading post, agreed to take us back with him so we could test the women and children at his house and commence our journey southward.

Gabriel was nervous about our departure. Although the Ilongots had not invaded the Lowlands for heads since their last trouncing by the United States Army some five years before, who was to protect the Lowland heads that ventured up to them? To make matters worse, Manolo arranged a feast for our departure and persuaded his Kalingan servants to stage a mock head-hunt for us. "I like to have one every now and then anyway," he said, "just to make the Ilongots remember that my own men can still take heads, and would be glad to do so if the Ilongots gave them an excuse."

Three of his older men had taken heads themselves. He asked Pangat Guhlu, the most famous of these, to re-enact his last successful expedition. They killed a pig for the feast, and the fifteen-odd adults and adolescent boys came rushing around the house in their full war regalia, carrying the pig's head in the conical bamboo head basket. Pangat Guhlu explained that there had been forty members in his last expedition, and he seemed dissatisfied that he had only fifteen actors to depict it with, but said he would do the best he could.

As soon as the head had been taken, Pangat Guhlu started home with it, the other members of the party keeping up a rear-guard action. As he re-enacted his return to the village, all of them dipped small pieces of bark cloth in the blood and ran off to hang them above the doors of their houses to insure good luck and good health, and to protect themselves from the vengeance of the slain man's friends and ancestors. Smelling his blood there, the *anitos* would think it was a house of their kin, rather than of an enemy.

While they were gone, Pangat Guhlu cut off the lower jaw, and then hewed off the skull of the head with his head axe and cut it into fourteen pieces, giving each member of the expedition a piece as he returned. Using the prong of the head axe, he scrambled up the brain; he poured *basi* into the skull, drinking of the mixture first himself, then adding more *basi* to it and passing it to the others as they arrived, the pieces of skull serving as loving cups. After all had drunk, four young men brought out *gansas*, gongs which they played with their hands. Each *gansa* was attached by a rattan thong to a human lower jaw, which served as handle. The men squatted on their haunches as they played, forming part of the wide circle of spectators gathering around the fire.

When the circle was formed, Pangat Guhlu, with a young man who posed as the victim, re-enacted the taking of the head, telling about every step in a piercing falsetto voice. His words were staccato and full of rage. They seemed sharper than his gleaming head axe. He had amazing agility for an old man. First there had been a spear fight, and the two parried each other's spears in a way which seemed to endanger both the duelers and the onlookers. At last the opponent was wounded in the thigh through the space between the prongs at the bottom of his shield, and fell, screaming for help. The old man was upon him in a moment, pressing down his arms with a shield. The axe descended. I fully expected the head to roll away from the body. The sharp, piercing cry with which the old man commenced each phrase of his account had an hypnotic effect. Manolo told me it was the actual war cry of the Kalingas and would paralyze an opponent if he was at all affected with *lata*, a type of hysteria which is common in the Malay-speaking countries.

Laughingly he told us that he had had a school teacher who went into trance whenever one of the students clapped his hands sharply or gave a sudden shout. The teacher, he said, would then imitate anything that happened, even to taking off her clothes. Of course, the head-hunter's prey who was a thrust behind his adversary would not have much time left for imitating. There was so much pent-up emotion in the voice and action of the old man that the whole thing became horribly realistic. There was a slight trickle of blood from the "victim's" thigh, where the victor's spear had made contact. Manolo said the old man would have to pay a fine to him to avoid a blood feud. Among the Kalingans even murder could be paid for, when it occurred between the lineage groups in a friendly territory. They had a system of fines on which the old men who formed a council for the territory in question agreed. The councilors (*pangats*) could call upon all the members of their various lineages to reinforce their decisions. They were usually chosen as *pangats* because they were feared and respected for the number of heads they had taken. Once having been chosen, they worked tirelessly to persuade the others to settle their difficulties by paying fines and inflicting minor wounds, rather than by taking heads.

Gabriel was ghastly pale. When the first encounter had been completely portrayed, Pangat Guhlu pulled a handkerchief-size piece of bark cloth from his girdle and handed it to one of the other old men who had taken heads, and another battle was enacted. This time, as he held his victim pinned beneath his shield, he called a younger man to wield the head axe.

Manolo explained that it was the custom to allow the younger men, who had not taken heads, this honor of enacting the actual head-taking, as it gave them prestige which the old men no longer needed. Then the bark cloth was passed to the third man, and the scene went on again pretty much as before, except that each performance became more lively and appeared more reckless than the previous one.

Gabriel became more disturbed with each performance and concealed his nervousness with difficulty.

After this phase of the program, there was a free-for-all argument in which everyone had a go at boasting about his bravery, his skills, his wealth, and his lineage. One of the young men boasted so often and so loudly that his uncle had seven wives, that I told Manolo to advise him that Brigham Young, headman of my group, had twenty-three. There was sheer disbelief on all the faces. The argument began to get out of bounds, and Manolo asked Pangat Guhlu to have the old women enact the ceremony which they had performed once a year in the head-hunting days to determine if it was necessary for the men to take heads in the coming year. The argument, he said, had reached a phase where the young men were insulting each other rather than boasting, and were berating the old men for their cowardice in allowing the institution of head-hunting to die off before they had had an opportunity to prove themselves. Such arguments are always highly dangerous with these people.

To commence the ceremony, one old woman stood up a half-dozen coconuts in as many conical head baskets, to represent all the imaginary heads which had been taken in the previous year. She stuck a spear into the ground to mark off a zone separating the women from the heads. They danced and sang for awhile, and at last the leader announced, much to the disgust of the young men, that no more heads need be taken to insure the harvest for the next year. Apparently the old woman found out through the ceremony whether or not the rice could withstand the ravages of a great mythical bird which had the power to eat it when it was in the milk stage. The women were experts on this bird because it also had the power to strangle babies or eat their spirits while they were in the womb.

The taking of heads was, therefore, related to both the fertility of the soil and the fertility of women. I had seen two bamboo poles, sharpened on the end and hardened with fire, sticking up from the rooftop of one of the houses. The woman who lived inside was pregnant. The long poles, which followed the slant of the roof and extended upward beyond the gable into space, would transfix the great bird if it fluttered too close. This was a necessary precaution since no heads had been taken recently.

I was tired. After eating the lavish dinner which Manolo provided for all I was unable to stay awake. But Gabriel felt like talking. Through the open door of the storeroom I could see Gabriel and Manolo in the yellow halo of a smoky kerosene lamp as I went to sleep.

Once I opened my eyes to see Gabriel explaining the labyrinths on the Porteus Maze blanks. Another time he was translating the dreams which we had collected. Later I heard his nervous treble laugh. The old man was showing him rocks, which I took to be samples of ore collected in the vicinity. Each time I saw him, Gabriel looked more excited.

At breakfast I was alarmed by the shrillness of his voice and the brightness of his eyes. Manolo was suspicious of the Ilongots and had filled Gabriel's mind with fearsome tales. What was worse, he was even more suspicious of me. No white man had ever come into these mountains except to seek gold. Gabriel's comments convinced me that the trader thought I was deceiving them about the purpose of my mission. He believed I had secret information about the location of gold deposits, which I had perhaps obtained through my contact with familiar spirits. He had convinced Gabriel that we would certainly lose our heads the instant we attempted to steal the Ilongot gold, and that, at best, we were in constant danger. I half suspected that he was exaggerating the danger ahead because he wished to sell us squirt guns, which looked like automatic pistols.

In Manila they sold for a peso, but Manolo asked two and a half pesos for them, and insisted that we should also buy a bottle of ammonia water to take along as ammunition for the guns. The Ilongots would think they were real firearms, and would not attack us while we were awake. Even if they attempted to attack us with their broad-bladed head knives, Manolo said, ammonia water squirted into the eyes would be more effective than bullets.

The squirt guns also offered protection from Ilongot dogs, which Manolo said were dangerous. But I bought the squirt pistols without enthusiasm since I knew they would be little help against ambush, spears, or the arrows of the Ilongots, if one was trying to escape through the jungle. The sales talk and the other things Manolo had said had unnerved Gabriel; he was close to the breaking point.

After breakfast Manolo gave Ijah, our prospective host, a talking-to. He sounded more like a Dutch uncle than a trader. Gabriel told me that he was explaining that Ijah's rancho would be wiped out by the United States Army if any harm came to us. Manolo would tell the constabulary exactly where we had gone and some of the police officers would soon be visiting us. Ijah seemed surprised and shocked that Manolo could have misgivings about his hospitality, and assured him that he would do everything in his power to make us comfortable and safe. But as Manolo said good-by to us with the customary, "God be with you," he was also muttering something about being sure that we were with the devil. I could see that his fiery lecture had still further aroused Gabriel's misgivings.

# THIRTEEN

# Hymns and Head Dances

As we left the road for the footpath leading to Ijah's rancho, Gabriel's steps dragged. It was difficult to explain to him why I wanted to collect the dreams of the Ilongots, why I wanted to give them mental tests and observe their ceremonies, and why the dreams of Lowlanders would not do as well. Manolo had raised some logical questions. Why was I more interested in the Ilongots' magical ceremonies than in their gold?

Each time we stopped to rest I attempted in vain to allay Gabriel's fears and put the gay smile back into his eyes. I expected him to turn back, but he could not do this without losing face. By evening I despaired of comforting him and decided that his fears would only be overcome when he found from actual experience that they were groundless.

That night we camped in a beautiful little grove of trees, where two streams came together in a rocky canyon. The climb from the valley had been delightful, and it was pleasant to be away from the Lowland heat.

Since noon I had left Gabriel alone with his thoughts, and we had scarcely exchanged a word. We made a tiny fire to boil our rice, and extinguished it before darkness fell. Ijah explained that we must not keep the fire burning at night, since there might be expeditions about in search of heads. Gabriel suggested that we each sit up half the night on guard, and I agreed to take the first half, but I could see that even after our hard day's hike he had got no sleep. When it was his turn to watch, I offered to continue instead, but he said he couldn't sleep anyway and insisted on taking over.

Ijah and the five younger men who were with him were sleeping soundly. Apparently they depended on the dogs to protect them from surprise attacks. I felt Gabriel's insistence on the watch was stupid, but I could not tell him so without offending him.

When I awoke the next morning, Gabriel looked hollow-eyed and still more tense. I fully expected him to refuse to go farther, but he did not suggest turning back. Again we trudged on in silence, but I was worried about him. He had the same brooding look in his eyes that I had seen at Bangued in the eyes of a lad who had run amuck and stabbed his school teacher.

Gabriel had given me his absolute confidence during the first few days of the journey. Now a suspicion that I had deceived him about the purpose of my mission was gnawing at him. I tried to talk to him, but he answered in monosyllables. If the Ilongots were like the Negritos, Gabriel's suspicion of me would be obvious to them, and his fear of them would be interpreted as unfriendliness. "Certainly Ijah will be afraid to attack us," I said, as we paused for breath. "Manolo told him that his group would be wiped out if he harmed us, and Ijah knows that his place could easily be found by the police."

"If they've cultivated all the land in the vicinity of their houses, they'll be ready to move anyway," said Gabriel. "Then they could take our heads and move off where the constabulary could not find them; and if we leave their group, Ijah will, as like as not, steer us to an enemy village which he wants wiped out anyway."

At last I asked Gabriel if he wished to turn back, but he could not admit that he did.

The sun was almost straight above us when we came in sight of the first Ilongot house. Ijah shouted and waved his arms. It was as though he had poked a stick into an ant bed. Barking dogs and shouting people poured out of the door and down the little causeway which led from the elevated entrance of the house to the steep mountainside on which it was built.

The house was a large, squarish, well-built structure, supported by the stumps of trees. The upper side was about six feet above the ground, but because of the slope of the mountain, the stumps on the lower side were some twenty feet high. The roof was thatched, and on all four sides it went up evenly from the eaves, without a gable, to within ten feet of the top. From that point on, two facing sides were left open for ventilation, while the other two continued to a peak, which formed a short gable extending out on each end to protect the open space. At each end of the ridge pole of the short gable, above the open space, a carved stick swept upward as though the ridge pole were continued out and up. From a distance the two carved sticks looked like the horns of a wild buffalo.

The various families which the house sheltered lived on a low platform extending about fifteen feet from the outside walls of the house. Cross walls divided the platform into stall-like compartments. A clay hearth in front of each compartment served the family within. In the center of the house was a large, square, open floor.

Our belongings were moved into a vacant stall reserved as a rule for visiting suitors. Gabriel immediately hauled out the horsehair and gave a generous portion to Ijah, asking him to distribute it according to custom. The gift was promptly returned in sugar cane and other foods. One look at the group made it obvious why horsehair was so treasured among them. It served as a part of the braided and woven designs on the handles of all their spears, knives, and other implements, on their betel boxes and baskets, and on the arm bands and earrings, leg bands and girdles of the women. The white color was thought to have a magical influence on the *anitos*.

The women and children of the household had no reticence about taking our tests and drawing pictures, and like the men we had tested at Manolo's, they came up to the American norms on all the tests but the Porteus Maze. They were equally willing to tell their dreams, and recalled them in abundance.

I had never seen a more charming and friendly people. The women and children had uncut hair like the men, but the women and the preadolescent boys did not wear hair nets.

The women and girls were no less spontaneous and self-possessed than the men. I concluded that they must have a splendid culture, so far as their social relationships with one another inside the group were concerned. I warmed toward them immediately, and felt very much at home.

As the afternoon progressed, however, their attitude toward Gabriel alarmed me. He was afraid of them and they knew it. Their gestures expressed contempt. I could see that Gabriel's fear was turning to hatred. He remarked to me at dinner that the Lowlanders were right in calling the Ilongots ignorant savages. I could see that he was contrasting his experience and accomplishments with theirs, and I tried to convince him of the danger of adopting a superior attitude. "We must make friends with them," I urged. "We must amuse them with stories of the world that you know and they don't. After all, they did not ask us to visit them."

After dinner I instructed Gabriel to ask the Ilongots about their dances. "Tell them we will sing songs and show them dances from other places," I said, "and that we would like to see their dances. We would also like to know about their magical ceremonies and medical practices."

Dancing was the chief pastime of the Ilongots. They responded to our request at once, hauling out drums and gongs, and primitive instruments which resembled the xylophone. Each of these had been made from a large joint of bamboo, eight to ten inches in diameter. When the wood was still green, the hard outer surface of the bamboo was slit into strings of various lengths, left attached at each end. A little wedge or bridge was inserted at each end of the slit to lift the string away from the wood. Then the instrument was allowed to dry, making the strings taut and tough. Each was played by a woman, who struck the strings with slender strips of bamboo, holding one in each hand. Her child, husband, or lover held the instrument. There were also Panpipes—mouth organs made of bamboo tubes about a half inch in diameter which were cut at different lengths, getting shorter and shorter, so that as they were passed along the lips and blown they sounded the various notes of a scale. These, with bamboo nose flutes, which were blown by the men, completed the instruments of the orchestra.

The music was excellent. Gabriel, now more at ease, translated the songs and talked with the old men about the meaning of the dances. The most impressive dance was performed by the men, who, with arms outstretched, danced in a circle, whirling and turning like hornbills in flight, while their women danced in one corner, in no particular formation, as though they were birds hopping about on the ground.

Gabriel did some steps of the *Rigodón*, the state dance of the Filipinos, and demonstrated other dances he had learned in the Lowlands. I contributed a shaman's dance, imitating a trance state at the end of it. Even before I arose from the floor, I realized I had made a mistake. Either the rhythm of the dance, or the trance, had thrown the Ilongots into a state of excitement. As the young men swung to the floor for their next dance, Gabriel turned pale and trembled.

"I have heard my mother sing that tune," he whispered. "It is the dance they do when they are going to take a head. We should not have come here without soldiers. Ijah has brought us up here as sacrifices. I was sure of it this afternoon when we arrived. They have harvested the rice, but have not yet put it into their storehouse. This means that they have not yet taken a head to pay the *anitos* back for the life force they will receive from eating the rice. When it is ripe, they cut the rice stalk by stalk and stack it up on bamboo platforms to dry until they take a head."

I tried to convince Gabriel that we were in no danger, but as the young men darted past us again and again, I became less confident that the dance was merely a friendly social gesture. As the pace of the dancers quickened, my companion's terror increased.

"You must stop them," he sobbed at last. "Everyone is looking straight at me as he passes. You must stop them quickly. They are going to take my head."

The change in the dancers was indeed alarming. They looked dazed, and had a piercing and set expression about the eyes. They were staring at Gabriel with a concentration that sent shivers down my spine. Unless I did something quickly, Gabriel would probably die of fear.

I stepped toward the dancers and clapped my hands loudly. Throughout the evening Gabriel and I had clapped at the end of each performance. Taken by surprise, the musicians ceased playing. The dance came to a standstill. There was only one thing left to do. I must sing a song that would quiet them.

Fortunately I had grown up in a religious community. I launched into "Nearer, My God, to Thee." It worked like magic. At first they listened with interest to the music; then they moved their heads to and fro with the rhythm. Then one of them yawned and the others took it up as though it were contagious. Their eyes began to droop, and when I could see they were starting to resist the drowsiness, I changed to another hymn. The same sequence occurred again. At dawn I was still singing hymns. I was astonished to find that I knew so many.

Gabriel's nerve was broken. He looked at me gratefully when I insisted that he return to the Lowlands and gave him the money to take him back to Bangued. I realized that if he spent another day here he would almost certainly run amuck. It was better to have no interpreter at all than to have one who awoke contempt and suspicion. Through Gabriel I arranged for one of the young men of the household to carry my pack and explain my drawings and games. The fee was to be a handful of horsehair every day. When the lad wished to go no further south, he was to hire for me, at the house where he left me, another assistant who knew the territory I was about to enter.

By concentrating on learning the language, in which Gabriel had been instructing me intensively since I first met him, I would soon be able to speak the dialect well enough myself to give the non-language tests at least.

An hour after Gabriel left, I set out for a clearing higher in the mountain, which could be seen dimly across the canyon. I might have stayed on longer with Ijah, but the cut rice drying on the bamboo platforms under the banana-leaf thatch bothered me. Probably I could find ranchos where the grain had already been put away.

With me was the young man whom Gabriel had engaged, and a half dozen of his friends. The trail led up the steep side of the canyon, then across some flats where the grass was so high that we walked through a tunnel. Here and there the country was cut by deep ravines, and we crossed them on huge roots and primitive suspension bridges of woven vines and rattan that made me dizzy. My guide carried my pack over these sections as though he were walking along a flat country road.

We arrived at the clearing shortly after noon. A shout brought men, women, and children around us in a moment. They appeared out of nowhere, and greeted their friends from the neighboring village with shouts and peals of laughter. I was much more of a curiosity here than I had been the day before. Apparently I was the first white man some of them had seen. The diversion was welcome.

Soon everybody was playing with the puzzles and experimenting with pencil and paper. Again, their drawings were excellent. They also made high scores on the puzzles, and they were not shy about doing them nor apologetic when they made mistakes on the Maze.

I was again given the compartment usually occupied by the young men who came to the community house to court the women of the group. The three suitors who were there when we arrived made arrangements to sleep in the already crowded compartment occupied by the young men of the house.

The air circulated freely through the chinks in the bamboo walls and under the raised floor of my room. The heavy thatched roof made an effective screen against the afternoon heat. I lay idly listening to the confused sounds without, in which were mingled children's voices, the birdlike twitter of the young women as they vied with each other for the attention of their admirers, the growling of dogs, and the ever-present afternoon chorus of the cicadas.

I was happy. What did it matter that it might take me a year or two to work my way to Manila, if I could live with these free and spontaneously friendly people? A couple of months of intensive work on their language and I would be able to learn about their institutions, their kinship system, their economy, and their magical and shamanistic practices.

As the preparation of the evening meal progressed, the chorus of household and jungle sounds was pushed into the background of my attention by the savory odor of food. In a slice of reddish sunlight, filtering from the eaves diagonally across the house, were tiny particles of blue smoke. Through the chinks I watched a wrinkled old woman as she moved into the beam and was lost again in the shadows from which she had emerged. The sun's rays revealed an expression of great patience and concentration. I marveled that a human being could be so completely absorbed by the simple task of cooking. On the coals of her slow fire I could see a half-dozen bamboo cylinders, olive green at the top, where the fire had not scorched them, and shading downward from tan through mahogany red to black, where they were charred by the heat. Deftly she plucked one from the coals, tilted it above the glossy surface of a traylike leaf, and removed the cover, made of a larger cylinder of bamboo. From the creamy throat came a cascade of dazzlingly white rice grains.

The woman was an artist. When I came to the evening meal I saw that each kernel of rice was as perfect as a snowflake, and as fluffy. From other tubes, laid on a number of fires, appeared a wide assortment of exotic vegetables and meats, including a tender mauve banana blossom, bamboo shoots, pale green tips of rattan plants, small boiled bananas with cubes of sugar-cane pith, squash, and several leafy vegetables and roasted roots which were strange to me.

In the center of the heap of food appeared the hindquarter of a giant tropical porcupine, which the men had been turning on a spit beneath the house. I was already dizzy with the variety of colors and odors when an enormous leaf was slid before me and I was told to eat. Was this my food for the week? I was surprised when, at the end of an hour, I had stowed it all away.

My desire to sleep after the heavy dinner was frustrated by my assistant, who told the gathering about the songs I had sung in his clearing the night before. From the interest he raised, I realized I could not escape another evening of singing and dancing. Bamboo jugs were hauled from under the house. They contained fermented sugar-cane juice, which the Ilongots extracted from sugar cane by crushing the stalks in a primitive mill.

I had seen the process in the afternoon. They had made the mill by laying a large log against a tree trunk. The top of this log had been hacked flat, except for grooves cut into it to carry off the sap. The roller was a round twenty-foot sapling, one end tied with rattan loops to the tree trunk, the other extending out over the flattened log. The stalks were fed in between the sapling and the log, one at a time, by a woman. A man standing at the small end of the sapling, twenty feet away from the tree, pressed down on the pole and rolled it along over the stalk. The sapling served as a lever as well as a roller. The juice ran off through the grooves to a piece of bamboo attached to the side of the flattened log, which funneled it into a pot. After extraction, the juice was boiled, cooled, enriched from jars already fermenting, and set aside until it began to turn sour, when it was considered ready for use.

On the previous night no wine had been served. Even so, the natives had appeared dangerously aggressive in their dance. I watched my new hosts now as they set out a dozen jugs before the fireplace of the oldest patriarch in the house. The young men who had come along with me were pleased at the prospect of an evening's drinking, but for me it brought back the picture of the Negritos at their feast, aggressively lashing out at their dogs.

As the contents of the first large jug was poured into coconut-shell cups, a foreboding of evil and danger, amounting to conviction, possessed me. The men produced their drums, and the old patriarch dug a battered bronze Chinese *gansa* from beneath his mats. It was very old and had a hoarse, deep ring. From among their possessions, the women brought out the bamboo mouth organs and xylophones.

Soon all the group were singing. The songs went round and round the room, each man taking a solo, which was then repeated in chorus. The excellence of the music and the warming effect of the wine picked up my spirits. The little mugs were circulated repeatedly.

Finally my turn came to sing. I had found that the Negritos liked the rhythm and the tune of "Jingle Bells." Now I tried it out on the Ilongots, with such great success that I sang it over and over again. At first the drums and *gansas* picked up the rhythm. Then, as I repeated it, the Panpipes, xylophones, and nose flutes came in. Before I finished, a chorus of voices joined me, supplying words of their own to the music.

The fires on the clay hearths flickered. In their rosy shifting light, white teeth, brown eyes, and lithe, handsome bodies gleamed or grew shadowy with the rising and falling of the evening breeze.

It seemed to me that I had no reason to fear these pleasant people, overflowing with music and good will. Now that they had shown they could appreciate my song and even sing it with me, I felt more easy about them. Surely my foreboding of evil was groundless. Soon the pulsing rhythm of the gong and the drums lulled me to sleep. The Ilongots dissolved into flitting dreamlike figures.

I opened my eyes; the fitful puffs of wind, which earlier had fanned the fires into rhythmic bursts of light, had now grown into a strong, steady current of air sweeping down from the east. It had blown the opalescent pall of smoke from the room. The bodies of the Ilongots stood out in bold relief against the red glow of the fires. An oily perspiration, drawn out by exercise, covered their skin, giving them a metallic sheen. They were no longer human beings filled with good will. They were sinister animated figures of bronze.

## HYMNS AND HEAD DANCES

All the younger men, including the lads from the near-by clearing, were dancing in a circle in the center of the room. They had only one face and one rhythm. The old men at their drums, and the women at their instruments on the edge of the dancing group, were tied into this rhythm by an invisible current. The slightest movement might hurl me into that mysterious vortex. I lay perfectly still, peering out from under closed lids, attempting to collect my thoughts. Fear to the point of panic had got hold of me, but I was not yet sure what I was afraid of. I needed time to decide which was the real world and which was the world of dreams.

I examined the sounds, colors, and shapes, and the quality of the dance movement. Suddenly I realized that they were singing the head-hunting song which had set Gabriel shaking the previous night. But now *I* was the object of that terrifying concentration. The rhythm of the dance had been set, its direction determined like an arrow in flight. And I was the target.

The benevolent old gentleman at the gong had undergone a mysterious transformation during the hours that I had slept. Now the hard lines of his face expressed cruelty and condemnation. Round and round moved the dancers, slicing the air with their broad-bladed head knives.

I could not accept the cadence of this ceremony as my destiny. The old men had known many men before and had controlled many situations similar to this. I would have to act differently from their previous victims. I would have to act now.

My body bounded from beside the hearth. I felt a roar in my throat, a sound such as I had never heard, which paralyzed the old man's hands above the gong and the hands of the men at the drums, and which froze the dancers.

For a moment even the flames stood still. Two long steps carried me to the center of that frozen circle of dancers. Before the old man or anyone else had found the will to act, my own body was doing a crazy, violent dance. A voice which possessed me—my own voice, yet not mine—was singing a crazy song. All around I saw the open mouths of the dancers, the women, the old men at the drums.

I watched the hard lines of the patriarch's face change from astonishment to surprise, and gradually relax into the good-humored expression of the day before. As my body bounced and my arms made motions which somehow were attached to that strange voice within me, the astonishment on the faces of the men turned into amusement. With the change in the audience, I felt my song and my dance changing. The bounce left my muscles. Soon I was dancing waltzes for them, as I had done the previous evening. As the blackness outside the windows gave way to sickly gray, I was again singing the doxology and "Nearer, My God, to Thee."

Roars of laughter gave way to snores, as the wine and the soothing religious music anaesthetized my audience. In the midst of a sleeping household, where only the children's eyes peeped at me, I softly sang Brahms' "Lullaby" as a finale.

When sunlight flooded through the glassless windows of the large room, dispelling the mist from the sea of bright green treetops below the house, it was difficult to believe that the mad dance of the night before was not just part of some nightmare I had had. In the jungles and mountains a great gulf is fixed between the night and the day worlds. My mind would not cross it now, as I watched the women laughing and singing at their task of preparing the morning meal. But here, as at Ijah's house, I saw the cut rice stalks drying on bamboo platforms under the banana-leaf thatch.

The afternoon before, all the members of the household had drawn their picture of a man for me, and had done my puzzles. I would not be able to collect their dreams or give the other tests until I learned the language, and I would have to pick that up on the trail. If I moved on, spending only a night in each house until I knew more about these people, I would not lose the advantage of the element of surprise, and their feeling of curiosity would not have time to give way to other emotions. The squirt gun in my pocket, full of ammonia, felt comfortable now, rather than heavy.

I woke my boy and pointed south. He declined to go farther, but a lad of the house helped to pack my things. After breakfast he set out with me for another community, which, from the angle he described in the sky, I judged we would reach by midafternoon. About noon we met a little group of men who were blacker than any mountaineers I had seen on this central range, and who were almost as small as Negritos, but more hairy than any Negritos I had met.

My boy talked with them and tried, by sign language, to tell me something they had said about the trail ahead, but I could not understand him. The travelers looked so fierce that I half wished the boy would refuse to go farther. But bidding them good-by, he picked up my pack and we set out up the trail.

# FOURTEEN

# MacGregor and the Enemy

THE air was warm and moist, and the trail hot, especially in the grass tunnels. About two o'clock, as we reached the high ground across the valley from the house we had left, we heard voices and thumps on the heavy packed earth, as though men were running. I wondered, with panic, why men should run in this peaceful wilderness. The sound grew louder. Three horses ridden by natives appeared around the bend. The men carried rifles in saddle scabbards, and wore pistols at their belts. They were followed by three pack horses, and a number of men on foot carrying packs. Near the rear of the procession rode a grizzled old man who looked like an American. He introduced himself as MacGregor, and explained that he was a prospector. I knew this territory had not been completely mapped, and I had thought myself to be the only white man within thirty miles. The old prospector was about as surprised as I.

"Well, Jesus, Joseph, and Mary!" he exclaimed. "What are you doing on this goddamned trail?"

I told him that I planned to travel south through the mountains to Manila, stopping at villages on the way to give my nonlanguage mental tests. Whenever I paused for breath, he shook his head. "Well, I'll be goddamned! Of all the crazy ideas! I never heard tell of such a fool!"

At last he asked me if I had had lunch. When I confessed that it had been limited to a sweet potato, he told his men to make camp and prepare a meal, also instructing them in dialect to transfer the load of one of the pack horses to the other two and to put a blanket over the empty packsaddle so I could ride.

"With any other group in the Philippines a crazy galoot like you might get away with such a scheme," he went on. "But if you try it among the Ilongots, the chances are ten to one you'll never reach Manila. And if you had enough soldiers to protect you, the people would get sulky and refuse to do your tests.

"I've got a camp in Abra and I'm going to take you along. We'll be going through some mountain villages where the people are as savage as they are down here, but you'll have a chance with them. If those people like you, they'll help you. Down here they'll probably kill you if they don't like you, and they're sure to kill you, to keep your *anito* with them, if they do like you.

"Just a few years back a man I met came here from the Field Museum to study these devils. They liked him, told him all they knew, and gave him everything they had. They had been drowned out by heavy rains for a couple of years, and good weather happened to start just about when he arrived. They thought he'd brought it. I've heard since that they loved him like a brother. He was part Indian himself and took to them. He must have been a great guy, but when he told them he was leaving, they snipped off his head like that." Grimly the old man snapped a dry twig.

"They've got you coming and going. If you act crazy enough, the Moros in the Southern Islands think you've come straight from God and treat you like a prince. These people think a guy is in with the *anitos* if he's as crazy as you seem to be, and they want to keep his spirit in the district. If they think you're wise, they kill you to keep your savvy for the tribe. If they think you're a fool, they'll kill you because you're in with the *anitos*. If they dislike you, they'll kill you because they think you're bad. You may get away with a few more nights like the last two, but the first ones who really like your singing will take your head and keep it as a spirit music box, and think they have honored you in the bargain. What's the use of taking a ten-to-one shot when you can find people just as good up north, where the odds'll be one to ten? I don't often feel so cussed strong about things," he concluded, "but I'm simply not going to let you go down among these devils, if I have to take you out hog-tied."

I really did not need such vehement persuasion to make me change my plans. Lack of sleep and the hard trail in the humid heat had made me submissive. But I was glad the old man took a firm stand, for I could now retreat without the feeling that I was running away from my own fear. I was about to give my bearer my remaining supply of horsehair, but the prospector objected on the ground that it would flood the market. Giving him a generous day's pay and explaining that I had changed my plans, the old man sent him back. He put the horsehair and trinkets in his own saddle-bag. "This will pay for your ticket back on my train," he said. "I'll use it the next time I come down."

For the next week I listened with increasing astonishment to MacGregor's accounts of his experiences during nearly sixty years of adventurous living. He had been on his present venture for three months and was glad to have someone to talk to. His most astounding tales concerned the thirty-odd native wives, from half as many mountain tribes, whom he had married during his life as a prospector. He was an authority on native marriage ceremonies and customs, and scrupulously observed the laws of courtship and the taboos of the native groups into which he had married.

"Pick out the one you like, give her old man a deer, sit through some ceremonies, and the girl is yours," he said. "She's bashful and sweet for awhile. When she starts to get grouchy and thinks she can rule the roost, you simply send her back to her family with another deer and a few silver pesos. This gives her enough wealth to insure marriage to some younger man, and everybody is happy. The old native leaders really like it. They think marriage to a white man, even for a short time, brings new *mana* into the tribe, for we whites are supposed to have strong spirits. You'd think they'd raised race horses and knew the dangers of too much inbreeding."

MacGregor possessed as strong a spirit as any I had encountered. In the villages through which we passed, everybody knew him and was fond of him. About the only thing he did not forgive in the natives was their habit of killing the younger of every pair of twins.

He was himself a twin. "What chance would I have had if I had been born to one of these devils?" he asked, spitting contemptuously.

MacGregor had been prospecting in northern Luzon since the beginning of the century, and before that he had looked for gold in Australia and New Zealand. I explained that I wanted to study the Ilongots because by learning to till the soil they had moved up the ladder of human progress, so that they were a step above the hunting-and-gathering Negritos.

Next above the Ilongots, who carried on only a shifting, dry-land cultivation, would be a people who also domesticated animals and irrigated and fertilized the soil, and who were learning to live together in territories where the rights of more than one kindred group had to be considered.

"I can put you down in just such a place—Bontoc—in the center of a people who've learned to live in cities," said MacGregor. "There must be almost three thousand in Bontoc and about two thousand in Samoki, its sister city across the river. They're not as dangerous as the Ilongots, because since the turn of the century, they've been in close touch with the American authorities and the Lowland Filipinos. There's a sprinkling of people up there who speak English, so you'll be able to get along without an interpreter."

Although I had not expected to go to Bontoc until after I had returned to Manila, the Bontocs were on my program. Now, as I sat in the humid jungle heat, Bontoc sounded like paradise. I tried to voice a grudging consent to go along with MacGregor, but he could probably detect a grateful eagerness beneath my feigned reluctance.

Four days of travel took us across the Magat River valley to the area northeast of Buguias. MacGregor kept to the high mountain trails. We were in the home country of his servants, inhabited by a people he referred to as Kankanai, because they spoke the Kankanai dialect. They were a branch of the Lepanto Igorots, and were called "enemy" by the peoples around them because they occupied the impregnable mountain heights and defended themselves resourcefully against the Bontoc, Ifugao, and Kalingan head-hunters. So far as was known, the Kankanai were not, and had never been, head-hunters. They were well-built, handsome people, heavily muscled like the Kalingas, but not quite as Oriental-looking. Many of them, especially the women, had the large lustrous eyes of the Ilongots. The men cropped their hair, and the women wore bangs in front, with long hair hanging down their backs.

The hands and arms of both the men and women were tattooed. On the backs of the hands of the men I noticed a circular tattoo which seemed in some way to represent or refer to the sun. There were also tattoos on tumors, goiters, and areas of the body which had been badly bruised or sprained. Tattooing had some religious significance, and when it was applied to the areas of the body in which there were blemishes or imperfections, it was thought to exert a therapeutic influence.

Most of the men, including MacGregor's servants, owned little toilet sets, including metal spoons for cleaning their ears and homemade metal tweezers for pulling out face and body hair.

The houses had high, peaked thatched roofs, which looked like square wigwams. There were many well-made stone pigpens, housing pigs which seemed healthier and larger than any I had seen in the Lowlands. Usually the trails leading from house to house in the ranchos were paved with flat stones, with rock gutters to carry off the frequent downpours of rain. Around the barrios were low terraces, flooded with water, in which the natives planted rice and taro. The terrace walls were usually built of clay and seeded with grass to keep the banks from washing away.

Near many of the houses were rock-fenced corrals for the horses which the Kankanai raised. MacGregor told me there were no other horses in the Philippines which could compare with them on the mountain trails for toughness, endurance, and sure-footedness. When I saw the eagles' nests in which they had been reared, and the way the natives pushed them up and down the slippery paths around their mountain ranchos, I could well believe him. Both the men and the women rode these sturdy ponies, bareback or with primitive leather saddles with slender copper stirrups which they made themselves, for the Kankanai had been mining and forging copper for hundreds of years, certainly before the Spaniards had entered their territory and made treaties with them about 1830.

After that they were famous in northern Luzon for the counterfeit Spanish coins they made and circulated throughout the territory. The Spanish never objected to these counterfeits, for currency was always scarce in northern Luzon, and the stream of Kankanai coins added to the metal supply of the island.

The native coppersmiths also made skillets, jugs, and other utensils which were highly prized throughout the island. MacGregor had never been able to discover the native methods of smelting the copper, and no one else had learned their secrets, so far as he knew. They also did hard-rock gold mining, attacking the narrow veins of native metal, wherever they were found, with their primitive iron axes and crowbars, following the veins along the steep cliffs, often hanging like spiders on slender strands of rattan. The gold-laden quartz they dug was crushed with stone hammers, ground fine between flat stones, and then panned so that the rock particles could be separated from the dust and nuggets.

The Kankanai also obtained gold from the stream beds in their copper pans, saving the finer particles of float, as well as the heavier dust. This skill at panning gold, which MacGregor said was greater than he had seen anywhere in the world, won for them his undying admiration. I was not sure whether it was the gold or the horses which had made him adopt the "enemy" as his family. He had always paid them fairly for their dust and nuggets, and seemed to have their absolute confidence. Their primitive knowledge of gold-bearing rocks and of formations in which gold was likely to occur, and their skill at handling the horses, accounted for the fact that for twenty years he had been using the Kankanai as servants.

"I feel at home with them because of their religion, too," he said one day as we feasted in one of the larger houses of a particularly high rancho, where his head boy lived. "Among all the mountain groups of northern Luzon, they're most like the Christians, since they do no head-hunting and believe in one god. They're superstitious about the *anitos* and the ancestors, but they don't regard them as gods, and they're no more afraid of ghosts or of death than most of the civilized people I've known."

He sent back the meat to be boiled by his own cook. "I'm never quite at home eating here," he admitted, "until all the meat has been cooked twice. We're having horse meat, and as likely as not, the horse died of distemper, or fell off a cliff and was not found for a day or two. Whenever an animal dies of sickness or accident, these people eat it. As often as I tell them how dangerous it is, they keep right on doing it. One of their favorite foods is dog meat.

They starve the dog until it's almost dead, then feed it a bucket of rice, beat it to death to make it tender, and cook it on a spit, with the half-digested rice as dressing."

The vegetables at the feast were plentiful and varied—squash, tomatoes, cucumbers, dry-land rice, and *camotes*, a kind of sweet potato, in abundance. We also had both mangoes and bananas, which abounded in the territory.

Apparently *camotes* were the mainstay of their diet. Wild pig and deer were plentiful in the territory, and eel was served at the feast and on several other occasions. I was told that few other kinds of fish could navigate the small mountain streams of the Kankanai territory. There was plenty of *tapuy*—rice wine—at this feast, and at the others we attended. It was served in carved wooden bowls.

The house posts and floor beams were not carved, as they had been in the Ilongot houses, but the walking sticks, spoons, bowls, and lime boxes were attractively decorated. I saw numerous carved statues of human beings. They were small in size, and rugged, but portrayed great vitality. Also, the likeness of a dancing man was carved on most of the shields. MacGregor had the impression that this dancing man, the sun tattooed on the back of their hands, and the little *anito* figures, were in some way representative of, or dedicated to, the high god, as were many of the songs and dances.

These people sang a lot, both at their feasts and on the trails. They had two musical instruments I had not seen before. One was a piece of bamboo, carved down the middle so it looked from the side like a tuning fork. The women played it by holding it in the left hand, striking it against their right forearm. Near the septum, at the closed end, was a hole which they thumbed as they played to change the pitch of the sound. This instrument had some religious significance and was thought to offer protection to its bearer. The women often carried it and played it as they walked along the trails.

At the feasts and ceremonies, the men played pairs of narrow, long-barreled wooden drums, which were so flexible that the player could alter the pitch by pressing the drum barrel under his arm or between his legs. The drumheads were made of well-tanned pig or lizard skin. The men played these with both hands, and obtained different sounds by striking the head at the center or on the side. The drums alone sounded like an orchestra. There were also brass gongs played with sticks, like those of the Negritos, but the sticks were not wrapped or covered with skin. The Kankanai too called these instruments *gansas*.

The men also accompanied their singing and dancing by striking a small stone on a steel bar. It sounded like the triangle used in American orchestras.

One of the most characteristic things about their ranchos was a low bamboo platform outside every house, on which they deposited offerings of food or flowers to the ancestors and to the high god, another step up toward the altar of the temples of modern man. Unlike the Ilongots and the Kalingas they did not have community houses for extra wives, for the Kankanai were monogamous. Their children were betrothed at an early age by the parents, and often set up housekeeping in early adolescence. Divorce was possible, but the divorce rate was not high. They attributed sickness to the *anitos*. Once it had arrived, both the high god and the ancestors would help cure it if they were asked to do so in the feasts and ceremonies.

"When a man dies," said MacGregor, "they have a funeral feast to which the whole community is invited. It continues until all of his accumulated property has been drunk or eaten up. It works like an inheritance tax, and shows their political foresight." Similarly, he felt that their making and circulating counterfeit Spanish coins when they were needed proved their flair for economics.

I had to agree with him that the greatest inventive genius of the Kankanai was expressed in their jewelry. He had mentioned their skill at casting and beating gold the first day I met him, and he had referred to it often even before we reached their territory. "They've invented something in the line of adornment for women," he said, "which, when it becomes generally known, will make them famous and blessed in every household throughout the world."

He would tell me nothing about it. I would have to see this primitive invention before I could believe it. I had begun to think there was some catch to MacGregor's story, that this invention was something like the wampas bird which flew backward, which I had heard about in childhood, when at the last rancho we were to visit before we reached the Bontoc country on our way north, he produced the goods.

There were three women and two adolescent girls in the household, all of whom were completely silent as they served us the evening meal. It was quite a change from the lively buzz of conversation which was usually stimulated by MacGregor's appearance and continued until he was out of sight. He watched me expectantly.

"Are these women deaf mutes?" I inquired at last. I was mystified, since I remembered distinctly hearing women's voices when we first reached the rancho before I entered the house. He spoke to one of them, and she smiled, revealing a solid, gleaming gold surface. I noticed that all the others held their lips open a little so that gold showed through from inside. So this was the great invention—a broad, flexible golden band which fitted inside the lips and turned woman's vanity against her loquaciousness, since when wearing the decoration the woman was unable to talk.

"Once you can afford one of these golden muzzles," he said, "you need have no fear of marrying a Kankanai woman. These ancient ornaments prove that to be what is regarded as beautiful a woman will even stop chattering."

Leaving the Kankanai territory we descended rapidly in a northeasterly direction toward Bontoc, going along ridges where the rank jungle growth gave way to fragrant pine forests. MacGregor's servants were no longer hurrying to see their people, so our journey was more leisurely. From day to day MacGregor went on with his task, long since accomplished, of convincing me that I should concentrate on the Bontocs and the Ifugao. Each time I tried to get his help in filling in the many gaps in my knowledge of the Ilongots, he showed his willingness to tell me what he knew of them and also used the occasion to go on persuading me that if I insisted on traveling alone, I had a much better chance of keeping my head among the more northerly groups which we were approaching. The Bontocs and the Ifugao are less dangerous than the Ilongots because their sacrificing of human beings is more conventionalized and is only a part of a system which also includes the sacrificing of domesticated animals. If someone has trouble with his voice, for instance, they can sacrifice a dog which is good at barking, growling, and baying at the moon. The Ilongots, however, would kill a man to get the power out of his voice and throat, instead of just sacrificing a dog. If anything goes wrong, the Ilongots kill someone to make it right, unless doing so is too dangerous for them. Their society is like a trigger-happy nervous person who has just had a gun put into his hands and shoots at everything that moves, even when he doesn't mean to. They are very much afraid of illness. When the *anitos* do not tell them in their dreams what to do for it, they stuff the sick person with food and leave him to survive or perish. When someone dies they do not take the trouble to bury him, but desert the house that he dies in, so it can become his sepulcher, whereas the Bontocs and the Ifugao can sacrifice animals and call down the thirty generations of ancestors who live in the Eastern Middle World, together with the sky god and the gods of the underworld, to help cure the sick person.

The Ifugao have an aristocracy or noble caste, a middle caste, and a serf or slave caste. The nobles cannot show fear in front of the people who are beneath them. Since they are usually the highest-ranking priests, they must act brave so the gods will not lose prestige. Every married man regards as his ancestors not only those in his own lineage, but those in his wife's also. It takes hours of rapid chanting for the noblemen of Ifugao even to mention all these ancestors. Before a conflict they make sacrifices and call on these brave ancestors, counting their deeds of valor until they are fully persuaded that there is no danger at all with such support. By the time they are ready to fight, each has a whole army of brave spirits at his command.

The Bontocs and Igorots eat dogs. Probably dogs were the first animals to be domesticated by man. MacGregor had also seen the Ifugao eat them on special occasions, if they were commanded to do so in a dream. They do not regard meat as ordinary food. Most animals are killed only as part of a ceremony. The ancestors and the spirits from the heavens and the underworld are always invited to eat the invisible soul or shadow of the food before the people eat the substance.

Every year after the rice is harvested, the men of Bontoc and Samoki line up on opposite sides of the dry river bed and attack each other with stones. They have shields when they start, but these are usually smashed up before the battle is half completed; if the men are lucky, they come out covered with bruises and bumps, if not, they may have broken ribs and fractured skulls. The next day they are all good friends again, but MacGregor said that at the time they look, and sound, as though they were trying to murder each other. They have to do this every year, or the rice would not grow in their terraces.

Every clan has a rice priest or priestess, usually chosen through a dream. After the old rice priest has died, someone of the proper rank always has a dream in which the gods elect him as the next priest. Everyone in the clan follows this leader in planting, caring for, and harvesting the rice. "You'll probably get to go to a rice-harvesting festival, as they're being held in Ifugao at this time of the year," said MacGregor.

I gathered that the United States Department of Agriculture, and all the accumulated scientific knowledge of the world, did not count for as much in Ifugao as the actions of these rice leaders.

The remaining days with MacGregor passed quickly, and I was sorry to say good-by to him when he set me down at the Lieutenant Governor's mansion in the city of Bontoc.

# FIFTEEN

# Bontoc

THE city of Bontoc, named after the subprovince in which it is situated, covers a territory about one-half mile square, divided almost equally into three parts by two gulleys which traverse it. It lies in a picturesque valley, with terraced slopes rising gracefully from its center like a park. Its 2500 inhabitants live in seventeen districts or wards (*atos*) which are presided over by councils of old men. A council is self-perpetuating, since its members decide when a man living in its district is wise, famous, or rich enough to be invited to join it and be called an *intugtukan*.

Before the American occupation, the *ato* council had the power to declare war on another group or challenge it to a head-taking contest, by sending a spear. If the dare was accepted by the challenged group, a spear or head axe was sent back in return, and there was war until one council or the other sued for peace by sending a present to the enemy group and asking on what terms peace could be obtained.

The old men of the *ato* council also had priestly duties to perform. The *waku*, the highest class of priests, decided when the citizens of Bontoc should celebrate holy days. The second class of priests performed a ceremony (*patay*) every new moon, in a sacred grove at the edge of town. Both of these ceremonies were dedicated to Lumawig, the high god of the Bontocs, who had a hand in the creation of all things. The third order of priests performed ceremonies to allay the *baguios*, or storms, to drive away cold or fogs, and to control the rains.

The *ato* council also exercised a judicial and police function in its community. The members were very diligent in collecting the fines—pigs, chickens, rice, and *basi*—they imposed for breaches of holy days, and for quarrels and grievances. Both the civic interests and the appetites of the priests accounted for this diligence, since whenever a fine was collected, they declared a feast and ate it up. Being priests, the old men had powers of divination to help them decide the justice of cases in which conflicting claims were made; they therefore felt no need for trial by jury.

One of the methods of deciding guilt between two parties, when testimony disagreed, was to have each chew a mouthful of dry rice and spit it out at a signal from the council. Since the guilty man would have a dry mouth, his rice would be drier than that of the innocent man. The priests also showed me a short, flat, carved stick, with the point of a nail protruding about one-eighth of an inch down at each end. Sometimes two conflicting parties were stood up back to back, and the stick was laid across their heads. It was then struck a sharp blow by one of the councilmen. The hot-headed man would bleed more freely than his cooler, more dependable opponent.

The old men were also experts in interpreting the actions of the omen bird and in making divinations from the bile sacs of the chickens and pigs which were paid as fees by the plaintiffs.

Each *ato* had three public buildings. One was the *pabafunan*, a clubhouse where all the men and boys over the age of four or five congregated, and where the unmarried men slept at night. The house stood in a courtyard surrounded by a fence made of phallus-shaped rocks and slabs of wood on which were carved crude human heads. In the head-hunting days these rocks and slabs supported the head baskets, into which the heads taken by the men of the *ato* were put when they were first obtained. Each young man who joined the *ato* was tattooed, progressively, according to the number of heads taken by his group, the tattoo not being completed until he himself had taken a head. Women were not allowed to enter the *pabafunan*.

Near the *pabafunan*, but with no adjoining passage, was the *fawi*, which served as council house for the old men. Unless a man was elected a member of the council, he could not enter the *fawi*. Beneath the stones of the *fawi* courtyard were buried all the heads taken by the *ato*, a few of which were sometimes dug up for ceremonial purposes.

The third public building of the district was the *olog*, the dormitory for the unmarried females of the *ato*.

The Bontocs traced their lineage back to a great flood. Fatanga and his sister, Fukan, were the sole survivors of it, and saved themselves by climbing up Mount Pokis, north of Bontoc. Lumawig saw they had no fire and went to a volcano south of Bontoc to get them some. Returning, he found Fukan with child. This made Lumawig fly up into the sky like a bird. My informants were not clear about why the god had left the first ancestors at this point, but I suspected that it was because Fatanga had broken the incest taboo and cohabited with his sister.

After the god's departure, the couple came down from the mountain and established the city of Bontoc. Their children intermarried and the population increased. After a time Lumawig decided to come back to earth to help his people and to look over various groups of Fatanga's descendants. He did not like the looks of the women any place but in Bontoc. Some had cropped their hair. Others were sickly, and others lazy. He met two sisters in Bontoc, however, who were just right. One of them, named Fukan after the first ancestress, so pleased him that he married her, after throwing a bean into her basket. Apparently he had brought the bean down from heaven, and this act was the beginning of the bean upon earth. He lived for awhile in Bontoc, taught the people there the art of agriculture, gave them patterns for their public buildings, instructed them in the proper ceremonies, and gave them names for everything, including the city of Bontoc.

I was led to a terrace in which a taro plant was growing which Lumawig was said to have planted with his own hands. The old men said that because Lumawig had brought this taro to the earth and planted it himself, it was eternal and would grow forever if you dug up the root for food and planted the crown again in the soil. Apparently there was a spring in this terrace which kept it always overflowing with water, so the taro had never died. The old keeper of the terrace told me that this water terrace was named *filang*, and that all the taro in the mountain country had been taken from this spot.

Lumawig was credited with establishing a code of ethics for the Bontocs, which was enforced by the *ato* councils. The Bontoc men were not to steal, lie, nor take more than one wife, and they were to be as brothers. Lumawig also gave them an economic system, in which the rice he had supplied served as currency in the exchange of all other produce. The smallest unit of exchange was a handful of *palay*, a small bundle of rice heads. The number of these bundles which could be carried conveniently by the average person was called a "burden."

The high-school students told me that the old people still translated Filipino and American currency into handfuls and burdens of *palay* whenever they carried on economic transactions.

The Bontocs lived in stone houses with roofs of thatch. The houses were neat and well made. By the side of each was a small, well-thatched, rock pigpen, with a level where the pigs slept and a level for collecting manure, which the Bontocs transferred to their rice terraces. Paved walks, in which the shape of each stone was defined by the bright-green moss and grass growing in the interstices, formed geometric designs around the houses.

I obtained drawings from the school children and pottered about the village for a few days, getting the men in the *pabafunan* to work on the mechanical puzzles, and quizzing the lads, who had been to school, about the Bontoc society.

After a child was four or five years old he no longer slept at home, but in a dormitory or clubhouse with other unmarried young men or women. Here the social life of the unmarried people was carried on. The boys' clubhouse was a meeting place in the daytime for the old men, who smoked, gossiped, and minded the babies while their wives worked in the fields.

I stayed with the American governor of the subprovince of Bontoc. He knew a great deal about the people and their history, and invited some of the old men to his house every evening to tell me about their myths and ceremonies. He was not surprised at my account of the spirit transformation of Ogong. He had often seen the Bontoc priest go into trance and speak with other men's voices, sometimes assuming the voice and facial expressions of a dead man he had known. The Bontoc priests, he said, had a well-developed tradition of spirit communication and spirit possession.

The Governor told me that the next village to the south was about a day's walk, and with my pack on a bamboo frame, I left the city. Carried on my head, the pack protected me from the frequent showers; when the weather was fine I slung it over my shoulder.

The ill-kept road along which I tramped was hardly more than a trail, and a pleasant quietness prevailed. The air was cool and exhilarating, and the round red mountains, with their vivid green foliage, were fresh and picturesque. On the trail I occasionally met girls, breasts uncovered, bright-red skirts reaching halfway to their knees, and feet bare, their bronze bodies glistening with perspiration from the exertion of carrying bundles of sticks, or leaves, or sweet potatoes, slung from a band across their foreheads. Usually they stopped to ask for a match and to pass the time of day, joking about me as they went on down the trail.

Toward late afternoon some boys caught up with me on their way from the sweet-potato land they were clearing. One of them, Tajo, had been to school and could speak English. He insisted on carrying my pack. He was the son of the Presidente of the village of Tapon, and said that while I was there I must stay with him in his clubhouse and take my meals with his family. When we arrived, his father confirmed Tajo's invitation and soon we sat down with the family to a steaming dinner of boiled rice with small, bright-red crabs (*agkama*), beans, and dried carabao meat which had been salted away in jugs. For greens we ate young sweet-potato leaves. The meat was high, but not objectionably so.

A drink, called *safueng*, was offered me at this dinner, but I declined it because it was served cold and smelled as though it contained a collection of all the germs in creation. With the Negritos I had made it a policy to eat everything which was offered me, but here I felt I must choose between certain death and displeasing my host. He was not surprised when I told him my stomach was too weak for such a strong drink, and admitted that to appreciate it a cultivated taste was required.

I inquired how the drink was made, and decided it would be more dangerous to a stranger than the Bontoc head-hunting. It was brewed with cold water, into which were poured spare cooked rice, *camote* peelings, cooked locusts, fish heads and skin, and all the meat bones left over from the dinner. It had to set at least ten days, but could be kept going indefinitely if it was put in a warm place and fresh ingredients and water were added from day to day to replace whatever was used.

Perhaps when the beverage got good and strong enough alcohol and lactic acid formed to kill the harmful germs, but nothing short of the prospect of losing my head could have made me take a sip of it.

After dinner Tajo took me to see the village and the places of interest in the neighborhood. It began to rain, and we ended up at the *olog* of the girl he was courting. It was a tiny structure, hardly high enough to allow a man to stand upright and not more than sixteen feet square. In the corner was a fire of fragrant pine boughs. The girls kept the baskets containing their possessions at their homes, where they ate their meals and lived in the daytime. Their sleeping boards were the only furniture in the little house. Twelve young women, varying in age from six to twenty-five or thirty, were gathered in the smoky interior. When we arrived, half as many young men were visiting them. The door was hardly more than a crack and I had to squeeze through it.

My entrance caused a great commotion. Some of the smaller girls whispered with terror and withdrew into the shadows, where only their wondering eyes were visible. Others tittered and sought refuge behind the older girls, who broke into a babble of excited inquiry. I had never been with so jolly a group. Waves of laughter swept through the cabin.

"What's all the excitement and laughter about, Tajo?" I asked, when a moment's silence gave me an opening.

"I'm explaining what a famous lover you are," he answered.

"But I'm a bachelor," I protested.

"That's what I said. Being rich enough to travel, you can have many lovers, but you are never chosen for a husband because you will soon be gone. I also mentioned the pictures you showed me of the places you have visited. They would all like to see them."

I hauled out my pocket photograph album. Most of the girls left the hewn slabs they used as beds and pressed into a half circle about the fire to look at the pictures. But recognizing pictures is an art which must be learned. They had great difficulty understanding the pictures. The trouble primitives have with photographs and diagrams makes it impossible to use them in intelligence tests. They overcame their embarrassment quickly, however, and were soon absorbed in what Tajo told them about the patches of light and shadow on the photographs.

Suddenly there was silence. Everyone turned his head to listen. A faint rhythmical buzz became audible above the patter of rain on the low roof. One of the girls sprang to her feet. Smilingly she admitted a young man. He slung the bundle of pine sticks he was carrying on the fire and stood by it to dry himself. Naked except for a loincloth, his rugged muscular body was studded with drops of rain which gleamed in the firelight. I liked this newcomer who surveyed me with steady eyes. These mountain people could respect a stranger because of the respect they had for themselves. Everyone talked at once in answer to his questions about me, and one of the older girls sat down beside me.

Presently the young man who had appeared so dramatically out of the wet night reclined on his lady's plank, and I learned the source of the buzzing sound we had heard outside. From his teacup-sized rattan hat, he produced a small bamboo jew's-harp. Holding it across his lips with the thumb and forefinger of his left hand, and with his right hand jerking a string attached to its bamboo tongue, he hummed the same song he had played at the door of the *olog* to announce his arrival. My subsequent attempts to play one of these little instruments ended in failure. The Bontocs always told me that my familiar spirit had given me no words for my songs.

One or two other lads dropped in as the evening wore on, and the gaiety of the party increased. The girl beside me offered me what I took to be dried shrimps to chew from a small bamboo tube. They were salty and tasted good, even after I learned they were cooked dried locusts. As the evening wore on we also munched sugar-cane pith, bananas, and other tidbits. The girls had gathered quite a supply of snails during the day in the rice terraces, and had them boiling in a pot into which everyone dipped, sucking the meat from the tiny shells.

My companion—called Betel because she had reddish hair which resembled the teeth of the Ifugao and the Igorots who chewed betel (both chewing betel and gambling were against the code of ethics left to the Bontocs by Lumawig)—babbled words to which I, not knowing her language, could attach any meaning I liked.

As the hour grew late, the younger girls curled up on their boards to sleep, or to feign sleep, while they watched the older members of the party. The smaller boys left for their clubhouses. Meanwhile the older boys and girls paid less attention to the group and more to each other. The embers in the fire burned low.

Tajo's girl had been sitting for some time between his legs, resting her head on his knee. Occasionally he stroked her hair or looked in it for lice, which he nibbled between his front teeth with a dreamy expression.

"Do you like those things?" I asked him, half disgusted, half fascinated, by the procedure.

"They are full of blood," he answered. "When you feel you will die if you do not own more of your lover, that blood will keep you alive; it tastes like air when you are choking."

The girl by my side had taken my hand in her lap and was playing with my fingers. Her sun-burned hair glistened red in the firelight. It was somewhat wavy, and I concluded that the Indonesian strain of her ancestry was more marked than is usual among the Bontocs. Her hands were rough from working in the fields, but I could feel the smooth roundness of her thighs through her thin skirt, woven, on a hand loom, of cotton grown by the Bontocs. Although there was more wood, no one moved to replenish the fire. The fresh smell of pine smoke was gradually giving way to the odor of expectant female bodies. The air was becoming chill.

My companion pulled me down beside her on the hewn tree trunk which served her for a bed. Her body, though muscular, also had a round softness. For a few moments we lay motionless. I was assailed by the old troubled feeling of perplexity to which the guest of primitive peoples is subject when, as so often happens, he must grope for a clue as to what is expected of him.

"How does one know what to do next, Tajo?" I asked into the semidarkness.

"You don't do anything unless she takes off your loincloth," he answered. "And then you may do whatever you like."

"But I don't wear a loincloth," I said.

The lad translated our conversation to the others. The *olog* rocked with laughter.

During the hours that followed, I found that Tajo's statement about doing what you wanted to had been most inaccurate. He should have said, "You may do what your partner feels will make a night of love last forever."

The muscular strength, flexibility, and dexterity which climbing the terraced walls and working in the fields had built into Betel's body, combined with the sharp nails of her toes and fingers, and with the sharpness of her teeth, made her dangerous. There was no freezing into immobility when I did not do what was expected. At least, whatever freezing occurred was in myself and was occasioned by pain. Betel seemed to proceed on the assumption that words were not necessary in love and that if a man could not know by instinct or intuition or from the subtle shadowlike movements and moods of his lover what was expected of him, then he should suffer.

I concluded that if Betel was any sample of the Bontoc mother the Bontoc children were not born in sin and conceived in iniquity, like the ancients of Judea, but fashioned in the art of subtle, wordless communication and conceived in the agony of interminable suspense.

As we walked home, toward morning, Tajo told me that he had first gone to the *olog* at the age of five, when he had donned his bowl-shaped rattan hat (*suklang*), and that he had been going there for twelve years. When he was nine, he had become interested in a girl and taken her presents—a flower, a bit of beeswax, an egg, a pretty rock. Occasionally he had also brought wood for the *olog* fire.

When he was twelve, his father had given him a *songkitan*, a girdle twelve to fifteen feet long, made of some dozen strings of twisted bark. Three years later he had received his *wanis*, the loincloth. The order of this progression—first the covering of the hair with the hat, then the confining of the belly in the girdle, then the covering of the genitals, seemed characteristic of the Bontoc culture, in which the individual exercised infinite control over his genital functions apparently without rejecting his impulses. It was as though the thoughts were trained first, the appetite for food second, and the sexual impulses last. Adults often quieted and soothed the children by stroking their genitals, and sexual play among children was encouraged.

Tajo said that the younger boys usually left the *olog* quite early, but by the age of nine they sometimes stayed all night. His girl had been very shy, however, and had given him little opportunity to experiment. At the age of thirteen, he had had his first love experience, with one of the older girls. She was some ten years his senior and had been trying for years to have a baby by every likely young man who came to the *olog*, so that she could be married. He slept with her off and on for a couple of years, and occasionally with some of the girls nearer his own age, before his present lover had made him into a monogamist. When I asked him if it was wrong to sleep with a lot of different girls, he was astonished by the question. "It's great fun to make love," he answered. "But when you find the girl you want to marry, you often have to leave the others alone or she won't see you."

The young girls were very shy and usually only let the boy whom they loved best court them; but if, as they grew older, they did not have a child, they accepted lovers more readily in the hope of conceiving. Even if these girls were not beautiful or rich, inability to have children brought them increasing attention from the young men not yet ready to marry. A Bontoc man did not marry a woman until she was with child, but a girl might choose any of her current lovers as a husband when she conceived. If she was sterile, she had many lovers and became a sort of educational institution. Usually when these women tired of being bachelor girls, they kept house for a man who could not find himself a younger girl to bear him children.

You might ask a girl if you could see her in her *olog*, or she might invite you to visit her; or, if the girl you wanted to see would not invite you, you could take a little firewood or some boiled eggs or tobacco to the *olog* and just visit nobody in particular. There was usually an *olog* in each *ato* and two or three *atos* in each village, and you could go to the neighboring villages if you liked.

Some of the higher-caste Bontocs arranged engagements for their daughters almost at birth, but if a girl was willing to lose her caste she could accept attentions from anyone she liked. She could sleep with the other boys first and marry her fiancé later, if he did not object.

Apparently venereal disease was unknown in the subprovince of Bontoc, outside of the city of Bontoc. Although divorce was easy, the couples, once married, usually remained together. From what I could gather, adultery was virtually unknown, and it was the only crime outside of murder for which a man could kill another man.

The blood feud was discouraged by the *ato* council, even in these extreme cases. The councilors tried to persuade the offended parties or their kinsmen to accept a fine, rather than to perpetrate a blood feud.

When we arrived back at Tajo's clubhouse it was after four in the morning, and he informed me that we would have to hurry over to his house for breakfast. It was still dark, but his father had already been up for half an hour and had the breakfast well under way. Soon a younger sister arrived from her *olog*, the mother crawled out of her sleeping box at the back of the house, and we sat down to breakfast on the earthen floor. The light was still poor, and we ate with the help of a blazing pine knot which rested on a flat rock.

There were bowls of steaming rice, which we ate with our fingers, and boiled eggs containing partly developed chicks. I had eaten these eggs both in the Lowlands and at Bontoc and was beginning to like them. Their complex flavor made them much more interesting than fresh eggs. We finished the breakfast with millet gruel sweetened by cubes of sugar-cane pith. Neither tea nor coffee was served.

When the sun came up at six o'clock, the family had been off to work in the fields for half an hour. I went back to Tajo's club, intending to sleep until noon, but it seemed I had just closed my eyes when I woke with a start. The villagers were running in all directions, shouting "*Cochon!*" and the air was full of bustle and excitement. I was certain we were being attacked by a head-hunting expedition until Tajo appeared.

"Come," he said. "There's a locust storm in the next hollow, and we must gather in a supply of them."

Each of the villagers was armed with a large funnel-shaped net, and carried on his back a rattan basket which resembled a large beer bottle. We ran up to the top of a small ridge, went along it for a quarter of a mile, and saw the swarm of locusts straight ahead, traveling through a ravine. Judging by their noise, it would have been more accurate to speak of a blizzard of locusts. The villagers, young and old, were dashing into the waves of pelting insects, swirling their nets in a whirling motion, and then stuffing the catch into the necks of their bottlelike baskets, plugging up the bottle with its rattan cover, then swirling the net again, screaming and laughing excitedly all the while.

Tajo had his basket full in half an hour, and when we reached the village again he emptied the locusts into a big earthen jar and went for another load. The women and children contented themselves with a basket or two, but he and some of the other men followed the locusts until sunset. I went to sleep, and when I woke in the afternoon, everyone in town was boiling locusts and drying them in the sun. When they were crisp they would be ground with uncooked rice and set aside in jars to make a special dish (*pinnatat*).

In the excitement of pursuing the locusts over the rough stones, one of the boys had bruised his knee. He came limping into town in late afternoon, and when Tajo returned, he told me that the boy was receiving the ministrations of a Bontoc healing priestess (*insupak*). I went along to see the ceremony. The priestess sat rubbing the boy's knee. At first I thought she was in a trance, because she was retching and spitting out saliva as she half mumbled, half sang, her prayers. Apparently the retching motions were a conscious device which she employed to build up a sort of suction, which she believed would pull the offending *anito* out of the lad's knee. She kept telling it to come out, to go away, to stop hurting her patient. After awhile the boy said his knee was easier, but I was curious to know if the priestess had stronger medicine. Tajo said that she did, and that she was willing to practice it if I would buy a chicken, a portion of *basi*, and a bowl of rice. But a member of the household or the priestess would have to go to the scene of the accident. If the priestess went, I would have to give her two handfuls of rice as fee. The chicken and wine cost a peso, and two handfuls of rice twenty centavos. I gave the money to the priestess.

Tajo and I and a boy who had seen the lad fall went with the priestess to the spot where the accident had occurred. She picked up a stick about a yard long, and pointing first north, then east, then south, then west, called on the sick lad's *tako*—his spirit or soul—to come home with us to the feast. She did not know whether the soul of his leg had been jarred out of his body by the accident, or whether it had been enticed out by the *anito* of one of his ancestors, or by someone who had known him and had died and wished to play with him.

In any event, the soul had got away. The Bontocs said it would be brought back by this ceremony. Souls, they said, were even more fond of chicken, *basi*, and rice than human beings were.

On the way home, as we crossed a creek which ran down through the bottom of a ravine, the priestess stopped and addressed another prayer to the *tako* of her patient: "Please come on home with us where it is warm. You will find it gets very cold here, around this water."

Tajo said that the spirit was not afraid to cross the stream with us, but that the souls of sick people were often fascinated by water and liked to play around in it as children do. When we got back to the patient's house, the priestess killed the chicken by beating it to death with a small hardwood stick. First she beat its wings, then its neck, then she banged on its head until it was crushed and the chicken was dead. Finally she pulled off the feathers, cut up the body, and boiled it for awhile, and we all ate.

Having financed the ceremony, I was given a leg. The portions of the others were smaller. I was told there was still another ceremony (*afat*) which could be performed for the lad, but this ceremony required sacrifices equal to the average yearly wage of a Bontoc, and the priestess usually did not perform it unless a man was near death, perhaps in a coma. This ceremony, too, was begun at the place where the illness or accident had occurred. A large hog was killed on the spot. A blanket, a bark girdle, a battle-axe, a spear, a live chicken, and some trinkets were all offered to the soul of the man who was ill.

Then everyone would return to the house of the sick man, where the hog would be eaten. The next day the chicken would be killed, and the priestess would recite a prayer claiming that the sick person was well, asking for an abundant harvest, and requesting that the spirit of the head-axe guard the door and that a spiritual broom of *palay* straw sweep away any words of black magic which had been said against the person who was ill.

This grand ceremony had never been known to fail, but there was a catch to it. Unless the spirits told the healer the patient would get well, no ceremony was performed. Like the old-woman healers of the Kalingas, the Bontoc women received their commission for healing in dreams, and they were often told in dreams what to prescribe for their patients. This Bontoc healing seemed to fall far short of the psychotherapy of the Negritos, since in Bontoc the offending spirits were simply invited to leave, and the absent souls asked to return. They were not communicated with, converted, and integrated, as the offending Negrito spirits appeared to be.

In order to get a more complete idea of the Bontocs' attitude toward the high god, Lumawig, I inquired about their beliefs concerning death, and about the prayers which were said at the funeral feast. They told me that often the person who is ill and about to die hears the *anitos* calling him, saying it is better in the mountains. When death occurs, the body of the deceased is wrapped in a blue blanket embroidered with white *anito* figures, and is set in a rude bamboo chair just inside the door of the house. Feasting and drinking begins immediately, and is continued for a length of time determined by the wealth and prestige of the deceased. During this time the old women sit watching, telling the deceased that people must die and must be placed in the earth. Each member of the family chants songs, saying how lonely he is and how much he will miss the deceased.

Before the burial takes place, the group chants: "You are dead. We are here to see you. We've done all the necessary things and given you a good burial. Do not come back and call on any of your relatives and friends." Off and on, the old people chant: "We are old and shall soon follow you."

Before the burial the property of the deceased is divided according to a rigid custom by which each of the children receives an equal share of the father's property.

The relatives also reason with the ghost, pointing out that he will have no one left on earth to make feasts for him unless he protects those who are living from other *anitos* who would kill them; their prayers tell of the good life in the mountains which the old men have seen in visions, and which the deceased can enjoy if he will go there to live and continue to co-operate on feast days with his living relatives.

After the dead man has been put into his coffin, he is rushed to the place of burial and covered up as quickly as possible. If a rooster crows, or a dog barks, or snakes or rats cross the trail before the burial is complete, it is a bad omen. After the burial, the men who assisted with it take a ritual bath, return to the house, and have a ceremony to propitiate the *anito*.

On the following day all the male relatives go to a stream and fish. That evening they have a "fish fry," to which all the ancestral *anitos* are invited. The relatives also spend the second night after the burial at the house of the deceased.

None of the prayers I collected invited the high god to intervene with the ancestors, as the Kalingan prayers had. But the *inpake* —the prayer which was said at the marriage feast when the couple's house was finished—was addressed to Lumawig. He was asked by one of the priests of the *ato* council to accept the union of these two of his children, to help them to be prosperous, to keep their animals fertile and large, to make the rice yield heavy, to give them large beans, and to help them to dwell together in harmony.

I was especially interested in this ceremony because central among the sacrifices which the priest offered to Lumawig was my old friend the egg. But now it was the sacrificial symbol of the perpetuation and growth of society.

Lumawig was also honored in the act of taking heads, since it was he who had introduced the practice, during his stay on earth. He had led an expedition against a neighboring village, and taking the head of one of the enemy, he had said that men would always take heads because he had taken this one.

The old men also told me a story about the moon, a story which, in their minds, supported head-hunting. The moon was making a pot one day when the sun's child came around to watch. The paddle with which she was moulding the pot slipped and cut off the child's head. The sun placed it back on, and said something about men taking heads because the moon had cut off his son's head. To me, however, it seemed that what had made head-hunting so important was the festival which taking a head initiated. When the head was brought back to the *ato*, it was hung for a day in the stone courtyard of the *fawi*, in a conical basket. A dog or a pig was killed and eaten at the first day's ceremony. The second day, the head was taken to the river and washed, and the jawbone was removed for a *gansa* handle. In the evening the head was buried under the stone floor of the *fawi* to initiate a month of celebration, during which carabaos, dogs, hogs, and chickens were sacrificed and eaten, and the men did no work except what was absolutely necessary.

After the head had been buried for three years, it was dug up, cleaned, and again hung in the *fawi*, with others dug up for the occasion. After a one-day ceremony it was reburied, this time for an indefinite period.

All the men in the *ato* shared in the victory, had a chance to boast to each other and to the men of the other *atos*, and had the record of the event tattooed upon their skin.

The most common answer when I asked the Bontocs, "What's the best thing that's happened to you?" was the same as it had been among the Kalingas—the attending of a feast ceremony. When they were asked to name the best thing that had happened before that, they often mentioned earlier ceremonies; they refused to leave the subject of feasts.

But the most direct connection between head-hunting and the high god appeared in their description of the fate of the spirit of the man who had lost his head. The spirit obtained a head of fire and went to the sky world (*chayya*). The *anito* or ghost of the beheaded man, who lived in the sky world where Lumawig resided, was called a *pinteng*. So far as I could learn there was no other way of getting to *chayya*. When anyone was inspired to take a head, it was the *pinteng* who gave him the impulse to kill. It was as though they wished to keep recruiting new members for their heavenly fraternity. But there was a note of morality in the Bontoc attitude toward head-taking which had been completely lacking among the Ilongots, and which I had not heard stressed among the Kalingas. The heavenly associates of Lumawig did not approve of the taking of the heads of women and babies. It seemed inconsistent that they should inspire all murder and then disapprove of the murder of women and children once it had occurred, but the *pinteng* were credited with punishing the murderers of women and children, whereas they completely approved the taking of men's heads in a fair fight, or at least in a fight in which the attackers risked their own lives.

The Bontocs did not expect to be either helped or punished by their high god under ordinary circumstances. Like Tolandian, Lumawig had created the world and society, put it together, and left it to shift for itself unless the earth beings got him into such a rage that he did not know what he was doing. Then he would not selectively punish the beings who had made him angry, but was likely to destroy everything. As long as the Bontocs had a ceremony each new moon and observed a holy day two or three times each month, he was satisfied. He had played a much more direct part in the building of the culture than had Tolandian, even materializing as a human being and living among them. He had sent his wife Fukan and her two sons to the downstream world in a coffin, setting on the coffin a rooster and a dog before he floated it down the River Chio.

The two groves of trees near Bontoc where the monthly ceremonies were held, were thought to have sprung from the bodies of the two sons of Lumawig, who were treacherously killed on their way back to Bontoc after they had been sent to the downstream world by their angry father.

Moving from the Negrito, who had no agriculture and raised no animals for food, to the Ilongots with their shifting agriculture, to the Bontocs, where kinship groups had learned to live together so well that blood ties were melting into political relationships and the blood feud was giving way to fines and punishments, I had noticed a steady growth in the interest in private ownership and private enterprise. However, the spirit of co-operation, which had impressed me so among the Negritos, was not lost in Bontoc society. All of the technology involving the building of rice terraces, the fertilization and cultivation of the land, irrigation, house building, and the caring for and slaughtering of animals, was interwoven with ceremonies which required the co-operation of kinsmen, in-laws, and perhaps *ato* members.

Each ceremony was accompanied by a feast, by drumming and singing, and by prayers. My father's old dictum that where work is concerned one boy is a boy, two boys are a boy and a half, and three boys no boy at all, was contradicted on every hand, making me suspect that the West had forgotten that work could also be fun if it was done in the spirit of festivity, and that we have become too lazy to motivate work and learning in a way which makes it interesting to the child.

What also astonished me was the sharp contrast between the work periods and the leisure periods of the Bontocs. The ceremonies which directed their work, requiring that every person act as though he were a cogwheel in a great machine, did not intrude themselves into the leisure periods of the children. At night and on the holy days which the old men declared two or three times a month the children were left alone and allowed opportunities for spontaneous activities and association among themselves.

The clubs in which the unmarried members of the society lived were as free from domination by the past and by the elders as the workaday world was full of it. Here the children could choose who would be their friends, could talk and amuse themselves all night if they wished, and could play at being old and responsible, or at being infants.

A tree, a rock, a spring, might have a spirit in it—the god-ancestor or the *anito* of a human being now inhabited a feature of the physical environment. But not all rocks and trees were thus animated. The souls of Lumawig's children were thought to animate the sacred groves of trees near Bontoc. The children of the sun were believed to dwell inside of hot mineral springs and volcano craters.

There were also some animals which were thought to have human souls or to have sprung, at some point in the past, from human beings. The rice bird (*tilin*), the serpent eagle (*coling*), and the monkey (*caag*), were supposed to have been created when various children felt rejected and unappreciated, or too severely or harshly treated. Two young men quarreled and lost their human forms, one becoming *finias*, the giant lizard, the other *cayyang*, the crow. There was a snake (*owag*) which attended a funeral and behaved so well that it became obvious that he, or one of his progenitors, had been animated by a human soul.

A selfish mother who gave her two sons only the food of pigs and dogs and yet criticized them and devaluated the wood they brought her, caused one of the sons to throw down his bones from a tree in which he was standing. Where he had been standing, there now appeared a serpent eagle, who said to the other brother, "Take these bones to our mother for her wood, and tell her that she only wanted my bones in the first place, and that now she can eat her own pig food and gather her own wood."

The two sons of another family were given no meat to eat and yet were asked to work all day protecting the rice crop from the inroads of birds and animals. At last, feeling that he was starving, one said, "I think I'll be *caag*." Hair grew on his arms, then all over his body, and he took to the jungle. The other boy was soon hairy too, but he went home, told his father, and then ran out of the house to the mountains and climbed a tree. The father followed, calling him, but the monkey jumped from the tree, struck out at him with his arms, and roared "Ha! Ha!" The father returned home and soon the mountains were full of monkeys.

A little girl was transmuted to *tilin*, the rice bird. She kept bothering her mother for *moting*—raw rice—and was scolded and told she should not talk so much. When the mother finished pounding the rice and went for water, the child, reaching for the rice, upset the large basket and was caught underneath it. When the mother lifted up the basket, a little brown bird flew out, singing, "Kingnik, Kingnik. Good-by, Mother. You would not give me *moting*."

All snakes were believed to have souls, and the Bontocs told me that since snakes know the bad *anitos* on every trail, it's best to be friendly with them. If you are in danger, a snake will crawl across your trail and you should pause awhile and let the danger get out of your way. If another crosses when you resume your journey, you should pause still longer. If a third one crosses, you should turn back and give up your project altogether, or at least wait for a better day.

The Bontocs had many other omens, and they were very important to them. The seeing of omens was mentioned most often in answer to the fear question of the Emotional Response Test, and dreams about omens were the most frequently mentioned of the fearful dreams. This was partly due to the fact that almost any fearful thing that happened to a Bontoc was regarded as an omen. Every snake he saw, and every snake dream, was an omen. Every crow he saw, every dream of big black birds, every dream of rats, was regarded as an omen. Falling stones and landslides were omens. The crumbling beneath one's feet of even a little fringe of earth seemed as important, and aroused as much fear, as an avalanche. A small reddish-brown bird, *ichur*, inspired as much confidence or fear as though it were the size of a guardian angel. Ghosts were also omens. Every dead person or stranger seen in dreams, every wisp of mist and phosphorescent stump, every unidentifiable sound or echo, every shiver, or flush, or inner pain, was an *anito*, a ghost, who was trying either to destroy or to warn.

*Anitos* were most likely to attack you when you were alone. Whenever your scalp crawled, your mouth got dry or your skin clammy, or you felt a shiver in your spine, you could be sure *anitos* were near.

I suspected that the girls of the *olog* talked of ghosts to discourage their lovers from leaving before dawn. Certainly they had an inexhaustible supply of ghost stories, all of which were said to be drawn from their own experience and that of their friends. Often they were corroborated by a number of witnesses, and the documentation could only have been improved by photographic films and sound recorders.

One night a group of boys arrived from a neighboring town. I could hear their bare feet on the trail as they approached, and their heavy breathing as they reached the door. They reported seeing the figure of a girl rushing along the trail to meet them. They had recognized her; she lived in the clump of trees below the trail. But they had not seen the girl herself—the figure had a phosphorescent glow and traveled with a sweep, instead of with jiggly steps. When she was face to face with them, her hands caught fire and she disappeared like a comet toward the mountain. Everyone accepted the fact that the real girl had not long to live. They knew she would die because they had seen the ghosts of other people who left their bodies at night to visit the *anitos* in the mountains just before they died. Soon a rock would roll on her, or she would be hit by a falling tree, or caught in a whirlpool, or she would fall from a rice terrace, or develop pneumonia. The boy who had planned to leave the group and visit her did not do so. He was already mourning her loss.

The next week two brothers coming down from a *camote* patch felt themselves grow faint and unable to move, and distinctly heard the war cry of the Bontocs and the war cry of the men of Berlig, their traditional enemy. Then they saw two fighting groups come together. The fighters rushed around, past, and over the boys. Then they realized that the raiding parties were only the *anitos* of the men of Bontoc and of Berlig, and that they had only the quality of coldness and the smell of dankness, with no other force or content. Even the blood that flowed was a ghostly red, like the color of sunset. The battle passed over them along the trail, and they were free to go. All of them thought it was a great portent, but nobody knew what it meant. Certainly the ghosts had come along to hear the story, if a dank smell, a freezing wind, and creeping skin were any evidence of their presence.

I had heard ghost stories before, and tales of supernatural things from the old Mormon pioneers, but never had I met the unnatural and uncanny at such close range as I did in the Bontoc *ologs*.

When I was ready to leave the village of Tapon, Tajo's father made me a short spear, which I could use as a sort of handle for my pack, and which he said would protect me from the *anitos* as I went over the mountains to Banaue. It had a half-dozen barbs on each side. *Anitos* were particularly afraid of the barbs on this type of spear, and would be less likely to make me lose my way or to push me from a cliff or a rice terrace along the trail if I carried one. On the morning of my departure, Tajo's father also killed a chicken and said a special prayer to his ancestors, who inhabited the mountains between the Bontoc and the Ifugao country, asking them to make my pack lighter, to keep the trail firm, and to see to it that my way was easy and safe.

# SIXTEEN

# Journey into Ifugao

WAVING good-by to Tajo who accompanied me to the main road, I started over the divide that separates the Bontoc territory from Ifugao. After walking for about two hours up the steep grade I was astonished to hear a motor behind me. There had probably not been another on that road for weeks. It was a Ford touring car. The back seat was full of five-gallon tins of gasoline. The driver, a Filipino in a khaki suit, pulled up beside me and asked where I was going. "Ifugao," I replied shortly, anticipating his offer to take me across the mountain and not wishing to admit that I could not afford to ride.

"I am going that way too," he said. "I'll take you over for ten pesos. It would cost you twenty-five if you hired a car." I thanked him and said that I preferred to walk.

"I'll take you for five pesos," he persisted.

Food alone had cost me over a peso a day among the Bontocs, and I had been told that it was equally expensive in Ifugao. I would have to stay there at least six weeks to get a statistically valid sample of test results, so I had decided not to spend a centavo for transportation until I was ready to go back to Manila. Since my plan of going back along the central mountain range had now been abandoned, my entire remaining capital of eighty-three pesos would be barely enough to get me back to Manila.

"No," I replied firmly. "I'm going to walk."

"Have you had lunch?"

"Yes."

Not at all taken aback, he produced a flask. "I can see you haven't had a drink," he said, passing the bottle to me. "You'd better ride up to the top of the hill with me, at least," he went on. "I have been driving alone all day."

Since the bottle was almost full, I accepted his hospitality. I got into the car and launched out into what proved to be an eight-hour nightmare. Julio Santiago, the driver, was such a storehouse of information that I simply could not stop talking to him, and he was one of those friendly people who must always look you in the eye as he speaks. I could not tell whether he was driving from the road he saw reflected in my own eyes, or whether he had been over this Bontoc trail so often that he could have driven it with his eyes shut, from the feel of the ground under the wheels. He had the kind of lean, wiry physique that looks grown-up at seventeen and does not age noticeably after that. He appeared to be in his late twenties, but I discovered that he must have been a great deal older than that.

When the Americans moved into Bontoc in 1900, Julio was already five or six years old. His people were Iloko, from the village of Bokai. His family had gone to Bontoc with Dr. Truman K. Hunt, the American who first set up a civil government there, to take advantage of the law and order established by Americans, and had set up a merchandising business. Julio clearly remembered Dr. Hunt and Ernest Jenks, who had lived in Bontoc in 1905 and had written a report on the Bontocs for the Bureau of Ethnology.

At about seventeen Julio had become a guide and bearer, helping to carry the luggage of American teachers and officials and of the Filipino constabulary through the steep, roadless mountains. When roads were built throughout the mountain province, he became a chauffeur. He had worked with United States Army officers and doctors, and with Dr. H. Otley Beyer, and he had taken the judges of the local courts from district to district.

Julio's accounts of the lives and policies of these American pioneers in Mountain Province changed the feeling I had had about

Americans as colonizers. When I was in Manila I had heard, with disgust, of American clubs to which no Filipinos were admitted and of other practices which smacked of a master-race outlook.

But the doctors, Army officials, and educators of whom Julio told me had obviously had an almost religious attitude toward democracy. With Julio, at least, they had left the impression that Americans were tough, fearless, fair, and just, and that there was not enough money on the earth to buy the slightest favor from them in the courts or in politics.

One of Julio's first memories was of four hundred Bontoc warriors who had been persuaded by the insurrectionists to take a three weeks' march to Manila, equipped with spears and head axes, to conquer the United States Army. At the second volley of shots from the Yankees, they turned on their heels and ran all the way back to Bontoc, never again to question American power or authority.

As a young man Julio had noticed the change which the introduction of guns brought about in the institution of head-hunting. The old practice of taking a single head in revenge abruptly disappeared. The guns enabled people to take a dozen heads as easily as before they had taken one. In revenge it was equally easy to wipe out a village. He told me of a conflict between Banaue and the down-river districts in which just that had happened, in defiance of the newly established American authority. The down-river people had come with seven guns to attack Banaue, but the Banaue men had thirty guns. After wiping out the whole raiding party, they had gone on to the village from which the raiders came, and wiped it out as well.

Julio told me of the great native leaders who had arisen to champion the new way of life which the Americans were introducing. One of these, a man from Berlig of mixed Ifugao-Bontoc parentage, who had risen to the status of a noble, had been killed by a member of an enemy group to settle a feud which had been raging before the advent of the Americans. The noble was offered a betel nut—a token of friendship—on arriving at the village. But his host let it fall from his hand as he offered it. Then, as the nobleman politely stooped to pick it up—in the democratic American way—the host struck off his head.

"In this territory, if anyone ever drops something as he is handing it to you, do not stoop to pick it up," Julio said. He glanced at the bulge in my pocket made by my ammonia pistol. "They know here that Americans carry firearms. They know that a man who is a good shot can kill a half-dozen men even when he is wounded with a spear thrust. But at close range, if your back is bent and your eyes are on the ground, the biggest coward in Ifugao is not afraid to snip off your head."

Julio stopped on a spur which commanded a superb view, and we again took a swig at the bottle. Since he had been looking at me most of the time instead of at the road, I was especially worried about his drinking. I took one long draught and emptied the bottle. The great green mountain took on a soft, hazy quality, and I got the feeling that the car would travel through the air as well as it did upon the road.

Julio's intense dramatic way of speaking, and his gleaming eyes, transported me to the scenes he was describing. Five thousand Ifugao in full war regalia, with their plumes and shields, their jawbone-handled *gansas*, their drums and bamboo clappers, paraded before me at the funeral feast of Bahatan. Bahatan's body, with the head sewn on to it, lay in a circular temple with walls of reed in a clearing on the top of a rounded hill. The priests chanted their prayers, and to determine when the revenge expedition should be undertaken, watched the sacrifices to see if the omen bird (*pitpit*) preferred the sacrifice dishes of pork, of chicken, or of rice. The noble, commoner, and serf moved about, each in his orbit. The body was carried to the tomb and buried, each priest-kinsman saying the proper thing, calling on the proper deified ancestors.

After the funeral, ceremonies took place in the houses of the nobles. The men and the women, facing each other across the fires, criticized each other in song, then sang about love and war, then broke the lines in which they were ranged, and in the true spirit of carnival acted out the love of which they had sung.

"Do you know," Julio said, as we topped the divide and paused to glance at the mountains rising tier on tier out into the province of Isabela and toward the seacoast, "I'd have paid you ten pesos to go into Ifugao with me. I don't like whiskey and only brought it to steady my nerves. These people are head-hunters, you know." He glanced at my unclipped fairish hair. No doubt he was thinking that no head-hunter would take an ordinary black Filipino head when he could have a prize like mine.

"I am going to stay in the house of the Presidente at Ifugao," he went on. "There will be a feast tonight. They invited me weeks ago, and when I accepted, I thought I'd take a police officer with me, but I'll have no time to get one tonight. Now, I'd feel a lot safer if you'd come along to the feast. The boys will be drinking rice wine and you can never tell what they will do when they've had a drink." I was watching the billowy treetops below the narrow dugway and paying him scant attention.

"The girl I sleep with when I'm in Ifugao," he concluded, feasting his eyes on my sun-bleached hair, "has a younger sister. I'm quite sure I can get her for you if you'll come along. Polygamy is the rule in Ifugao, and it doesn't matter if you have a wife elsewhere."

We left the divide and started down the canyon of Ifugao. As we rounded the bends, I wished that I had drunk all the whiskey. Now it was raining and the road was not visible fifty yards ahead. I wondered how such a reckless man could be afraid of headhunters.

Now he was telling me about the religion of Ifugao. It seemed most appropriate to be speaking of gods at a time like this, when skidding an extra foot on any turn would bring us face to face with them. Apparently, in Ifugao it did not matter whether we skidded to death up, down, or to the side. The gods were everywhere—in the sky world, in both the upstream and the downstream regions of the middle earth world, and in the underworld. There was even a subbasement, where you would find the gods if you happened to go over an extra big cliff and fall through both the land and the underworld.

The four layers of the universe were inhabited not only by gods but by their wives and children, each with his rank and status, arranged like the Ifugao society. Each had appetites, likes and dislikes, and a predilection for flattery. The favor of each could be bought, or wheedled, or cajoled. All came down daily and possessed the Ifugao priests in their ceremonies, spoke through the lips of the Ifugao, drank through their stomachs, and danced with their legs. Each of them was jealous of the others, and of the power, luck, success, and wealth of mortals. Their minds were full of schemes, plots, and intrigues.

It was obvious, as Julio talked to me, that the Ifugao did not have the freedom and spontaneity of the Negritos, the Ilongots, or the Kalingas, and that they lacked the stability and philosophic maturity of the Kankanai and the Bontocs. It was as though Tolandian had, like Brahma, split up into layers of gods, ancestors, and men, and was no longer in any way supreme. But no Buddha had arrived to condense and simplify the endless ceremonies which the gods required of the Ifugao as he carried on his agriculture, his animal husbandry, his manufacturing, and his social intercourse.

# SEVENTEEN

# The Rice Terraces of Ifugao

In the late afternoon we slid to a standstill beside the large white stucco schoolhouse at Ifugao. Julio switched off the ignition and took a small satchel from the back seat, and we set out for the house of the Presidente. Our path led across a wooden footbridge which spanned a small river. Before us in the fog and rain there loomed a stone wall with a ditch at its base. The path turned sharply left and followed the bank of the ditch for a hundred yards. The wall was some thirty feet high, with neatly clipped grass between the large stones. Halfway along, a little waterfall cascaded down into the ditch from the top of the wall. Julio crossed a large, flat stone slab over the ditch and disappeared in the mist.

I had fallen a little behind at the waterfall. When I reached the rock bridge, I was completely at a loss to know where he had gone, since the trail ended abruptly against the wall. The bridge looked wet and slippery. "Julio!" I called out, wondering if he had fallen into the ditch. His answering voice came down from the sky. Looking up, I saw him almost at the top of the wall. He seemed to cling to its smooth surface.

"How the hell did you get up there?" I called out.

"Just climb up the rocks which stick out from the wall," he answered. "You'll see them when you cross the ditch."

I walked across the flat rock, and there, leading up like the rungs of a one-sided ladder, was a series of variously shaped protruding stones. Julio waited for me at the top. "It's not nearly as difficult to climb as it looks," he said. "But you will feel safer if you take off your shoes. The steps never cave in. Hundreds of people travel them each day, and once you feel your bare feet on the rocks, you'll have no fear of slipping."

I took off my boots. The rocks did feel much more solid then, and the depressions, worn where many feet had fallen before, gave assurance that the ascent was not impossible. "Keep looking up and in toward the wall," said Julio, when I'd climbed half the distance, "and you won't even notice that there aren't two sides to the staircase."

The feeling of relief I had on finishing the climb was short-lived, for now the trail continued along the top of the wall, with a thirty-foot drop to the left, and a pool of water to the right. "Look into the terrace paddy and not down at the ditch," said Julio, as we started along. "Step on the boulders and not on the grass, and you won't lose your footing. You'll soon get used to the trail. If you slip, don't forget to fall up the mountain into the pool. The water isn't deep."

The rain had abated somewhat, but the visibility was still poor. We climbed one perpendicular terrace wall after another. All the walls were built of the same kind of uncut boulders, and down each came a tiny waterfall like the first. Always the trail followed the tops of the walls, forming a narrow slippery path, with the muddy water of the terrace on one side and sheer space on the other. The mist which had hidden the top of the canyon when we began to climb soon filled the bottom, and we were clinging to the side of a terraced world without beginning or end. As we climbed, the walls loomed higher and higher. Once or twice Julio had to ask his way. I did not blame him for wanting moral support on such a journey.

But his conversation as we walked along bolstered up neither his morale nor mine. The first man who directed us along the way made him think of a man condemned to ten years at hard labor by one of the judges he had recently chauffeured. Three of the man's children had been chopped to pieces by one of his fellow tribesmen, who had run amuck. When the man found his children dead, he had taken his dog and tracked down the murderer, only to find that others had robbed him of his revenge by killing him before he arrived. There was nothing left for him but to kill the sisters of the dead man whom he found weeping over their brother's corpse.

"The judge simply had to lock him up," Julio said, "because he had killed only two of the murderer's sisters, and he had lost three children, so he would not have stopped until he killed another member of the murderer's family. All the Americans say that Ifugao is the worst place in the Philippines for running amuck. Down in the Moro country, men will bind up their bodies, so they won't bleed to death quickly if they're wounded, and then go out after Christians, with no regard for their own life. But in Ifugao, they kill everybody when they run amuck, even members of their own family."

I had not heard of a Negrito or an Ilongot running amuck. I had never heard it even mentioned among the Kankanai or the Bontocs, and I suspected that Julio's preoccupation with the subject was due to a case or two in which he had been involved as the judge's chauffeur. But as we went along, I was soon disabused of this idea. Twenty years as a guide and bearer in the mountains of Ifugao had furnished him with accounts of amuck for every terrace we were traversing, until I expected every innocent passerby we met to stab Julio and push me off the terrace.

The stories Julio told me as we threaded our way along the slippery walls, every boulder of which seemed like the trigger of a death trap, were more like the bad dreams I had collected than like stories I could have made up myself.

I sighed with relief when at last we arrived at a little clump of houses, each standing on four wooden pillars and roofed with thick, overhanging thatch which made it look like a great toadstool. The canyon was almost blotted out in darkness as we climbed the ladder of the house belonging to the Presidente of Banaue. Inside the single room a dozen people reclined or squatted on the floor of hewn planks worn smooth by naked human bodies. The women were lined up on one side of the central fireplace. They wore the same type of short skirt that I had seen among the Bontocs, with no clothing above the waist, and bare legs and feet. The men wore loincloths. Each man's spear rested against the smoothly worn plank walls of the boatlike dwelling. But the spears were not accompanied by the head axes which I had seen in the Bontoc houses.

Large portions of a pig, killed and cooked for the feast, lay on leaves in the middle of the floor. "The Americans would have roasted the pig whole," said Julio, "but here in Ifugao, before it is cooked, portions of it must go to the priest who butchers it, to blood relatives who are not bidden to the feast, or who are unable to attend, and to the local politicians and the in-laws of the host."

I was ravenous after the long climb. Even the bitter viscera soup and the musty sour rice wine tasted good. Our host was hospitable to a fault. I had to admit to myself that the younger sister whom Julio had mentioned in the car—and spoken of as we climbed the terraces, whenever he thought I was getting discouraged with the project—was a devilishly attractive girl. But to stay awake after the wine and huge quantities of food, and the fatigue of climbing, was more than I could manage. It was warm in the overcrowded little house, and the air was heavy with the odor of roast pork, rice wine, and human bodies.

I could catch only a word here and there of the conversation, and not a word at all of the songs in the queer religious language, in which the men and women took turns criticizing each other, as was their custom in this type of social gathering. Even Julio did not know the words of the verses well. "In their songs the men are saying something about the women eating the crabs and snails they gather at the terraces, rather than bringing them home to their husbands," he said, when I questioned him about one of the verses. "In answer, the women are singing that the men eat up all their catch of the delicious fish on the banks of the stream, and do not share it with the women." He did not know when they would start singing about love and war, causing the men and women to break up their lines and intermingle. Knowing the respect that most primitives have for a sleeping person, I was certain that I would be left out when the intermingling began, for the monotonous chants, on top of the food and wine, were acting on me like a field of poppies. Even the occasional sidelong glances of the younger sister failed to keep me awake. Julio noticed me drowsing and suggested that I retire. He said he would bring me the younger sister later if he could.

The Presidente led me to a near-by bamboo shack which he

## THE RICE TERRACES OF IFUGAO

used for a storeroom. I unrolled my blanket, and lulled by the steady patter of rain on the roof, was soon asleep.

Later I was awakened by the full moon shining on my face through the partly open door of the shack. The rain had ceased, and the clouds, which on our arrival had been low, sodden, and slate-colored, were now lofty, white, and flocculent. The mysterious muffled roar in the air, which had formed a background to the sound of the rain as I climbed the terrace walls, was now clearer. The terraces were so constructed that the water from each one overflowed into the one below, making thousands of miniature waterfalls. The roar had a ghostly quality since it came from every side at once rather than from one particular spot.

I looked out. In front of the door the muddy water of a miniature rice terrace reflected a giant tree full of fireflies, startlingly bright, like the winking lights of a city. As I looked, the pool changed into a shadowy silver stairway. The separate steps were laced together with strips of shiny white ribbon. I had a chilling sense of unreality until I realized that a cloud had drifted past the moon, lighting the terraced hillside above and reflecting it in the pool. Looking more sharply I saw that each of the terrace walls up the canyon formed a step of the stairway. In the reflection the giant stairway seemed to go down into the pool until it reached the edge of the world, ending in clear sky surrounded by clouds. The waterfalls formed the silver lacing on the terrace walls. At the bottom of each was a cloud of spray—marking the tangible source of the roar.

The view was stupendous. For miles up and down the canyon the terraces rose in endless sweeping curves. I felt impelled to survey it from above. Scrambling up a zigzag row of protruding stones, I turned again to look and marvel. From this height a thousand terraces were visible below and their glistening surfaces were even more startling than the stairs above. I scrambled up another wall and then another. There was a ridge ahead, past which the hill fell away into a side canyon. I followed the narrow terrace path of slippery stones. The side canyon was deep and almost circular. Breaking into full view at the point of the ridge, it had a breath-taking beauty.

There was a weird, crazy, jumbled quality about the scene which suggested violent emotion, as though the mistress of a divine boudoir had flung her mirror down from heaven in a rage, to be shattered on the earth's uneven floor. My sense of time and direction was vague as I stumbled across the dappled expanse of subterranean sky. The thought of the moon's mirror crashing into my skull stunned me, and my breath came in gulps or not at all. I could not tell if it was fear or ecstasy which bound my ribs.

Suddenly I found myself in a clump of trees like the one in which the Presidente's house stood. I walked quietly, hoping not to disturb the dwellers in the toadstool buildings. The moonlight scene was like a picture torn from a book of fairy tales. Halfway through the little cluster of trees and houses I stumbled on a pig. It started up with a sleepy grunt. From under one of the houses came the yelp of a startled dog. The next moment the stillness was slit by furious barking. Pulling the ammonia pistol from my pocket, I retreated backward down a narrow path, wondering if I should waste my supply of precious liquid at a ten-foot range, or if the ammonia would stop him once he had decided to charge me. As I felt for the trail with my heels, afraid to take my eyes from him, I vainly tried to quiet him with soft words.

The trail ended abruptly in a low clump of bushes. To my left was a round sweep of terrace wall which dropped for fifty feet; to the right there was a tiny pinnacle of rock, up which I scrambled. I could go no further.

In one of the houses the flicker of a fire, visible through a crack in the door, was fanned into flame. In a moment, it was burning brightly. The door opened and a ladder was let down. A naked man descended. The firelight glinted on the broad steel point of the spear he carried. Seeing me there at bay on the rock, he walked warily toward me, carrying his spear in readiness for instant use. I hid the pistol under the corner of my pocket, fearing that the sight of it would trigger his spear. He spoke to the dog and its deafening din ceased. I glanced down the sheer face of the cliff and then back at him. He was speaking to me in the native dialect. I answered in English. Neither of us understood a word the other said, but his voice was friendly, and I tried desperately to conceal the tension and quaver in my own. There was a moment of silence. Then, using his spear as a staff, he clambered onto the rock and sat beside me. Relieved, I slipped the pistol into my pocket.

Fires were being lighted in some of the other huts. I could not help admiring the lithe, powerful body of the head-hunter, even as I wondered if he was about to transfix me with the spear. I pulled a pack of cigarettes from my pocket and held it toward him. He accepted one, and his eyes smiled up at me as I lighted it for him. A breeze stirred the leaves of the trees into a low murmur. The dog cocked his head to one side and looked at us inquiringly. I pointed to the crest of the hill which towered above us, scarcely lower than the white cloud banks, for which it might easily have been mistaken. My companion pursed his lips and shook his head in the direction of the bottom of the canyon.

By turns, we talked and we smoked in silence. Neither understood a word the other said, but nevertheless we argued stubbornly for the virtues of the top and the bottom of the canyon. The terror which had welled up inside me as I retreated before the dog's flashing teeth and as I regarded the gleaming spear point, was changing into a glow of exaltation. But remembering Julio's story of the hero who lost his head as he stooped to pick up the betel nut which had been offered him as a token of friendship, I leaned in from the edge of the precipice, determined that I should not alone fertilize the plot below, if my host should suddenly decide to make me a sacrifice.

But no fear could long withstand the force of the light filtering down from the lofty canyons of churning clouds and up from their bottomless reflections in the pools. The little pinnacle on which we sat became a world lost in limitless space. Nothing but the rock and the man beside me had any solidity. All else was expanding clouds and weaving patterns of dark and shine. At last my companion was convinced that I was determined to go on, and commenced, in pantomime, an unmistakable series of final instructions. Pointing to the dog, he clamped his hand on the calf of his leg. My pistol would take care of strange dogs. I nodded knowingly. Then he seized a twig, and bending it over, placed the butt end of his spear against it. He was telling me to beware of spear traps set along the trail for wild pigs. I had seen many of those since I had first joined the Negritos, and by now considered myself an expert on them.

I made a sweeping gesture toward my own thigh to convince him that I understood. Then he walked his fingers down his arm from his elbow to his wrist, and as he touched the back of his hand, he allowed it to drop. He was warning me of a pitfall. I was familiar with those, too; they were not so dangerous as a spear trap, but uncomfortable if you had to spend the night in one, and perhaps good for a broken leg. I jumped from the rock pinnacle to show him I knew what would happen if I stepped into such a trap. He grinned and nodded, and stepping down beside me, led me to the upper path.

The walls were higher now and the strips of level water narrower. The side canyons were precipitous and the trails not as well worn as those below. I plunged repeatedly into the icy terrace pools to keep from falling down the man-made cliffs. Even the earth and hard rock walls had lost their stability in this crazy diagonal world. The winding terraces writhed on every side, like snakes of quicksilver, each time I caught a slanting glimpse of them while staring at the trail.

At last I reached the topmost level and limped up a grassy mound, sitting down at the very top on a little bald spot where there were small rocks and debris. The moon's power was fading, as though its effort to drench this leviathan of man's handiwork with silver had drained its life force. It grew rapidly wan. The stairway, a specter of its former self except for the white skeleton of falling water, disappeared. A deathly stillness brooded over the canyon, and the gray terraced rims became wrinkles on the visage of a mummy. I could feel the damp chill in the air now that I was no longer kept warm by the effort of climbing. I shivered in my wet clothes. Something rough I was sitting on became uncomfortable. Shifting my position, I noticed that what I had thought to be a stick was actually a bone. Looking more closely I saw more bones and bits of dried flesh and hair, partly covered by some sort of matting. I realized I was sitting on a grave, and found my feet. In the afternoon, Julio had told me that the Ifugao always buried low-caste members of their own group on a mountaintop when they were victims of head-hunting. People who had died a natural death were buried beneath the houses in which they had lived. This grave must have been dug long ago, before the terraces reached so near the top.

I stepped down, hoping that no one had seen me at the top of the knoll. At least, no one could accuse me of the anthropologist's sin of hunting skulls there.

For a moment the world hung in the balance between night and day. As if in answer to the signal of a bird's sleepy chirp, a string of clouds on the horizon caught fire.

The gray of the canyon softened. Other clouds glowed low on the horizon. The mist on the opposite wall of the canyon separated into layers, which thinned steadily and were dragged out by the morning breeze into long, ribbonlike wisps. The shiny rim of the sun appeared. Its rays lit red patches of ground on the hillside across the canyon, and picked out countless designs on the sparkling rocks and grass of the terrace walls. The sun trembled for a moment like a red plate on the green shelf of the distant hill. Muffled sounds of life burst up from below. The world of Ifugao had awakened.

I knew I would be looked for at the Presidente's house. With a last glance at the enchanted canyon, I started down, having no idea of the route I had taken the night before or of the location of the house of the Presidente. As I descended, women, naked but for their bark girdles, appeared on the terraces, clipping the leaves and grass from the walls with long hooked poles, and trampling them into the mud of the terraces for fertilizer. They stared at me, startled, as I passed. Some reached for their skirts when they saw me coming, or tucked the ends of branches or grass beneath their girdles, to serve as skirts. Others watched me, legs apart, mouths open, with an impudent expression on their faces, as if to say, "He who disturbs a lady at her work is worthy of no consideration whatsoever."

Far down the canyon I met a delegation from the Presidente's house. They had been scouring the mountainside for me, and were immensely relieved when I appeared. It would be a great disgrace to the Presidente if his American guest were to have his head taken.

The return journey took three hours. I was given a very welcome breakfast, served by the younger sister, who watched me demurely as I ate. Julio insisted that I was mad. He had found the moon shining squarely on the blanket where I had been lying when he returned from the feast. At least that was comforting since it held out the hope that the madness might be only temporary. As he guided me across the canyon to the provincial schoolhouse, where I took leave of him, he told me to what great pains and expense he had gone to find me a wife for my stay in Ifugao. He kept mentioning the stupendous figure of twenty-five pesos.

"Anyway," he said with a sigh, "I've done all I can. Younger sister was insulted when she found you gone. The girls gossip in their clubs and news of it will spread. Now you'll probably have to content yourself with a bachelor's lot while you are in Ifugao."

"The Lord giveth and the Lord taketh away. Blessed be the name of the Lord," I said to him consolingly. But he refused to be consoled. In my behalf he had employed his resources, used his contacts and his knowledge of the Ifugao, and spent at least a little money for the privilege of bringing an uninvited guest to the feast. He had served me as a guide and a go-between, functions for which he was in the habit of being well paid.

By all rights I should have paid him twenty-five pesos for his efforts in my behalf. He explained that just for his successful efforts in obtaining me a mistress the legitimate fee was much higher than the figure he was asking, which included paying for me at the feast, giving the younger sister a present, and wasting half a day of his time wandering up over the rice terraces to look for me.

"But, Julio," I said. "I'm not one of those rich Americans you've been in the habit of serving. I'll need at least fifty pesos while I'm in Ifugao, and another twenty-five to get back to Manila, and I have no way of getting any money until I'm back there."

Then he hit upon a scheme. He could take me back to Manila in about six weeks, and would consider the twenty-five pesos a fair payment for the obligations I had already incurred and the transportation back. If I finished my testing in Ifugao in about a month, as I planned, I could hike over the mountains to Bokai, where his mother's people lived, and I could stay with them until he came along. He would be through with his work up north in about six weeks and was planning to stop at Bokai anyway on his way back to Manila. He pulled out a road map. When I was through testing in the Banaue school I could walk across the mountains to Loo. He marked off a route on his map. I was to cross the canyon at Banaue and pick up the trail to Hapao, following it as far as Kinga, a distance of about fifteen miles. From Kinga, I would go down to the Asin River Rest House.

"That's a good day's hike," he said. "And from the Rest House you cross the high divide between Mount Abao and Mount Tabayoc to Loo, a distance of about ten miles, and another hard day's hike." From Loo I could catch a bus to Cervantes, twenty miles distant. Then I would be forty miles from Bokai, an easy three-day hike to the North. "There's a good trail all the way," he said. "From Cervantes on, the trail follows the Abra River. You can hike the whole distance in a week. I've done it myself with a heavy burden. For a peso you can hire a pony most anywhere along the way, if you get tired or if the heat becomes too oppressive."

I agreed to his plan, and he thought I should pay him the twenty-five pesos on the spot to bind the bargain, but I gave him only ten, with the promise of the rest when we reached Manila. I could get back from Bokai by bus for about fifteen, I thought, but the hard bus seats, and the frequent stops in the Lowland heat, made the thought of riding with him in the car very attractive, even though I knew he would look at me instead of the road every mile of the distance back. He then introduced me to the high-school principal and took his leave with a promise to pick me up in six weeks at Bokai Abra.

The Filipino principal of the school received me kindly and put himself out to help me obtain dreams and tests from his students. Judging from the test results, I might as well have been testing in an American or an Hawaiian school. In all of them the children scored near the American norms. They had the same tendency to draw men in action and large feet which I had noticed in all the other mountain groups. Among the Ifugao I again found participation in feast ceremonies named as the best thing that had happened. I also found the fear of ghosts very frequent.

A large number of the children had had fearful experiences with men who had run amuck. Amuck behavior was a runner-up in their fear dreams, but the man who had run amuck and been killed was always described as an *anito* or ghost. Like the Bontoc dreams, the fear of animals was largely crowded out by the fear of ghosts, but the dream ghosts of Ifugao were still more violent than those of Bontoc.

In contrast with the Negrito lack of memory, among the Ifugao memory seemed to be the supreme function of the mind, apparently as a result of the practice of learning, almost from birth, genealogies and details of ritualized procedure. This capacity to remember things and put them into categories made their scores on the Emotional Response Test largely incomparable with those of the other groups. They appeared to remember an endless number of experiences of all types.

The best thing that could happen, they thought, would be to get wealth and power and caste, and more wealth and power. The worst thing that could happen to a high-caste Ifugao was loss of his wealth and power. Low-caste Ifugao thought the worst fate would be hunger. After that, loss of one's kinsmen, then one's own life, especially at an amuck's hand, were considered disasters.

The fear of this insane amuck behavior, which came out in their recall of incidents, in their dreams, and in their negative fantasies, was of special interest to me. Certainly, the Ifugao child was given no assurance that the men who surrounded him would act toward him constructively, or fairly, or even predictably. The people who taught him about the gods and who interpreted his dreams gave him no help in changing the behavior of the images he acquired, and no assurance that the gods would behave differently from, or better than, the men who surrounded him.

The attitude of the Ifugao seemed to be feudal in the extreme, with everyone struggling to become a nobleman and every nobleman struggling to gain altitude by cutting down others, or by climbing up on them, or through extortion, through intrigue, through marriage, through magic, through violence, and through prayer. The gods would help those most who gave the biggest feasts. After the gods had feasted on the essence, the substance went to the priests, relatives, and politicians. Like the gods, these powerful human beings were with you only as long as the gift which accompanied your request for favor was bigger than the gift of the others who wished the same favor, or as long as you could inspire more fear than those who opposed you. When the Ifugao traveled back in time, they remembered the names, status, and prowess of people for thirty generations. This brought them to the first ancestor, Balitok, who with his sister-wife, Bukan, was the only survivor of the world flood.

All these thirty generations of ancestors had to be approached and called upon in the proper formal manner. The same was true if one traveled in space to the sky world or to the underworld, or if one traveled into social space to learn to do things by oneself and to co-operate with others. Everywhere one had to learn the rituals and find his place in the hierarchy of the authorities who passed on the ritual and the technical knowledge. Man could not be spontaneous or capricious in any direction unless a ritual or ceremony required him to. In the past most of the ceremonies which had periodically released the population from all restrictions had been associated with head-taking.

The amuck type of murder increased the tension of everyone. Since the Americans had blocked the blood feud but as yet given the people no philosophy which would help them restore balance and order, they were often preoccupied with this amuck type of behavior, which could upset their inner universe much as the typhoon upset the universe of the Negrito.

It was easy to get information about the religion of the Ifugao. There was a sprinkling of men, now middle-aged, who as adolescents and young adults had studied English with Dr. H. Otley Beyer and Dr. Roy Franklin Barton, who had been educational directors of the subprovince of Ifugao. There were also Ifugao who had served as interpreters and assistants to Lieutenant Giles and Captain Jeff Gallman, and to governors, judges, and officials. Most of the Ifugao had the encyclopedic minds of college professors. For once, I did not have to ask for information, but found myself in an avalanche of it.

The Ifugao had deified almost everything. Like the Ilongots, the Kalingas, the Kankanai, and the Bontocs, they thought that illness and death were caused by supernatural beings, and that these spirits could be persuaded to leave the body of their patient, or to give back the soul of their patient, with bribes of pork, chicken, carabao, rice, and wine. If a direct appeal to the offending spirit failed, the ancestors might help to restore the missing soul or to banish the possessing spirit if they were called in and fed, flattered, and cajoled by the proper authorities.

Among the Ifugao I found neither the healing ceremony of the Negrito, which assisted the patient to go back in trance to the origin of the illness in his personal world, and to struggle with and transform the offending spirit; nor the powerful god of the Kalingas, who was always being told how powerful he was; nor the high god of the Kankanai and the Bontocs.

There were forty-odd classes of gods, with an established order in every class. All of these gods had the power to cause man illness and bad luck. They could also cause death, but not without the consent or co-operation of the ancestors. Some of these classes had no other function than causing illness, so far as I could learn, and they were named after the type of symptom which they caused.

No one seemed to know exactly how many gods there were, but

I was told that Dr. Barton had listed twelve to fifteen hundred of them when he was studying the Ifugao religion, and that he had not yet finished compiling the list. To appeal to all these gods when someone was ill would be impracticable, if not impossible—it would take many priests many days to accomplish and would be fantastically expensive. The process of divining what deities were causing the illness was therefore an important aspect of healing.

The method thought most reliable for this divination was to set an egg on the blade of a knife, mention the name of a god who was suspected of causing the illness, and ask the egg to grip the steel if this god was responsible. If the egg balanced, the sacrifice was performed to the god named. Balancing the egg on the knife seemed to require some abnormal power or skill. At least, I could not do it myself even after a good deal of trying.

The Ifugao had great confidence in this egg method, paying for this service according to the reputation of the practitioner, which was gradually built up by the success or failure of the sacrifices he recommended. The diviners also used this method in locating lost or stolen property, detecting crimes, and spotting sorcerers responsible for illness and misfortune. The young people called them detectives.

I heard many stories which credited the egg diviners with supernormal extrasensory powers. In Ifugao every normal male adult became a priest and some of the women became priestesses or mediums. But the people believed to be gifted at performing this special type of divining were few and received very high fees. They charged all the way from five to twenty-five pesos for a single séance.

With the coming of the Americans more than twenty years before, Western medicine had been brought to the Ifugao. Not many, therefore, were in need of my home remedies. The few who did take my medicines and go into trance at my bidding looked for the cause of their headaches or stomach-aches, or rheumatic pains, and found, like the Bontocs and the Kalingas, earlier and earlier incidents in which they had been attacked by gods or ancestors for failing to provide the proper sacrifices.

Speaking through the trance, the ancestors agreed to stop bothering the subjects if I would furnish the pigs and chickens for a suitable feast, but due to my rapidly dwindling supply of money, this was out of the question. It was evident that it would be neces-

# THE RICE TERRACES OF IFUGAO

sary to work through many layers of socially acquired images before they could respond to psychotherapy as the Negritos did.

After three weeks of testing in the school and the vicinity of Banaue, I mailed most of the material I had collected to Hartendorp, to lighten my pack. I kept only the data on the Emotional Response Test to study on the way, and set off for Bokai on the trail which Julio had marked for me, staying where night found me in the small communities perched on the tree-clad hill crests above the endless terraces.

I traveled at a leisurely pace, as I had an invitation to stop at Hungduan, a village near Kinga, where some of the students at the high school lived. One of their number, a boy called Chirp (because he had been named after a cicada), was the son of a famous old priest. Chirp said his father was too old to work, and being very bored with life, would welcome the opportunity of telling me about the ceremonies and ideas of the Ifugao, without charging me the usual informant's fee. If I arrived there on a Friday night, I could spend ten days talking to the old man and still get to Bokai at the appointed time.

# EIGHTEEN

# The Rice-Increasing Ceremony

THE second day out of Banaue, when I arrived at Hapao en route to Hungduan, I was invited to participate in a rice-increasing festival. All night long the men of the village sat in a circle around a dish of rice on the floor of one of their toadstool houses, chanting rituals in unison and drinking sour rice wine. At dawn, in a drizzle of rain, the animals for the day's feast were sacrificed, and the blood was collected in wooden bowls. The local old men and a famed priest were in charge, and from time to time, one, or the lot of them, delayed the procedure with tedious chanting. The chief priest wore an old-fashioned sunbonnet, to the front of which a green china parrot had been sewn. I suspected that the bonnet had been taken along with the head of some missionary's wife or Lowland woman. When the priest was excited, the parrot bobbed up and down, adding emphasis to his falsetto voice.

The proceedings opened with the solemn bleeding of a number of chickens. Then a pig was thrown on its back, secured by cords extending from its legs to stakes driven into the ground, and decorated with wreaths. The old priest led a procession of villagers

## THE RICE-INCREASING CEREMONY 213

round it again and again, chanting as they went. Now and then they took rice paste from a bowl and dabbed it on the pig. At last they made a small incision at the lower extremity of the ribs and thrust a bamboo stick into the animal's lungs and heart. After collecting the blood in vessels, the old men spent some time examining the bile sac and arguing about what predictions could be made from it. These were determined by the size, shape, and color of the sac. Some of the blood was used to douse stones and objects which had been arranged in carved troughs, and the rest was boiled in clay pots under the houses. The pig's hair was burned off with long wisps of grass, and a ceremonial division was made of the meat. The slaughter of two more pigs followed, with similar ceremonies. A great deal of bickering accompanied the division of the carcasses. The disputes were settled in due course by Old Green Parrot, who took a lion's share for himself.

Since dawn, a half-dozen old men had sat apart under one of the houses. A gaunt old water buffalo stood before them in the rain, while the old men maintained a steady, mournful chant. Gradually, as the other animals were sacrificed, more men joined this group. The dreary dirge they were chanting grew in volume.

The scene was bleak. Dejectedly the buffalo stood in the drizzling rain, swaybacked, with a pathetic head that sagged under the weight of its enormous horns. Since daylight it had slowly chewed its cud, waiting patiently in the midst of the feverish human activity.

At last Old Green Parrot approached the buffalo and harangued it with great vehemence. Then a huge wooden bowl was placed on the ground beneath the buffalo's neck. All the men lined up, holding their long knives in readiness for a signal. With a quick sweeping blow, one man brought his knife down on the back of the animal's neck. The head sagged forward. The buffalo kicked convulsively with its hind legs, while remaining on its knees as though to accommodate the natives. After a few tense minutes, the squirting blood lost its force, ran lazily for awhile, and began to drip. The china parrot hovered over it for a moment, as the priest moved the bowl and gave a signal. The waiting crowd charged upon the body of the still-quivering beast.

"Each man will get whatever he can cut loose," a little boy explained to me.

The men hacked frantically. In a short time the buffalo was

a mangled mass of red flesh. Still they tore at the meat, getting in each other's way, shouting, jostling, cutting each other with their razor-edged knives. At last the constabulary officer, fearing that someone would take advantage of the confusion to settle an old score with a fellow tribesman, said that the remainder of the carcass would have to be divided in some other way. The men fell back and the green parrot again dominated the scene, but now it had a red bonnet.

Many fires were burning, with pots simmering above them. The men drank freely from great jugs of the vile-tasting but potent sour rice wine. Wounds received in the fray over the buffalo were washed. Drums and brass gongs were brought out, and the crowd congregated in knots beneath the houses, singing, talking, and eating. Young girls in bright-red skirts and heavy beads formed circles and did a simple dance, pulling their feet along by doubling up their toes.

Later the men danced in circles by themselves. Someone said that I must do an American dance, and I offered to show them a waltz, explaining that men and women danced it together. A lengthy discussion took place while I waited for the drumming to begin. Then the small boy told me that the old men had decided it was immoral for men and women to dance together. Having seen the liberal attitude toward sex maintained in the *ologs*, I was startled by this aspect of Ifugao morality. Grumbling to myself about the difficulty of becoming acquainted with the mores which determined what was good and bad in human behavior, I racked my brain for a dance which would not flaunt the "degeneracy" of the West in the faces of these conservative, puritanical old men. I performed some hula steps I had learned in Hawaii. They were received with wild acclamation by the young people. The women tittered, but the old men did not look pleased. I later learned that my dances were not acceptable because of the avoidance taboos, which forbade any reference to sex when certain relatives were together.

Borrowing a small drum from one of the boys, I did a shaman dance I had learned from the American Indians. The old men approved of this and applauded so heartily that I went on and on, with such fervor that I fell into the fire and burned myself. I was afraid that the delight of Old Green Parrot could only express itself by the gift of his parrot. Instead I was deluged with rice wine.

## THE RICE-INCREASING CEREMONY

All day long we feasted, danced, and dozed by the fire, and wakened to feast and dance again. By nightfall the gods had so increased the rice in the granaries that there was no danger of hunger before the next harvest. At least, the protruding bellies of the Ifugao told them so.

I had been greatly impressed by the desperate manner in which they had divided the sacrificial beasts. It was further evidence that most of the people never had quite enough to eat. Yet they planted only one crop of rice a year. Two crops would have provided a surplus with which to buy meat. For years the United States Government had been trying to convince them of this, so that they could live in plenty, but their forefathers had planted only one crop and they did not wish to offend them or the gods. Their economic practices were inseparable from their religious beliefs, and they knew that as long as they performed the ceremonies directed by the prophets of the past, their one crop would be enough. Emotionally, they lived secure in this knowledge. It was a sin to count the bundles of rice in the storehouses before the rice-increasing ceremony. It was a sin to measure the rice in any way. If it ran short, they had incurred the displeasure of the gods and would have to atone for their sins by fasting. Some of the natives felt that plenty would never come again because an ox's head was now substituted for that of a human being in their ceremonies.

In view of this childish slavery to tradition it would be easy to call them "stupid savages," but such a judgment could not be reconciled with the evidence of culture provided by the rock walls of their fertile terraces. These astonished me more and more as I made my way toward Hungduan along obscure foot trails, which led through chasm after chasm into which rice terraces had wormed their way like the roots of some colossal plant.

The grandeur of these terraced carvings on the rugged canyon walls filled me with superstitious awe. To look at the stones piled row on row was like thinking of traveling in a straight line forever. It seemed incredible that men should build a wall a hundred feet high, hew miles of canal through solid rock, and convey mountains of earth in small handbaskets of rattan, to form a strip of land thirty feet wide on which to grow rice. My reason disputed the evidence of my eyes, giving me a constant sense of unreality.

These terraces were not monuments to death built by slaves

under the lash of the whip, nor monuments to war erected by teeming millions spurred by fear; they were monuments to life and love, each one a story wrought in stone of a father's love and ambition for his child, of a boy's yearning for a girl and a home.

The population of these mountains never exceeded 150,000. The people for generations were menaced on every hand by tribes less settled than themselves, glad to rob them of the fruits of their toil, and by interminable blood feuds. What a grueling trial they must have endured through the ages, fighting man and beast and the restless tide of the tropical jungle which, if their vigil relaxed, would smother their cultivated plots in half a year. Even the mountain wind was pregnant with the seeds of destruction for these mighty walls, the seeds of unnumbered jungle plants ready to thrust their roots like disintegrating wedges into every crevice along their vast frontier. And the relentless rain was forever tugging at their foundations. Often, as I trudged through the intricate maze of terraces toward villages perched like eagles' nests a thousand feet above me, I heard it roaring down from sodden, low-hung clouds.

The night before I was to arrive at Hungduan to keep my appointment with Chirp, I sought shelter from this rain in a deserted shack where a missionary had lived. I awoke in the gray half light of dawn, with a startled awareness of another's presence. The merciless din of the rain on the thatched roof, which had pelted me to sleep, had ceased.

Since I had talked to Julio of the amucks and the headless bodies which had been found in the irrigation ditches of Ifugao, a part of my mind had stayed awake on guard every night. Now it was warning me that another human being was very near. A flush of terror tightened my skin. Taking stock of my position I found my left hand resting on the jacket under my head. Slowly I gripped it to parry a possible spear thrust. My right hand grasped the ammonia gun. Now, triggered for action, I could wait for some move from my adversary.

But there was no sound in the deserted house. Then directly beside the house, outside the paneless window, I saw the silhouetted figure of a naked girl standing out black against the slate-colored sky. She could not see me in the gloom of the house, but I was afraid to breathe lest the sound should startle her out of balance and make her fall from the terrace wall on which she was standing. She was bathing in the water cascading from the terrace. When she had finished, she took a glowing ember from a clay pot, which she had cached upon the side wall, and blew a handful of dry rice straw into flame, making a tiny fire. In it she burned a bundle of straw, stalk by stalk, until she had accumulated a pile of charcoal. I was transfixed by the beauty of the scene, feeling no power inside to move even when the flames of the little fire illuminated me to the point where she would have seen me clearly if she had turned her head.

Then, grinding the charcoal between the fingers of each hand, she polished the long strands of her uncut hair. She was singing softly with a happy air, as though the little spot of rock and water, air and mist which she occupied were, together with her own beauty, the only thing in the world to be desired. At last she wound her long hair into a bun, secured it with a comb, scoured her teeth with the remaining charcoal, and rinsed her hands. Putting on her short red skirt, which lay folded on the intersecting wall, she placed the pot with the burning stick upon her head, turned her back on me, and disappeared into the mist which shrouded a clump of houses farther up the mountain.

At noon, as I made my way to the eagle's nest of a village which was pointed out to me as Hungduan, I found Chirp. He had been on the lookout for me and met me halfway up the terraced mountainside. His father, Amambay, was waiting for us on a carved wooden bench beneath the house. His name, I was told, meant "That's true." I never did learn if this was his real name or a nickname given to him because of his reputation as a teller of tall stories. He was not a native of Hungduan, but came from the vicinity of the village of Kiangan, said to have been established at the beginning of the world by Balitok, the first ancestor of the Ifugao. This village was thought to have been the gateway to the sky world, the village to which came Lindum, the Giver and the other gods who gave the Ifugao their domesticated animals, their technology, and their ritual.

I suspected that his family had had less wealth and rank than that of his wife, for whom he had left his native territory. Since he came from Kiangan, however, people respected him highly as a priest and teacher, much as the Mohammedans give deference to a native of Mecca. He was now so old that Chirp's brother had to carry him about on his back if the ceremonies he attended were at any great distance.

Amambay greeted me warmly, speaking in pidgin English, and soon I was installed in the little house on the compound, and was launching into a ten-day period of the most strenuous talking I had ever done. Amambay proved indefatigable and his store of knowledge inexhaustible.

One day I asked him about the meaning of the ceremonies at the rice-increasing festival I had attended at Hapao, and about what was said during the hours of interminable chanting.

"If there were twelve priests at the ceremony," he said, "and you watched them for a day, it would take me twelve days of steady talking to tell you what they said. Explaining things in English through my son, it would take me twenty-four days just to repeat the ritual of that day's feast."

I explained that I did not have that much time. Could he give me a sample of what was happening here and there, tell me about the trance behavior of the old men when they seemed to be in a state of spirit possession, and about the figurines and stones which were drenched with blood, washed with rice wine, or smeared with the pasty cooked rice?

"The names of the gods, and the recited myths in which they play a part, and the prayers said to them, explain all that is to be known of the ceremonial," the old man said. "So I'll have to tell you their names. First the messenger deities are contacted. They assist the priest in calling the ancestors and the other gods. After the ancestors are bidden to the feast, the Matungulon are called."

Amambay launched out into a recitation of the gods of the Matungulon, describing the action of the priests in the ceremony as he proceeded. "In this first order of gods," he said, "there are a hundred and sixty-eight living in the four quarters of the sky world, in the upstream and downstream regions of the earth, in the underworld, and in the vicinity of Kiangan. Matungulon means 'pay back' or 'pay up.' The sacrifices are offered in payment for the gifts which Lindum, the chief of the order, and his descendants, bestowed on the Ifugao.

"The second god is called Haver-and-Giver of Dreams. The third god, in each of the four levels, is called Like-a-Vision and gives men visions. The next one is named Covered-Up."

## THE RICE-INCREASING CEREMONY

Amambay said it was like planting a problem in your mind and leaving it until it sprouted. To me he seemed to be describing reflective thought.

The next god was named after a fluffy seed, like a milkweed pod, which breaks open. He was especially important in the miraculous fluffing out, or increasing, of the rice. Then there were a few gods the names of which had no translations, and there were Stir-Upper, Forgetter, and Betrayer, who were asked respectively to stop stirring up the Ifugao and to stir up the enemy, to help the Ifugao to forget unpleasant things and remember important things, and to cause the enemy to do the reverse, and to stop betraying the Ifugao and to betray the enemy.

Then the names of the gods trailed off into the technology of weaving. Apparently the Ifugao had deified all the steps in the process of weaving, and many of the features of the loom. Not wishing to become a weaver, I asked Chirp about the second class of gods. They were called the Napulungot. Like the Matungulon they were "Pay-backables," but they were described as living in a cluster of villages down-river from the Ifugao, rather than in the sky world and the underworld.

The locusts and grasshoppers were the chickens of the Bugan, the wives of these gods. The gods were asked to stop their chickens from feeding on Ifugao crops and to pasture them on the crops of the enemy. There were thirty-four of these gods, the chief of whom, Binonbong, was sort of a personified dam who stretched himself across the rivers leading out of the Ifugao territory. He caught up the released souls of the domesticated animals and of the rice, and returned them to the Ifugao.

There were also four gods of this class, called Scatterers, whose sacred object was a bamboo clapper much like the clappers the Kankanai women used in their singing, and those which the dryland rice growers used in the planting of their rice in various areas surrounding the Ifugao territory. These clappers were included in many of the agricultural ceremonies of the Ifugao, as though to acknowledge their debt to the more primitive methods of growing rice which had preceded the use of terraces.

The Napulungot gods had a special attachment for the granary idols, which the Ifugao usually carved out of the trunks of tree ferns, and which reminded me of the *anito* guardians of the Ilongots. When these granary idols were dedicated or activated, the

Napulungot were invited to possess the officiating priests, causing them to run around on all fours and to bite the ears of the pigs tied up for sacrifice.

By dinnertime Chirp's father had named off the two-hundred-odd gods in these first two classifications of "Pay-backable" deities. It appeared to me that this portion of the rice-increasing ceremony was an effort on the part of the Ifugao to express their appreciation for everything which had come down to them from the past, the accumulated knowledge of human beings. Through the names of the gods they not only honored and expressed appreciation for the art of animal husbandry and agriculture, for the technology of weaving, pottery, and housebuilding, and for the efforts their ancestors had actually expended changing the face of the earth, but also made a bow to the vision, the dream, and the reflective thought which had made it possible for these ancestors to invent and build their civilization.

When I had been on the trail with the Negritos and we stopped to leave a shred of tobacco at a tree or a rock or a river crossing, I had had the feeling that the giver was offering an honest gift to something which was primarily outside himself. But the Ifugao gave their rice, wine, pigs, and chickens to gods who existed as names in their own minds. And then they ate the sacrifices which they had dedicated to these names of gods and ancestors.

It was a "have-your-cake-and-eat-it" society, so far as the religious ceremonial was concerned. They did not pay an honest fee of tobacco to the tree or the rock, or an honest fee of blood to Tolandian, as the Negritos had. But the people who paid for the feasts only got a fraction of the meat and wine themselves. The high-caste priests and their relatives and families got the lion's share. On the face of it, the major motivating drive in the Ifugao religion, so far as I had seen it, was the emotion of guilt. They said, "I am in debt to the gods and the ancestors, and I must pay this debt with animals and rice which I have grown."

For the average person this was a legitimate type of social activity, which should help him feel he was paying back a debt to god, nature, or society, like the sacrifices and the magical hunting-and-gathering dances of the Negritos. But for the authorities, who consumed the major share of the payment, it seemed spurious and should have, it seemed to me, the reverse effect. The priests were not giving, but only collecting from the other people in the name of the gods, and were consuming what they collected.

At dinner, Amambay wreathed with fern greens the sweet potato he was eating, and told me what the priests had said to the pigs at the feast. Chirp explained that his father's mind was not as good as it used to be, and that he could trust it to recall the ceremony better if the sweet potato was made to serve as the pig.

"Now he is summoning the *linauwa* or soul of the Monlapu who was head rice priestess of the district of Kiangan before he left that territory," said Chirp. "She is now dead and another Monlapu has taken her place. Now the soul has possessed him and he is doing the chant that all do together at the feast: 'Oh come, Bahiwag of the underworld. Drink the rice wine, speed the multiplication of the rice. Oh yes, that's it, the *bagol*—deity. Make the rice grains as numerous as the grains of sand. Miraculously increase the rice. Oh, do grant it, please. Make the rice heads heavy so they bend the stalks. Oh yes, that's it.' "

Now Amambay was swaying in his chair and shuffling his feet. With his finger, he was tracing counterclockwise circles around the sweet potato, as I had seen the priests encircle the pig at the feast, when they poured wine on it after the completion of each round.

"Get the pig, you spirit," Amambay was saying. "Oh, that's it. A libation has been made." Again he quivered and shook his head slightly as though he had received a blow.

"That's to show the arrival of Bahiwag," said Chirp. "Sometimes I think my father is possessed, just telling of a ceremony. Now the possessed dancer speaks with the god's voice."

"I came up from below," said the old man in a changed voice, dramatizing the chief messenger god, Bahiwag. "I, Bahiwag, behold, with favor, that you are making a rice feast. Drink, all of you, because I give you to drink. I taste the pigs, and chickens, and the rice, as I have been accustomed to do in times past. Thus, I drink in your dwellings and in your granaries. I desire it so, year after year. We are the miraculous increasers of the rice. We are the slowness of the rice to be used up. We are the harvest knives and ties."

Chirp interpreted, and then went on to explain that his father had shifted to the role of Tinukud, another god, who is usually invoked later on in the feast, and who honors the process of cutting and tying the bundles of rice, as well as increasing it. "Now he is doing the *Monjua-Aa* chant to dispatch the pig's spirit after it is killed," said Chirp, translating the prayer. "You are enwreathed, Pig, because you were used at a harvest feast, in order that all of you—rice, death, stick, and pig may stay together and keep company. Rise up, all of you, into the sky world. Arrive in the quarters of the gods there. Tell them, Pig, that men killed you. Do not remain speechless. Do not tarry, Sleeping Pig. You are enwreathed."

At this point, Chirp's mother broke in on the account of the ceremonial, ordering us all to eat. "She says my father will be in the spirit world soon enough, without us asking him to go there at mealtime," said Chirp.

After dinner, Amambay went on with his account of the ritual, but he no longer confined himself to the ceremony I had seen. As soon as he mentioned the Deceivers (the Manahaut), the third class of gods, he became excited, seemed younger, and launched off into a description of the head-hunting ceremonies. "The Deceivers are the major gods of war," explained Chirp, "and there are nine long head-hunting rituals in all. There are sixteen gods of war and sorcery, and Manahaut, the Deceiver, has twenty-four deified descendants. Also, the Sun has twenty-eight descendants, and the Moon has thirty-one, all of whom must be honored in a full ritual. Like the others, they live in the sky world and in the underworld."

After awhile, he got his father to dramatize the sacrificing of the pig to Manahaut. At the climax of this ceremony, the priest, possessed by the Deceiver, raises his arms above the pig. Another priest, possessed by the spirit of the sun, spears the bound and decorated animal; and the third priest, possessed by the spirit of the moon, rushes up and drinks the blood which spouts from the wound.

Acting out the roles of the three priests so exhausted the old man that he was willing to leave head-hunting and go on to the description of the fourth order of gods, the Gahidu. These gods activate the snakes, the birds, the insects, and the other things, such as the bile sac, which supply the Ifugao with information about the future through their many omens. They, like the Deceivers, were invoked in all the ceremonies, and they were depended upon more than any of the others in the head-hunting rituals. Then came the fifth order,

## THE RICE-INCREASING CEREMONY

the Reproducers (the Maknongan), who took care of fertility and birth.

The symbolic allusions and the indirect way of talking of and representing these important human functions, made me think I was back in Sunday school or listening to a mid-Victorian father discussing the facts of life with his family. Chirp's interpretation of his father's veiled similes, of his description of the activities of the reproduction gods, pictured what Westerners would think of as orgasm and conception in terms of a fish darting with supreme effort up the froth and foam of a waterfall, an aggressive, driving rain making love to the expectant, thirsty earth, and the evening mist penetrating and filling up the jungle.

As Amambay went through the first seventy gods in this order, who lived in the downstream world, the upstream world, and the underworld, I began to understand why my mention of men and women dancing together, and my exhibition of the hula dance, had received such a chilly reception at the rice-increasing ceremony, where there were people together among whom the mere mention of sex was taboo. The nearest mention of sex in the ceremony was found in the names of the reproduction gods themselves—Investor, Earthquaker, Giver, Closed-in-a-Basket, and Shaky.

The only actual recognition of the result of birth was in the name of one god—Quiets Babies.

From about the eightieth god on, I got completely lost in a maze of gods who were the actors in a series of myths called *Hudhud*. Some of the characters of these myths did, at least, have a little to do with the preliminary emotions leading to reproduction. They were named Lover's Harp, Affection, Charity, Comfort, Consolation, Charmed, Made-to-Chuckle, Make Anxious, and Coax. But the myths in which these characters played a part were sung not only by the priests in connection with the invocation of the gods of reproduction, but also by the women at their work, and by the whole group at prestige feasts.

Even the ceremony performed while the mother was in labor —dramatized for us by Amambay—was still on the level of the birds and bees, since it had to be performed before relatives in whose presence the mention of sex was taboo. This ceremony, which Chirp told me was supposed to give aid and comfort to the woman in labor, again sent the old man into what appeared to be a trance. He acted out the myth of an ancestor named Gold, who was possessed by Skillful Giver. The god said to Gold, "Come to the top of the mountain and we will find Friend." At the mountain, Gold chopped down the highest tree, peeled it, and turned it loose to roll down the side of the mountain. Its slippery sap made it slide easily down to Gold's house. Then he threw down the bark and said, "So will Friend arrive easily in the house and his blanket will soon follow."

Amambay chopped vigorously at the imaginary tree and threw it down the mountain with such fervor that he dropped exhausted on the floor.

# NINETEEN

# Lost among the Gods

It was late, and Chirp's mother took advantage of the momentary pause to shoo us out, so her aged husband could get some sleep. Before sunrise, we were called for breakfast. While we were still eating, Amambay started his account of the sixth order of deities, the Halupe, the Convincer deities, who were believed to control social relations among the Ifugao, especially those which enabled the giver of the ceremony to collect his debts from his debtors and to avoid paying them to his creditors. These gods also played a great part in the head-hunting ceremonies, by causing the adversary to forget about vengeance, bringing him out of his house where he could be easily taken, and causing him to feel pity if he got the advantage.

I had a hard time keeping my mind on the gods. The whole thing seemed like magic rather than religion, and like suggestion psychology slanted to overcome anxiety even more than magic. It was like the Lord's Prayer said backward: "Forgive me my debts and make my debtors remember to pay." In the West if a man who is in debt suddenly claims to be John D. Rockefeller, we put him in a hospital and mourn his loss to society. These ceremonies were psychological in that they aimed to make the people feel secure when they were not secure, but they did not quite create an insane attitude because the priests prayed that the outside debtor would also be affected, along with the inside images. There was still a realization in everyone's mind that this desirable state of affairs might not quite come off. Apparently, there was an appeal to the most powerful forces in nature to help it along.

The chief god in this category was Kidul, Thunder of the Sky World. His son was Bagilat—Lightning. Then there were gods having the names of several different kinds of thunder and of several different kinds of fear. There were gods of relaxing, of soft words, of agreement, and even one named Dumb, whose function was to prevent the adversary from answering. Another one was named Slowness, and was supposed to make the adversary slow-witted. Then we again ran into the characters of the *Hudhud* myth, and Amambay sang about their activities and adventures until almost noon.

The seventh class of gods were the Hidit, who regulated the relationships between enemies. They were invoked to blow the odor of the Ifugao's wine and food into the nostrils of the enemy so he would breathe it in, thus breaking the taboos of ingesting enemy food and drink, and bringing down disaster and illness upon himself from all the gods.

The eighth were the Pili, who guarded the rights of property and punished those who did not have the proper respect for the prestige of the nobles.

I had heard stories from the Kalingas at Manolo's compound about the *anitos* who guarded the property and privileges of the nobles. The stalk of the *runo* reed, with the two top leaves tied into a loop, was used there to indicate private ownership, as a "keep out," "hands off" sign. The Kalingas had told me that anyone could put such a sign on anything which was in the public domain. But if you did put up such a *runo* stalk and did not have the courage or the kinship backing to force others to stay away from the property you had claimed, you laid yourself open to the contempt of both gods and men. The *anitos* were especially prone, the Kalingas said, to give you elephantiasis of the testicles, if you made a claim which you could not force others to respect.

In Ifugao the *runo* loop was called a *pudung*. There was a whole class of gods, some sixty-nine or seventy in number, to enforce private ownership and to punish those who did not respect the *pudung* or used it when they did not have the prestige to force others to respect it. The Ifugao often reinforced the strength of the *pudung* by building little Pili shrines near the *runo* stalk, and inviting the gods to inhabit idols carved of stone or wood, which they deposited in the shrines.

Amambay told us his favorite among the myths used for inviting the Pili gods. Apparently there were quite a number of such myths. Halfway through his recitation of it, he again went into trance, and seizing a carved wooden spoon, danced around with it, singing words which Chirp said would so activate the spoon that nobody could use it for ordinary eating. His mother was very disturbed, until I said I would buy the spoon and keep it to guard my pack.

The old man was now speaking in the first person, saying, "I, Tan Amud di Pudung, activator of the *runo* loop and the idols of the *runo* shrine, enter this image to guard and keep watch over your property, and the dignity of you and your kinsmen." He went on with an account of the frightful things he would do to anyone who broke the taboo for which the *runo* shrine was set up. At last Amambay came out of his trance and looked at the spoon with a vague expression, asking how he had got hold of it. The others explained that Amud di Pudung had possessed him and put a Pili into the spoon. But Chirp said that it was all right, as I wished to buy the spoon to guard my pack when I went on my way.

This occasioned a long discussion. Once my pack was guarded by Amud, who now inhabited the spoon, he might bite or give illness to innocent people who happened to touch my pack without meaning me any harm. This would be all right as long as I was in Ifugao, since Amambay or some other priest could relieve any illness or pain which the Pili caused to innocent people. But once I was out of the territory, it might cause people damage which I could not relieve even if I wished to, since I was not a priest and could not call Amud down to take away his curse from innocent people or from the culprit, once he had confessed. I assured him that I would send the spoon to a museum, where it would be in a glass case so that no innocent person could touch it. But I asked him also to instruct Amud, next time he had occasion to call on him, not to bite any innocent people very hard, just for the safety of the postal authorities and the museum curator.

We did not get around to the ninth order of gods, the Makalun, the messenger deities, until after lunch, and they occupied us for the rest of the day. There were not as many in this group as there were in the other categories, but they overlapped with the ones that had gone before and with other classes which we had not yet discussed.

In order to call the gods from the sky world, the downstream world, the upstream world, or the underworld, the priest apparently had to be possessed by one of the messengers. Even the gods who inhabited various localities in near-by parts of the known world were represented by messengers of the flying-monster type.

The most exciting information I gleaned that afternoon was the fact that the messengers were the first gods to possess the Ifugao priests, and further, that possession was not the result of initiation when the priest was first ordained. The spirit possession had to be sought by each individual priest, and although every normal male Ifugao became a priest when he got married, some of them never advanced to the rank or status attained through spirit possession.

This possession was sought through the good offices of older priests, and entailed a fee. It was attained through a procedure similar to hypnosis and often required months of co-operative effort. Unless driven to seek possession through chronic physical, or mental illness, all but the wealthiest priests usually neglected this type of training.

Here I had found a true branch of psychotherapy, almost an exact replica of the spirit possession which the Negritos sought through the older shamans. There was, however, an important difference once the possession state had been attained. Among the Negritos, the possessing spirit became the personal property and constant companion and servant of the shaman, whereas among the Ifugao, the priest became the servant of the possessing messenger spirit and of the class of gods whom he represented.

Instead of moulding the god to the therapeutic needs of the shaman and organizing him as a part of the healer's emotional and intellectual resources, the Ifugao trance populated the priest's mind with gods, each more important than the priest himself and open to the bribes of all his enemies. Furthermore, each god was thought to be subject to all of the negative moods and vindictiveness of the extortionist and the opportunist in Ifugao society.

After dinner, Amambay dramatized the calling of the tenth order, the Pouk—wind deities. Four classes of these lived in the downstream and upstream regions which lay to the east and west, and two others lived in localities roughly north and south of central Ifugao. These deities were invoked in all the major feasts and were asked not to take the life out of the rice, but to increase it, and not to blow over houses and granaries, but to exercise their violence on those who opposed the givers of the feast.

Amambay chanted softly, almost in a whisper, the words of his invocations to the wind gods. Thinking that the old man was getting hoarse from his hours of singing, I suggested that we go to bed. Chirp informed me that it was not wise to speak the names of the wind gods loudly. If their names were not spoken softly and with deference, they were likely to descend upon the priests as typhoons rather than as possessing spirits.

After the old priest had whispered his way through the forty-six gods, a good number of whom possessed him as he went along, he asked Chirp to bring him the store of beeswax which was kept in a rattan basket under the eaves of the house, just outside the door. Then Amambay lit a portion of the beeswax, reciting incantations as it burned.

Chirp explained that this was an added precaution in case any of the winds had been aroused by his father's recitation of their names. Beeswax was a sort of chloroform to the Pouk, whom the Ifugao thought of as having human form and as releasing the winds by lifting their arms and thus opening the armpit caves in which the winds were generated.

The next nine order of gods, which Amambay described the following day, were of quite a different nature. All the deities we had previously discussed might cause illness, destruction, and even death if they were angry or felt themselves neglected, but the next nine orders of gods had no other function than the causing of illness and death. There were the Umaladang—the spiral-uppers who came up from their house in Dagahna, the subbasement of the universe, and bored their way into men's bodies, causing mysterious ailments; the Pumihdol, who caused boils and tumors; the Liblibaiyu, who carried spears and hunted with dogs, stabbing men in the back and causing symptoms of the liver; the Tinikmal, who caused headaches; the Bulbulnit, who caused wounds, bruises, and fractures; the Baiyan, who caused arthritis and rheumatism; and the Bayiad, the payment deities.

There were myths connected with all these orders of gods, but Amambay refused to recite them unless we offered sacrifices. One did not lightly bandy about the names of these illness deities. Amambay had great respect for them. But the payment gods of illness were so much like the Pay-backables, toward whom the Ifugao felt obligated for their technology and their ritual, that I decided to hear the myth and the names of the payment gods, even though I had to buy a chicken for the sacrifice.

The myth he recited, after sending the messenger deity and being possessed by the deity Pati from Humadol, told how Pati long ago went to the downstream region to trade with a character named Bumabakal, who apparently had all the diseases of the world locked up in bamboo tubes. Bumabakal agreed to give Pati these diseases in part payment on a transaction they were negotiating. By pulling out the stoppers, Pati would be able, henceforward, to cause men any kind of disease which he liked. In order to get well they would have to make sacrifices to Pati, not because he had given them anything useful, as the Pay-backables had, but just because they wished to recover from the illness he had given them to collect the sacrifice.

It seemed like taxation without representation to me. But the Ifugao apparently saw nothing wrong in it, although usually the payment deities were not invoked until all other treatments and ceremonies had failed. If the Bayiad ceremonies did not cure a person, hope for him was abandoned.

The meanings of the names of the gods who were invoked in these ceremonies made me think I was back in a pathology class at medical school. There was Smallpox, Headache, Flux, Constipation, Rheumatism, Chicken Pox, Malaria, Spit, Fever, Inflammation, Mumps, and a few others. The names of these gods included all the known diseases not covered in the other disease-producing classes of gods, and some that were.

Again there was no attempt to convert the illness deities into healing spirits, as there was in the Negrito ceremonial.

The eighteenth order of gods were described as harpies. They were called Gatui, and were supposed to look like winged dogs with human faces. These, like the other disease-producers, would cause illness and misfortune if they were not remembered with sacrifices now and then.

After these came the nineteenth order, the Bumugi, the Spitter deities. They searched out the souls who had recently left the bodies of men, before they had learned their way about in the spirit world. The Bumugi tricked these innocent souls into betraying their children or loved ones. Once the newly dead had admitted a relationship with a living individual, thus bringing him under the power of the Bumugi, these deities could victimize the living person by spitting or pointing at him.

This stress on the spirits of the newly dead, the danger they were in, and the way they endangered their living fellows, was upsetting to me. I felt that unless I could figure out some reason for such ideas, I would soon run screaming out of Amambay's hut. The image of the newly dead in the mind of the survivor was dangerous in all societies. Even to think about it seemed to endanger my own mind. The social policy of the Negritos, which encouraged the survivor to go on communicating with this image in his dreams until, in the funeral feast, it could be made at-one with him and the rest of the community, seemed much more sane than the approach of the Ifugao, which put both the image of the newly dead and the survivor under the power of spiritual monsters which, to me, symbolized the fear of death. The Ifugao had climbed the ladder of technical progress, but they had stepped down psychologically. At sometime in the past they had probably written into their culture the neurotic mechanism of one individual, and they were imposing it, generation after generation, on the entire group.

In the next two days we covered the remaining twenty or so of the forty-odd classes of gods in the hierarchy, of which I had heard in Banaue. Amambay no longer followed the sequence in which they occurred at the ceremonies, but grouped them according to his interest in them. Seven of these classes had to do with death and the fate of the souls thereafter. The Taiyaban—flying monsters— whom he mentioned as the twenty-sixth order of gods, devoured the souls of the dead and the soul-stuff of the living, causing blindness, paralysis, deafness, and the like. I was surprised to learn that the names of these gods were taken from the various trees and other features of the Ifugao territory. Sink Hole, Landslide, Weir,

Thorny Thicket, Tributary Streams, Tree Fork, Gravel Bed, Rock, Terrace Bank, Nightflyer, Water Place, Mountain Pass, and Mountain Peak were among the names Amambay recited.

I was getting weary of the gods of the Ifugao, but I could not stop writing down their names and Amambay's descriptions of them. At last, I decided that I was hypnotized and that each of the gods was possessing me, along with the old priest, as he proceeded. The central mind had built Amambay's body out of the elements of the earth, and his personality out of the elements of this Ifugao culture. Each god he spoke of was a center in his mind. This center had a name and a form or pattern of action which, in their ceremonies, various priests had dramatized for Amambay as he grew up. The dramatizations had enriched the form and name with Amambay's emotions. As he witnessed the ceremonies from his earliest childhood, he had responded with feelings of awe, guilt, anger, fear, love, or hope to the name and the action pattern which depicted the role of each god.

Now, as he told me of the gods and acted out the roles, he was allowing me to travel like a pilgrim through the vast interior of his personality. Each center of his personality was like a terrace in the unfathomable maze of terraces which covered the mountains of his homeland. Each terraced center of this vast inner world where now I found myself had trails leading to higher and lower terraces, and to either side. They were related to the central mind of Amambay, and were avenues through which this central self could reach his fellows, his land, the elements of nature, and even me. In fact, these endless patterns had not only reached me but engulfed me like a net. Now I could find my way out of them only by following them back to the simpler Negrito patterns and forward to the ways of thinking of my own society. I had to listen to the end to Amambay's descriptions of his gods and determine where each section of his network attached to the world that I already knew.

As Amambay acted out the various roles, he felt he was serving as a vessel of the god whose tendency and will he was dramatizing, but to me, each of his gods was a vessel or vehicle through which the center of himself found expression. Each was a vessel of his own heart, as long as he stayed within the framework of the ceremony, a vessel through which he expressed his fear of death or failure, his hope of success, his feeling of possession or power over animals, people, and things. But I was uneasy as I watched him dramatize the gods, lest he should slip out of the framework of the ceremony, or slip back to a time before American law had put an end to Ifugao head-hunting. If this should happen, one of the gods might command him to substitute my head for that of the ox, or he might run amuck and play the role of one of the ghouls whose only desire was to absorb the soul-stuff of as many human beings as possible, leaving them cold and dead.

The dazed look which came into his face as one god left and another entered into his body reminded me of the expression on the face of the small, scrawny lad in Bangued who had run amuck, stabbed his teacher, and sliced up half the school and the police force with his stubby-bladed pocketknife before he could be brought under control—had stabbed at everything alive as though he had no sense at all, but with cunning for his own protection and the destruction of others. But neither boredom nor fear, nor the desire to be on my way, could break through the net of gods which Amambay had thrown around me. I had to tread my way over the knots of the mesh until I reached the end of his gods. Mechanically I went on writing.

The Poglan deities, the twenty-eighth order of beings, the ending deities, were the gods of death.

The Imbagaiyon, the twenty-ninth order, were the conductors of souls that had died, carrying them where the gods or ancestors wished them to go, and assisting the priests to bring them back to the death rites.

The Angob, the thirtieth class, were ghouls who ate, married, or enslaved the souls of the dead. They were also thought to possess the living in an attempt to hasten their death. Among the names of these gods were Rat, Cat, Dog, Python, Carabao, Civet Cat, Wild Boar, Pig, and Cobra. Sacrifices to these gods were made at midnight at whatever spot they took possession of an individual. Ghoul possession was indicated by the arrival of a heavy, damp feeling. As the ghoul spirit left, one was supposed to see the kind of an animal it represented scurrying off into the darkness.

The gods of the thirty-first class were called the Banig. They were the actual ghosts of people who had failed to leave the earth because they were earth-bound or who had not yet found their place in the spirit world.

The Pahang, the thirty-eighth class of gods, were soul-stuff stealers, like the flying monsters, but they inhabited the sky world.

The Kibkiblu, the fortieth class of deities, were invoked in the postburial funeral services.

Altogether, there were more death rituals than any other single type of ceremony, seventeen in number. In some of these, all of the deities, not just those of the classes especially associated with death, were invoked.

Some of the remaining orders of deities seemed like subclasses of the gods already described, and some were deified ancestors.

The thirty-sixth were ancestors who were credited with actually building certain terraces the Ifugao had inherited, as well as obtaining the art of terrace-building from the sky world.

The thirty-ninth order, the Pahiu, were ancestors claimed by some of the lineage groups to have somehow intermarried with the gods, resulting in children who were both divine and human. To me this seemed like an extension or elaboration of the Bontoc myth in which the high god came down to earth, married the namesake of the first ancestress, Fukan, and had children.

These gods brought some warmth to my heart, and dispelled the numbness which was settling on my mind. They, at least, were germs of yeast which might eventually break up the stratification imposed upon the personality of the Ifugao by the layers or castes of his society and the many strata of his gods. Any of these descendants of the gods would become a commoner if he married a commoner, so they were being diffused through the layers of their society, and being relatives of the gods, they could invite the low gods up to the earth, and the high ones down. If they got them to rub elbows often enough, a democracy might result, where at least the heart of every man would be equal to that of his neighbor.

The thirty-second order of beings, the Pumupud, were the obstetric deities. Judging from their function, they might be described as a subclass of the gods of reproduction. The Pumupud blocked or helped with the delivery of the child. Dam-Builder, Plaster-Upper, Tear-Downer, Vagina-Blocker, and Shifter were some of the individual gods in this class of deities.

Then there were also four classes of gods devoted to activating talismen. The Kawil activators had been invoked mostly to enliven charms used in head-hunting. They were the twenty-first order of gods in the hierarchy.

The Bulol, the twenty-third order of deities, were specialists in granary-idol activation, whereas the Hagaiyup—the thirty-seventh order—were an order that was invoked to activate the charms used in love and hunting. In my own mind I classed all of these talisman activators as gods having an outgiving psychological function, like the war gods and the Convincers already mentioned, and like the minor war deities, the Hipag—the twentieth order.

There were a number of myths connected with the Hipag. These were stories about a stronger and weaker contestant, a hard stone and a soft stone, and a fledgling who fought a losing battle with a full-fledged cock. Chirp told me that the stronger contestant was entreated to stay on the side of those giving the ceremony, and the weaker to go to the side of the opponent. These gods were also talisman activators. The cock image, along with the hard river pebble, was usually covered with the blood of the sacrifice during the ceremony, as I had seen in Hapao. These Hipag deities were thought to like raw meat, and an offering of it was made to them before the meat was cooked. They were most often invoked in conflicts with kinsmen and in sorcery. They were of interest to me because they represented aggressive forces in conflict, gods turned against the gods, the way the good in man is often turned against the bad in him. But according to the myth, the stronger was always the good. The reasons underlying a disagreement were never even considered.

The Hawat-Buyan, who came thirty-fifth on Amambay's list, were the diviner deities. They did not represent an outgoing function like the talisman activators and the war deities, but were receptive in nature, like the omen activators through whom the Ifugao learned the will of the gods, or at least their intentions. They were invoked whenever the diviners wished to balance the egg on the steel blade, and in other types of divining. They were most often appealed to when people were ill and when things were stolen or lost.

The sun, moon, and stars were prominent among the gods in this class. In telling people what was wrong with them and warning them of misfortune, these gods, more than most of those in the other classes, seemed to act like Western gods. But even they had to be paid well by sacrifices if they were to function.

The Makiubaiya, the thirty-fourth order, Fond-of-Sugar-Cane gods, were almost the exact opposite of the disease-producing deities. They were believed to gather about the altars leading in and out of the Ifugao village, to eat the sacrificed sugar cane, in swarms so thick that the disease-producing deities could not get into the village.

The gods most exciting to me were the Pinading, the twenty-seventh order. They were said to own all the game in the area where they lived and corresponded almost exactly to the local place spirits of the Negritos.

The hunting deities—the Bakaiyaawan—the twenty-fifth order; the mountain spirits—the Monduntug—the twenty-fourth order; and the deities of the chase—the Alabat—the twenty-second order, also corresponded very closely to the Negrito spirits. The names of the Alabat deities sounded like a Negrito magical dramatization of a projected hunt. Hunter-at-Starting-Place, Encourages-Dogs, Hurls-Spear, Holds-Quarry, Spurting-Blood, Staining-Vegetation, Cuts-Off-Head, and Shares-Carcass were among the deities who were invoked to attend the Ifugao on the hunt.

The Monduntug, who were also asked to attend and protect the hunter, had the function of making the snags and thorns soft. Like-Straw, As-If-Rotten, Like-the-Soft-Flopping-Doo-Dad-on-a-Woman's-Headdress, Puddle-Maker, Soft-Like-the-Down-of-a-Runo-Plume, were among the gods invoked. The Bakaiyaawan had a similar function of protecting the hunter from thorns, snakes, and wounded animals and carrying him along to the game, as the magical hunting dances of the Negritos were thought to do.

The thirty-third order of beings, the Binudbud, with which Amambay finished his account of the gods, were invoked to affect the game, to wrap or tie the animals so they could not escape from the hunter. Wrapped, Get-Between, Covered-with-Vines, Caught-in-Trap, Stinginess, Fasted, and Pacified, were some of the individual gods in this Binudbud class.

These wrapping gods were invoked in all the ceremonies for one reason or another. In the rice-increasing ceremonies they were asked to wrap up men's stomachs, so the rice would not disappear so fast. At the prestige feasts they were encouraged to wrap up the aggressive emotions, so fights and quarrels would not develop, since the giver of the feast is responsible in Ifugao for the welfare of his guests. They were also invoked to tie up the anger of creditors, so their demands for payment of debts would not be harsh, and even to tie up the sexual force of men, if their kinsmen or wives thought they were unable to direct their love into the proper channels.

Like the other gods, the Binudbud were encouraged to have a baleful effect on the enemy, especially to tie up his bowels and to make him sexually impotent.

# TWENTY

# Spiritualism in Ifugao

THE five days I had spent with Amambay, Chirp, and the Ifugao deities left me in a state of confusion about the structure of the mind and personality of the Ifugao. Apparently there existed in the mind of the Ifugao the same kind of mosaic arrangement as I had observed in the mind of the Negrito, with the image of every stone, animal, tree, force of nature, and human being possessed by, or inhabited by, a spirit. Both of these peoples credited these spirits with strength comparable to, or superior to, their own. The main difference was that among the Ifugao the mosaic was infinitely more complicated, containing such a great number of individual beings identified by name, that systems of classification had grown up, perhaps out of the sheer necessity for a method of remembering them.

Obviously, the Ifugao had to absorb more images than did the Negrito in order to perform his ceremonies. Obviously, the gods in the mind of the Ifugao had to get along with each other and to help the individual adjust to the group and to the environment through the ceremonies. When the gods failed in these two functions, there was physical illness, insanity, or amuck.

## SPIRITUALISM IN IFUGAO 239

I knew that if I could pay for the sacrifices, it would be possible to arrange for some healing ceremonies. I could then see how the ceremony operated on the individual who became ill in spite of the fact that a thousand-odd gods were frequently invoked and bribed with sacrifices to keep him well.

The next morning I told Chirp that I had developed a headache and a stiffness in the neck, and asked him if his father could perform the healing rites for these ailments. Amambay said that he should have a priest or two to help him with such serious symptoms, and that there should be at least one chicken for each symptom. This was out of the question in my impoverished state, so I explained that the symptoms were not serious and that my head hardly ached at all. At last we settled on a small chicken for the stiff neck, and a duck, cheaper than a chicken, for the headache.

It took Chirp and me all morning to round up the sacrifices, and buying as economically as possible, we still spent three pesos.

The ceremonies performed that afternoon for my ailments were not very different from the god-calling, or god-pushing, and the possession states I had seen at the rice-increasing ceremony. The names of the gods recited in the ceremony were interesting—Headache, Not-See-Straight, Sunken-Eyes, Red-Eyed, Hiccuping, Kicking, Sweating, Struggling, and Vomiting.

The small duck sacrifice entitled me only to the recitation of one headache myth. Amambay told how Balitok went downstream with his companions and speared the god Montinig. They cut off his head, but it went right on laughing and jeering at them. Terrified, they buried it and went back to their village. A year later, as they went along the same trail, they found a coconut tree growing over the burial spot. Thirsty, they drank some coconut milk, and all had headaches, so Balitok made a sacrifice to Montinig, whose head had grown into the tree. The god blew him a cure.

Chirp told me there was another myth about a fight between the sun and the moon, which would have been recited if my headache had been more serious.

The ceremony for the stiff neck was much more dramatic. The Baiyun gods which were invoked bent Amambay and the other priest almost double as they possessed them. In the chant the priests told the arthritis gods that they, the gods, were afflicted, bent over, stiffened, and swollen up, but asked them please not to swell me up, since I had bought the chicken.

"But do not affect us who have returned vengeance. We are dear to you. Those enemies of ours started the feud. They speared us first, anyway," said Amambay.

The myth told how Wigam of the sky world came down to Ifugao and cut a *mara* tree for the girder of his house, into which the avenged and the returners of vengeance might enter. The myth made it appear that I had a stiff neck because I did not express my rage by taking vengeance on my enemies. It indicated that the tree demons, like the earth demons, had originally demanded sacrifice, preferably human, for the lives of the trees which were used up in building the house. The priests had not asked me about my frustrations and quarrels, but the ritual declared to the gods that my enemies were all in the wrong—"They speared us first."

The words of the myth also indicated that these Baiyun gods were Pay-backables, and that the sacrifice was a sort of interest payment on the debt which man owed to the gods for the technology of housebuilding. Further, it showed that arthritis and rheumatism were believed by the Ifugao to be the result of unexpressed aggression or revenge, and that these symptoms were imposed on men who failed to take revenge on their enemies, especially when they did not fulfill the blood feud. I inquired of Chirp about this, and he told me that you might get arthritis if a distant kinsman were killed or wounded even if you did not know the wrong had been committed. It was not, therefore, necessarily a matter of lacking courage to take vengeance, or of failing to follow your conscience in the matter.

If the symptom was stubborn, the diviners would have to be called in. If the laws, or one's resources, did not permit the revenge the diviner gods prescribed, then a man would have to resort to sorcery or black magic for his revenge, until the symptom disappeared.

It seemed to me that here the Ifugao were only one step from the realization that the enemy which had to be destroyed was inside the individual who had the symptom. Once they had taken that step and come to see that the arthritis gods were dream characters or facets of their own personality, they would not perpetually have to complicate their social life by attacking their fellows merely because the diviner said that they were enemies.

In the morning, while we were buying the fowl for the ceremonies, Chirp learned of a sick woman in a near-by village. We obtained permission to visit the healing ceremony which was to be held for her that evening. Chirp thought that she was mentally deranged. She was a young married woman and came from a poor family. In order to avoid the expense of a ceremony which involved the priesthood, she was to be treated by some woman healers.

In this type of ceremony, dried pig jowls, which no one could eat because of a taboo on them, and the essence of clothing and beads, were offered up to the gods. These articles were not destroyed in the ceremony and could be used time after time. Therefore the price of the ceremony was negligible. In order to make ourselves more welcome, we offered to bring along a jug of rice wine.

On the way to this ritual, Chirp told me that the female priests were called *halag*, and that women became practitioners only as a result of illness which led to dreams in which they were commanded to become healers. This indicated that the elaborate ceremonial and ideology of the men had not crowded out the more primitive dream-inspired shamanistic healing, which both the men and women practiced among the Negritos, and which the women practiced among the Ilongots, the Kalingas, the Kankanai, and the Bontocs.

I was most anxious to learn if these *halag* operated on the offending spirit as the Negrito did, forcing it to serve the patient, or if the Ifugao healing ceremony resembled that of the Kankanai and the Bontocs, where the offending spirit was only asked to leave or to attack someone else, instead of being transformed into a servant of the patient.

There were four *halag* assembled in the patient's house when we arrived. Each, with closed eyes, was squatting on the floor chanting over and over the names of her own ancestors in a monotonous singsong voice. How many times a *halag* would repeat the name of each ancestor, before passing to the next in the lineage, was apparently determined by her feelings as she said the name. Chirp said they would continue to name the ancestors until they got back to Balitok and Bukan, the first ancestors. Then, in a like manner, they would recite the names of the gods, especially those in the Hudhud myths. Sometimes it took an hour or more of this monotonous chanting before one of them was possessed by a god or ancestor whose name she was repeating.

Tonight we were fortunate in not having to wait so long. All of them stopped the chanting to take a drink of the rice wine as it was passed around. Then, about five minutes after the chanting had been resumed, one of the *halag*, a cousin of the woman who was ill, went into trance. She leaped from her squatting position high into the air, and catching hold of the boards of the side of the house, agilely climbed up into the rafters, announcing with a gruff voice, "I am the grandfather of the sick one." The possessing spirit also happened to be the grandfather of the *halag*, but this did not seem to be important. Then one of the other *halag* asked the spirit why he had climbed onto the rafters. The gruff voice explained that there was a stranger present whom he did not know, referring to me. Another *halag* told him that I had bought the wine and invited him to come back down and have a drink of it.

A little persuading, and the possessed woman returned to the floor as agilely as she had climbed, and accepted another bowl of wine. The grandfather's voice asked why he had been called, and the third *halag*, silent until now, explained that the hostess was ill and wished to know from him what she must do to be cured. The grandfather spirit admitted that he was causing the illness and that he would not allow the patient to rest easy until she had arranged a second burial for him.

Apparently this had been a bone of contention in the patient's family for years. The other mediums, speaking to the spirit through the possessed *halag*, pointed out that the patient had already decided to have a ceremony for him as soon as she could get the rest of his descendants to co-operate. It was not her fault that his son, her father, had neglected this very important rite. They would have the ceremony as soon as possible, but was there nothing that could be done now to pacify him until a really good and satisfactory second burial could be arranged?

At this point the medium's voice shifted to a higher pitch. "I'm cold," she said. Her teeth chattered. "I'm so cold. Can't you bring in more wood? Tell your father to bring in more wood." Now she was shivering and bending double, with an expression of pain on her face.

A Negrito shaman would have said she had met the spirit of cold, and would have tried to help her to get a song from him, and to

## SPIRITUALISM IN IFUGAO

make him one of her spirit assistants, but the other *halag* simply ordered the patient to put more wood on the fire as a sacrifice to the ancestor. The possessed woman went on mumbling about hot broth, more blankets, and special foods, doubling up every few minutes and writhing as though with pain, as she had at first. But the others did not encourage her to build the writhing movements into a dance, or to weld the scattered phrases into a song. Instead, they went on adding to the pile of sacrifices, to which all those present were contributing, knowing that the spirit would only take the essence and that after the ceremony they would get back all their belongings.

"This storm," said the spirit voice, jerking as though listening to thunder.

What an excellent opportunity to get a drum rhythm! But the assistant *halag* did not ask her to beat out the sounds. Instead, they said that as soon as the patient could afford it, a sacrifice would be made to the Pouk, the wind deities, so they would blow away the storm.

After awhile, the grandfather spirit left, and the ceremony came to an end. The patient said she felt better, but Chirp told me that she could not expect a cure until the reburial ceremony had taken place and the Pouk had been invoked. These ceremonies would require real sacrifices of pigs or chicken, not just the spirit from the pig jowls, blankets, and wood which had to be burned anyway to keep the house warm. This part of the healing procedure would be a regular ceremonial, performed by the priests, not the *halag*.

I had a chance to ask the *halag* about their calling to the profession of healing. All of them had been forced into it by a series of dreams and by illnesses which did not clear up until they had been possessed. The patient had also had dreams encouraging her to become a medium, and had been told, through the diviners, that she must seek possession through the messenger gods, but so far neither the priests nor the *halag* had succeeded in bringing her to a state of possession. At least these spirit ceremonies made her the center of the social group, and therefore helped to keep her in contact with social reality.

It occurred to me that the *halag* who attained possession in these séances in attempting to help the patient was probably receiving a much higher degree of therapy than the patient herself. If the spirits that had expressed themselves were, as I believed, parts of the medium's personality, this was certainly an opportunity to allow them expression. Through this expression these fragments could become better attached to the images of the members of the social group who were assembled at the ceremony for the purpose of helping to cure the illness of their friend.

The next day was Thursday, and I busied myself with preparations to leave. Amambay insisted that Chirp go along with me as far as the Asin River Rest House. Because I was his guest, he was responsible for me until I was out of his territory. In the outlying districts American influence was not as strong as it was around Banaue and Kiangan, and a stranger traveling alone might be in danger. Amambay did not regard the inhabitants of these borderline districts as quite civilized. When he had told us the day before of the Hagaiyup, who activated love and hunting charms, I had asked Chirp if I could get a love charm for myself. He had heard about my failure to keep the date with younger sister that first night in Ifugao, and said he had been thinking that I needed a charm to change my luck and to interest me in something besides gods and ceremonies. A year before, he and some other boys had killed a crocodile on the Kinga River and he had obtained its testicles, planning to have a love charm made of them for himself, later, when he needed it. But his glibness and gift of persuasion, so highly valued in Ifugao, had won him so much attention from the women that he had never felt impelled to arrange the ceremony which would make his crocodile glands a love charm. Knowing that he did not need them as much as I, he offered them to me as a parting gift.

We were planning on spending the evening in the village of Kinga. Chirp thought that if I would have a ceremony to activate the charm the Hagaiyup were certain to give us luck in love on my last night in the territory. I felt compelled to arrange a ceremony in appreciation for what I realized was a great sacrifice for him, but I knew it was expensive, otherwise Chirp would have already had it performed for himself. His older brother had looked admiringly at my silk tarpaulin and had even borrowed it to throw over himself and his father when he carried him about. I had had the feeling at the time that I could not take it with me when I left. I told Chirp to ask his brother if he would like to have the tar-

## SPIRITUALISM IN IFUGAO 245

paulin in exchange for the chickens I would need for a charm-activating ceremony. He was delighted, and an hour later turned up with three large chickens and three priests.

One of the old men he had brought was the love-charm expert of the district, and had with him the ingredients necessary to complete my talisman. He ground up herbs in a small wooden mortar and smashed out their juices. Into this mixture he ground the dried brain of a kingfisher (which looked like half a walnut), coconut oil, and the precious gonads of the crocodile. This was poured into the open end of a tiny gourd.

By now my gift, the silk tarpaulin, was spread on the *runo* mat beneath the house, and the invocation of the Hagaiyup deities began. It was a beautiful ceremony. The four priests chanting together tickled the ears of many ancestors and gods with their invocations. These, half prayer and half command, would make me irresistible to the ladies and the ladies powerless to withstand my words of love. They would also make all my rivals dumb, impotent, and unattractive.

Off and on through the ceremony, my mind returned to Mrs. Hartendorp. If, as she thought, I was running away from a fear of love, or of my own inadequacy, I had certainly run to the right place.

When each of the thirty-nine Hagaiyup gods had possessed the priests and each of the priests had danced, elevating the talisman so the gods could pass into it through their hands, the talisman-activating ceremony came to an end.

Then the priests invoked the other classes of gods of the Ifugao hierarchy, requesting that they accompany me on my journey. The tears welled up in my eyes as Chirp translated the prayers and the persuasive arguments which the priests were having with the deities in my behalf: "Surely it will be good to turn all pestilence, famine, witchcraft, and villainy aside from the path of thy son, as he goes on his journey; protect him from the landslides, from falling trees, from thorns and stones, along the path between Mount Tabayoc and Mount Abao; save him from the cataracts and whirlpools of the Asin River and the Abra River, as he travels to Bokai, to Manila, and to his native place; protect him from the Upstreamers, and turn against themselves the spears of all those who would molest him; make each step on the trail as safe and familiar as the path of his own backyard at home; allow him to get very drunk without committing violence; permit him to talk much and talk straight, to ask for what he wants from strangers and to get it; compel all his creditors to extend the term of his debts, but let his debtors hear his voice as that of a commanding deity; inspire all his kinsmen to give him their rice, their pigs, their death blankets, and their rice wine in abundance. He shall stand up straight and remind all of the tail feathers of the full-fledged cock. To those who know him well, he shall be as gold that does not tarnish. Throughout all his journey, until he returns to us, his head shall toss proudly, like the *runo* plume in a breeze, like the seed of the cogon grass riding free and high on the wind. He shall go forward, even like the waters of a mighty river that cannot be halted in its course."

It was well on into the afternoon when Chirp and I took leave of his family and the priests, and set out for Kinga, the last outpost of the Ifugao territory. Chirp insisted on carrying my pack. I felt as though I were walking on air. Word had been passed along to his mother's brother, whom he referred to as Uncle Dalum (Upstream), that we were coming, and we received a warm welcome on our arrival.

I did not have a chance, however, to test the potency of the love charm, which had been plugged up in the gourd with dry sugarcane pith and sealed with hot beeswax, so it could be conveniently carried. There was a postburial funeral service for a girl who had recently died in the village, and all the young ladies in the vicinity were attending it. We went along.

The officiating priest had already invoked the ancestors when we arrived, and the Imbagaiyon deities were conducting the soul of the girl back to the priest, so she could talk through him to her relatives and friends assembled for the ceremony.

"The priest is possessed with Monunglub now, the facer or director of souls or forces," said Chirp. "He's talking with the voice of the god, and is describing how he's directing the girl's soul back up from the downstream region to the ceremony. She is nearly here."

The priest shuddered, and the right side of his mouth twitched violently. His facial expression changed and his voice lost its deep guttural quality and became falsetto. "Now he is talking with the girl's voice," said Chirp. "She is explaining why she died. She says she had nothing against her friends and family, but she was very tired, and her lover, who died last year, kept calling for her. It was he who permitted the Angob (ghoul) to push her off the terrace. The ghoul took the form of a civet cat and jumped at her, so she lost her footing as she was returning from working in the terrace. She says that civet cat, the ghoul, has made her his servant and will keep her always if a pig is not sacrificed to him in her behalf."

Then she left, and the old priest went on invoking the other classes of gods, whom he charged with the responsibility of helping him to free the girl's soul from the servitude of the ghoul.

When the ceremony was completed, I realized that this was the first formal religious ritual I had seen in which a priest had become a spirit medium for an ordinary mortal. Always before it had been the gods and the deified, or partly deified, ancestors who had spoken through the priest. These spirit beings spoke in a formalized way, with the voice of authority. Speaking through the priest, the gods were given a chance to express themselves. The facets of the priest's personality through which the gods spoke received exercise or release in the process. If the health of the individual priest was, as I suspected, dependent on the expression of these parts of himself, the ceremonial would function as psychotherapy for the priest. This would hold both while the priest's personality was being moulded as he learned to undergo possession and when he later performed the ceremonies which released or exercised the patterns established by this possession training.

In this postburial ceremony, as in the healing ceremony of the women mediums, there was some opportunity for spontaneous expression on the part of the priest.

It was already late when the ceremony was completed, but the priest consented to stay on and answer questions if I could supply more rice wine. I gave one of my remaining three pesos to a man who lived near by, and he agreed to bring a jug of wine. Two pesos would have to do me for food until I got to Bokai.

We launched into a discussion of the dangers of love between the living and the dead. Some of the dead accepted the help of the Spitters, the harpies, the ghouls, and the local place spirits, or the other disease-producing deities, when they wanted to bring their loved ones across the barrier of death. In the opinion of the old priest, all ghosts who accepted such help were dupes. The living who consented to be taken before their natural time to die were also cheated, since they would be enslaved by or married to the monsters who had helped with the process. They therefore would not reach their loved ones or kinsmen in the afterworld for a long period, if at all.

The same dangers applied to suicide. To be safe, one had to love and serve the living people who surrounded him until he had repayed the Pay-backables for the gift of life and for the gift of the accumulated wisdom of the past. Then he might go to his loved ones who had died.

The Ifugao had a ceremony in which a man could tell the gods that he felt he had paid up his obligations, and that he was weary and wished to die. But it was extremely dangerous to speed up the process of dying with the help of the ghouls.

I was interested in this philosophy of life and death, and poured the wine freely in the hope of learning more. I instructed Chirp to ask the priest to shut his eyes and see if he could travel back to other postburial ceremonies at which he had officiated, and see again or listen to the other spirits which had spoken through him. The pictures and conversations he described, once he had got well started, convinced me that the spirits who had spoken through him and told how they were being eaten, enslaved, or raped by the cat gods and the cobras, the wind gods, the flying monsters, and the harpies, were not very different from those which spoke through the Negritos when they were in trance.

When first contacted, the horse-faced dwindis and the pain-producing spirits which possessed the Negrito shaman were much like these returning spirits of the dead. So were the nightmare characters which attacked the dreamer and his friends in the bad dreams of both the Negritos and the Ifugao. But here again I could find no evidence that the Ifugao attempted to transform and utilize these spirits or dream characters, as the Negritos did. The Ifugao priest hoped that the offending spirit would release the image of his friend, or patient, and withdraw into the shadows. The priest made no attempt to transform and utilize the spirit.

# TWENTY-ONE

# Spirits of the Mountain

It was getting light when we left the cabin, and Chirp suggested that we should be on our way, as the trail to the Asin River Rest House was steep and rugged. By eleven o'clock we had said good-by to the last rice terrace and plunged into the jungle. The next morning at dawn, across the Asin River valley, I left Chirp and started over the divide.

My pack was light now, as I had given him my blanket as a parting gift. It would help to keep the mountain cold out of his father's bones, and I would soon be down in the Lowland heat, where I would not need it.

Chirp had given me a bag of parched corn, just in case I sprained my ankle on the trail and had to spend a few days waiting for someone to come along. "Drop me a line from Loo," he had said. "If we don't hear from you in a week, my father will insist I come over the trail looking for you. He will consider you our guest until you are in Loo."

As I lost sight of him down the trail, I suddenly realized that for the first time I was on my own in the jungle. The idea of traveling with no one to show me where to step and where to rest my hand was terrifying. The trail led along through massive hardwood trees. The rising sun glittered on the thorns, spines, scales, hooks, and tendrils which made the underbrush into an armory of desperate plants, striving to protect themselves as they climbed helter-skelter over the palms and tree ferns and onto the hardwood giants of the sky to seek the light of the sun. I recognized the rattan creeper, the thorny bamboo, and the spiny ficus. The priests had warned these plants not to harm me.

Each time I sat to rest, my eyes followed the rays of the slanting sun on past the thorns and spiny leaves to the rotting floor of the jungle, where I saw a deeper world, inhabited by the wood scorpion, the giant caterpillar, the grub, the iridescent beetle, the centipede, the lizards, and the lizardlike gecko, clinging to glassy bark with suckered feet. Amambay's parting prayer had also made all of these my brothers. He had especially instructed the gecko to warn me if there was danger about. Looking closer, I could find the twiglike praying mantis and the spider. Even turtles were there, and flying frogs, to cheer me on my way that morning as I trudged upward toward the lofty pass between Mount Abao and Mount Tabayoc.

Two hours of sunshine, and then the Pouk gods, who also had been asked to help me on my way, brought clouds as black as twilight to conceal the beauty of the path, and rain which roared in the upper branches and dripped like a million leaky faucets on the trail. Another hour in the gloomy sodden depths, and the jungle ended abruptly in a wildly swaying field of cane which looked like cogon grass but was heavier. It was like marching through the beating, tossing branches on the top of the jungle; the long, ribbonlike leaves streaked across the trail and vibrated with the singing sound of band saws. In some places the cane leaned so far over that I was forced to crawl on hands and knees through tunnels black as night. Where the wind was not steady, the leaves swirled and cracked like bullwhips. Above it all, there was the thunder. Soon I had picked out the muttering thunder, the rolling thunder, the clapping thunder, and the sobbing thunder, of which I had heard so recently in the ceremonies.

Often the lightning played about on the tossing plumes and leaves of the cane with a crackling sound, filling the air with a sulphurous odor. At times I even felt it playing in my hair like ants. Progress was slow, with the drooping wet leaves even more slippery than the mud, sometimes blocking the trail completely. I had to step back and throw myself upon them, crashing them to the ground and measuring my headway against them only by the length of my body. It was afternoon before the wild sea of cane leaves gave way to a scaly, mossy growth of gnarled, stunted trees, and still the trail led upward, even steeper than before.

The Rest House keeper had told me that noon should bring me to the summit. But the storm in the cane belt cost me an hour or two, and what is more, I was exhausted. Steadily the air grew colder. The soaking rain came down so hard I could not see for twenty yards, but now the trail held underfoot. The blanket of moss seemed inches thick, and was tough enough to hold firm under my weight. As I gained altitude, the gutlike roots of the trees became more and more exposed, as though the top of the mountain had been washed away from under the trees, until, at the summit, the forest had a crazy two-story appearance. One story was made up of the twisted, tripodlike, obscene roots, and the other of the trunks and gnarled branches.

As if by prearrangement, at two o'clock, when I reached the top of the divide, the rain stopped. The sun burst through the clouds, filling the air with a profusion of rainbows from the drops of water clinging to the twigs and tendrils and strands of moss. The myriad moss-draped caves in the roots of the trees lost their yawning gloom, and each became an Aladdin's treasure cave. The upper branches of the humpbacked trees sparkled with orchids and other flowering plants. The scene was terrifying in its splendor. No wonder the priests had named one of their flying monsters Mountain Pass.

My smarting cane-leaf cuts, fatigue, and clammy clothes were forgotten in a moment, but I could not have endured the consuming desolation of the scene for long. I drank the little gourd of *basi* which Chirp's Uncle Upstream had given me to sacrifice to the flying monster of the pass and which he had charged me not to drink at any other place. Then I started down, half afraid to look back upon its writhing, insane splendor. The moss-carved troughs, flumes, crosses, gibbets, towers, and grottoes soon gave way to ferns and pine trees, and the springy carpet underneath turned into slippery mud. By three o'clock the cold rain again fell in torrents.

Where the trail crossed a little spur, I caught a glimpse of the country below and saw, a long way off, what I took to be the village of Loo. The rain had delayed me at least three hours. If it swelled the streams below, I would have only a slim chance of reaching Loo by nightfall. The thought set me off down the trail at a dogtrot. At least now when I fell, which was frequently, I could slide along toward my destination, instead of back toward my starting point.

The flying monster of the pass seemed responsible for this added speed, and I only wished the priests had thought to soften the snags I sat down on, as well as those on which my foot trod in my journey.

Sometimes I had to vault the stray limb or creeper which barred the path, sometimes I slid under it. Cutting was too slow. At other times I had to stop against it or twist loose from it, leaving bits of my clothing if there were thorns. Once I felt the ground tremble under my feet. The idea that there was a ghost flashed across my mind. I whirled and grabbed an overhanging bush. The soggy trail under me gave way for thirty feet, sending rocks and logs booming down the precipitous canyon. As I crept along above the place where the trail had been, I hardly knew which god to thank that I had not been carried down with them. With rain like this, no wonder the Ifugao mentioned landslides, rocks, and falling trees in their prayers when they thought of traveling.

It was getting dark when the trail leveled out and I was confronted with the first stream of any size. It was so wide I could not see the opposite bank, but it appeared shallow. With the first step into it, however, I sank breast-deep. There was nothing to do but wait for daylight. The Negritos would have built a shelter, but in the darkness, I was not equal to it. Munching the parched corn, I found the partial shelter of an overhanging rock, wrapped the tent around me, and soon shivered myself to sleep.

The next morning I found a trail that led upstream to where the small river split up, and was able to cross on fallen trees and rocks. The downstream crossing could not be used when the water was high. By ten o'clock I limped into Loo, hardly like the *runo* plume waving in the breeze which Amambay had described in his prayer, but glad to get there all the same. At the local store, where tinned motor oil and gasoline were sold, I inquired where I could find a barber, and was directed to a bamboo shack near-by. The barber was out in the fields, but his daughter set out at once to get him, and his wife agreed to mend my torn clothing. So little of the cloth was left on the seat of my riding breeches that we decided to cut off the legs to mend the seat.

Everything worked out smoothly. Since I had to retire to the bathhouse to give her my trousers, I was able to take a bath and attend to my many scratches while I waited. There was no tub, but I did find a big earthen jar of clear, cool water, a bamboo dipper, and some yellow laundry soap. Soon the barber came and helped me out with the scratches I could not reach and trimmed my hair. By the time we had finished, I looked like a mercurochrome-colored Indian from head to foot.

By noon I was back at the store, dressed in shorts which made me look a little as though I were a yogi and had sat on my legs so long that their imprint had been indelibly stamped on the seat of my pants. As I waited for the one-bus-a-day, which was supposed to leave for Cervantes at noon but which I was assured was always an hour or two late, a prosperous-looking American drove up in a shiny car, with a smartly dressed woman at his side. A mining engineer from some near-by American property, I concluded. It seemed ages since I had seen an American. I wanted to caress the shiny car, to shout for joy and throw my arms around its occupants, but I felt shy, as though they were the high priests of a ceremony, and I was just a casteless urchin. I spoke to the man, as the contents of a five-gallon tin of gasoline were transferred to his tank. He was going to Cervantes. The back seat of the car was empty and looked smooth and very soft.

"I've got a ticket for the bus," I remarked casually, "but it will probably have a cushionless wooden seat that's very hard."

"If you hadn't already taken the precaution of having the seat of your pants half-soled, I'd insist that you come along with us," he said, with an amused smile. His wife shot me a sympathetic glance, and then they were swallowed up in dust.

I found myself murmuring, in reverse, the Ifugao prayer about landslides, rolling rocks, and snags, to help him on his journey.

When I arrived at Cervantes, I got a lift on a battered pickup truck bound for a plantation in the vicinity of Angaki, which was on my route north. The ride was almost as wild as my trip down from the divide the day before, and left me bruised in a lot of new places. Twice we forded a little stream, which the driver told me was the Abra River. Even in the five miles between our first and second crossings it had grown noticeably. The second time, the four assistant drivers and myself had to struggle with poles and ropes to get the truck across and then had to fuss with it for an hour, drying out the carburetor, to get it chugging again.

As I crossed and recrossed the Abra River in the next two days' hike to Anopel, it seemed to increase miraculously in size at every mile of the twenty which I covered. At a ferry near Anopel, I ran across some men who were cutting bamboo poles which they floated down to the village of Patoc, some five miles away, for housebuilding. They made the large thirty-foot-long poles into six pole rafts, laying them flat on the riverbank and boring holes through them at each end, through which they passed heavy rattan loops which they lashed to short hardwood crosspieces. Two men, with long poles, had to ride each raft to steer it away from the rocks in the rapids and to push it along in the quiet stretches of the river.

For half a peso they agreed to build a little bamboo frame in the center of one of the rafts, on which I could sit and rest my pack. Since I had caught glimpses of the growing river a hundred times and longed to see its banks from the center of the stream, I was very pleased with the project. The ride was exhilarating, and more lovely than I had imagined it could be, but the extra weight on the raft made it more difficult to manage than the rest. In the rough water the waves began to lap against my little platform, and the boatman lashed my pack to it to prevent its being washed off; but this was a fatal error. Before we had gone another mile, the raft caught on a rock in the sweeping curve of the river and overturned. All three of us were able to catch hold of the sides of the raft. Released from our weight, it slid along the rocks, but when it scraped clear, the platform and my pack were gone. In the muddy water, we never even caught a glimpse of it again.

I had lost my tent, the medicine kit, the knapsack, and all the data on the Emotional Response Test from the Negritos on, except for the compilations I had already made in my notebooks.

We climbed back on the raft. The vine-covered shores of the river took on a sinister aspect as I philosophized away the loss of the hundreds of hours of work that the river had swallowed up.

We landed without further mishap. The next day I reached Bokai and was welcomed by Julio's relatives. They informed me that he had been delayed and would not be back for a week or two, but had made arrangements for me to stay with them until his return. He had met Dr. Perez, who had been north on an inspection trip of the vocational schools, and had mentioned that Perez had inquired about me. Apparently this had made a deep impression on his aunt and uncle, and I was accepted as an honored guest.

The villagers had heard of my dream collections and mental tests from relatives and from the children who had attended the high school at Bangued. By the afternoon of my first day's stay, neighbors and friends of the family were dropping in to tell me of strange dreams they had had, of spirit possessions, and of miracles that had happened in the vicinity.

The next morning, Philipe and Christopher, two boys of the household, brought me a lad named José from a near-by village. He was about seventeen years old, and so weak and emaciated that he had to be supported as he walked. They told me that he was a victim of black magic. They had heard from Bangued of my "possession" by the sopot demon, and Julio had told them that I had charms of my own by which I controlled familiar spirits. They appealed to me to help the boy, who was a retainer of their half uncle. A few months before, he had lost his appetite and his ability to retain what food he did eat. He had always been shy and more interested in working than in playing with the other boys. Everyone thought that he was possessed by a mountain spirit, for he had a habit of going to the mountains alone, with his water buffalo, to bring down wood. When his friends went to the witch doctor who had cured me of the sopot, she told them that a certain man in a neighboring village had cast a spell over the lad. For a fee she agreed to break it. But in spite of her countermagic, the boy had become steadily worse.

They were looking to me as a last resort. Fortunately, José had been to school for four years and had a fair knowledge of English. I asked him to close his eyes and see a picture of something that was good to eat.

"I am not hungry," he answered promptly. "I hate food. I cannot swallow."

The Negrito shamans would have said that this was the boy's demon talking, since he was obviously starving. They would have labeled it the "not-hungry demon," and asked it to give him more words for a song, to furnish the steps of an accompanying dance, and to keep on repeating it until he had memorized it. Then they would have asked the spirit for more verses of the song. They would have invited the spirit to stop squeezing his stomach and become his spirit guide. They would have threatened it with attack from their own spirit guides if it did not co-operate.

"Sing the words you just said, and the spirit will give you more words of its song," I said.

He singsonged the words a time or two, writhing and trembling, then cringed and relaxed as though a blow had knocked him unconscious. Now he failed to answer me. He had gone into a deep trance. If I had not seen the Negrito shamans lose contact with their subjects in a similar manner, I would have thought he was dead. Patiently I went on suggesting that he would see something for which he was hungry. At last his lips moved. "He sees a coconut," said the boys excitedly.

"Your mouth is beginning to water," I said. "You are hungry for the coconut milk."

José gave a loud scream and his deathlike body came to life. "Save me! Save me!" he moaned. "She is going to eat me. A snake is growing from her breast. It is wrapping around me. It is a python. It can crush out my life and cover me with spit and swallow me up."

"Let it swallow you," I urged.

The writhing motions gradually quieted. Now he was whispering phrases which made no sense even to the boys. I kept urging him to speak louder, to sing the phrases and develop the jerky spasms into a dance. The phrases became more singsong, but he failed to control the spasms which accompanied them.

Perhaps the many trance states the Negritos saw as they were growing up prepared them, as suggestion alone could not, to get music and rhythm for the spirit words.

Gradually José's words grew from disjointed phrases into sentences. The boys said that the python was letting go of him. He kept calling out the name of a famous midwife in his village. Now he was pressing his hands against his head, pushing on his chin, clawing at his throat, and opening his mouth as though trying to cry out or struggle for breath. The Negritos would have said he was emerging from the spirit cave.

"Where is the woman now?" I said. "Please tell me about her."

"She came out of the coconut when I cut off the end of it," he said. "At first I liked her, but then I saw a worm coming from her left breast. It got bigger and bigger until it was a python."

"The native women sometimes tell their children, when they wean them, that there are worms in their breasts," said Chris. "José is having a dream, but he thinks he is seeing the spirit of the coconut tree."

"You are stronger than the spirit, José," I said. "You can make it your servant. Drink the coconut milk and listen for the spirit's message."

His face wrinkled. "The milk's bitter," he said.

"There, you see," said the lads. "He is dreaming. He is tasting the pig's gall his mother smeared on her breasts when he was weaned."

I looked at his lips. He did look as though he were nursing. "Please make friends with this dream woman, José," I said. "She will give you words for a song."

"I hear the goat," he moaned, wringing his hands.

"Sing the goat's song," I urged.

Tears gathered under his closed lids and ran down his cheeks. "My poor little goat," he wailed. "They are going to kill it for the festival. It is crying. It is afraid." Again he screamed, and his heart made a tom-tom sound against his ribs. He mumbled and fell back into his native dialect.

"What is he saying?" I asked the boys.

"His mother has killed his goat," they answered. "She is cutting off its head. The smell of the blood is making him sick."

José's body stiffened. His stomach kept knotting and a pale-green ooze came from his lips.

"Let him cry and vomit as long as he likes," I said. "Then he may feel hungry."

Gradually he quieted down and his tortured expression became tranquil.

"Please see something that is good to eat," I suggested again. "You are very hungry."

"Now the woman is giving me milk from the coconut as she sings to me," he said.

"Remember the song," I urged. "And you'll feel hungry when

you wake up." Turning to the boys, I asked them to fetch a coconut.

We woke up José a half hour later. When he opened his eyes, he looked around him for the coconut we had set by his side, and drank the milk. When the lads asked him what had happened, he told them what we had already heard and described the songs the coconut woman had sung to him with his grandmother's voice. We agreed with him that from now on he would be a medicine man. People would come to ask him about planting coconut trees, and he would make coconut charms against all demons who upset man's stomach.

I did not see José again, but a few days later, I suddenly thought I was looking at his ghost. Walking with a soft-footed tread, an old woman approached the table where I was having lunch. Her agile movements and her long skinny arms gave her the appearance of a gibbon. She was scarcely less thin than José, and she looked enough like him to be his twin, except for the appearance of great age. Across her skinny shoulders she was carrying a huge stalk of bananas, which she set on the floor beside me. Then she jabbered at me in dialect, struggling harder and harder to put her meaning into her eyes and gestures, with an expression which seemed comical to me.

Everyone around the table spoke at once. She was very poor. This stalk of bananas, which she had brought as a present, was all she possessed. She was giving it to me because I had changed her starving son into a medicine man. She had walked for miles carrying the bananas and was making a great sacrifice.

Her tears had washed little rivulets through the dirt on her sunken cheeks. She stood sniveling, arranging the rags that furnished scant covering for her emaciated body. Between the ragged folds of her scarecrow costume appeared the pendulous end of one sagging breast. Shocked, I looked back at her face. The curious expression of her eyes, peeking at me through her skinny fingers, made her appear incredibly funny. But I simply must not laugh.

I bowed my head and murmured, "It was nothing. It was nothing." I had said the wrong thing, only spurring her efforts at pantomimed communication to still greater heights. Fortunately, at this moment a servant appeared with food for her. With fantastic, loose-jointed gestures, she grasped my hand and covered it with kisses and muddy tears.

Two days later I set out with the boys for the climb to the top of the crag above the Abra—the expedition that ended so dramatically when I was caught by the river current and hurled through its rapids and whirlpools to the quiet pool below.

# TWENTY-TWO

# The Trail Back

As time passed and I became more convinced of my own sanity and was able to view the events of the expedition in the perspective of my total past, I became convinced that I might never find any direct reasons for the guilt I had felt in the rapids. The feeling itself was too vast, too difficult to get a grip on. But the vision of my mother, the hallucination which was part of the event, might lead me to some understanding of it. A number of experiences came to mind which might explain or lead up to the radiant face I had fashioned from the pattern of the cloud. The moonlike transformation of the face of the Negrito shamaness, the white marble into which Olan's figure had been changed, my conviction that the actual moon had become enraged and smashed her miror into the rice terraces, and the cloud witch Jabon had seen in possession of me, now appeared to me as steps which had led to the discovery of this avenging-angel image of my mother, the focus of my feeling of self-rejection. The cataract of blood I had seen in the early morning from the granite cliff, the fatigue of tramping through the bottom mud, the bat stench of the gloomy interior of the cave, and the crazy excitement released by the increasing roar of the river as we traveled downstream, might well have served as further steps in preparation for the hallucination which I had experienced.

But I would have to search deeper than any of these to find the reason for the disproportionate sense of guilt, to explain my overwhelming conviction of unpardonable sin. And now there was a further mystery as I remembered emerging from the eternity of blackness into the bubbling water of the river pool called the Mother of Fountains. As the memory of that blackness had been swallowed up by the light of the afternoon sun, like the tail of a snake disappearing down a hole, I had felt an utter and complete freedom from any sense of guilt at all.

Now I knew that, like the Negrito shaman, I would have to search for the answer to these mysteries inside myself, beyond the events in my past life which had an obvious connection with them. I would have to search deeper and deeper into the store of experience I had accumulated since my creation or conception as an individual.

When I climbed from the pool below the rapids and began to walk slowly back toward the village, wearing the banana leaf which I had secured about my middle with a bit of vine, and with my bare feet digging into the moist, warm earth of the trail, I felt at one with the sky, the trees, the air, and the sounds that came through the afternoon haze from the jungle and the distant village. The whirlpool had broken down some barrier inside me. For awhile, at least, I was free from that merciless drive to grasp for the unknown, as though to escape something inside myself. Perhaps I had always been afraid of hearing that deep earthquake sobbing which had come up to me from the bottom of the rapids.

Just the memory of it, and I was sobbing now. Suddenly, I knew that that sobbing in the river had almost caught up with me in the typhoon, that I had wanted to cry with the Negritos as they looked at the seemingly artificial sun and cowered in the cleft to escape the flying limbs and crashing trees. Instead of accepting my fear and expressing it as they did, I had allowed it to accumulate inside, causing the inner shock and breakdown which showed up as sopot-sopot. As I had listened to the Negritos and felt the tingling shock of the lightning that came too close, I had been aware of no tendency to cry with them or to recall any of my sins, as they did.

The mere possibility of dying at any minute had not made me remember, let alone regret, any sins that I had ever committed. It had taken the certainty of death to unleash the sorrow for sin that I had felt in the rapids; and even then I repented only one sin. The sobs said, "Why do you thus murder yourself?" Even then I had felt not sorrow or regret, so much as hatred and self-loathing. I had got myself in the rapids and thrown away a lifetime, past and future.

Now I found myself crying as though all the sobs I had ever heard had entered me and frozen inside, and were melting one by one. Remembering the primitive ceremonies, I concluded that every man must put his life in jeopardy—by taking a head, or mutilating his body, or symbolically dying in ceremonies or in dreams—and must then experience rebirth, to neutralize the sins and sorrows of the world which he absorbed or internalized, along with the images of things and people, as he grew up.

Certainly I had learned something about revelation on my journey, as I had listened to the dreams and trance experiences of the people I had met. But only the experience of revelation, the hallucination of the faces in the cloud and the voices in the rapids, had succeeded in forcing the vastness of the dream world up into my fully wakeful mind. Here I had learned something about man's inner state of balance that tied together many of the things I had seen on my journey. Although man could exist with some of his inner systems out of balance, resulting in tensions or physical illness, there was a point of imbalance where he would break apart and cease to function as a rational human being.

In the typhoon the Negritos had become irrational. They had been certain that their god, Tolandian, was angry at them. By tearing their hair and slashing their thighs they expressed the anger of their god, as though the deity were inflicting his punishment through their hands.

Using the accumulated experience of their respective groups, the various peoples I had seen strove in the best way they knew to maintain their sense of inner balance and to grow in their powers to deal with people and things from day to day, and to meet crises. The Negritos cut themselves and tore out their hair, the head-hunters took a head, to avoid the kind of shock that I had suffered in the rapids.

These ceremonies gave them a way of releasing inner pressure, gave them something to attack when the real source of their misfortune was unknown to them or out of reach. The ceremonies of the Negritos, however, directed them to suffer pain themselves, to sacrifice their own hair and blood, while elsewhere the ceremonies led to the torture and sacrifice of animals and other men.

As a social mechanism for restoring inner balance, the simple little ceremony which the Negrito originated when he stubbed his toe on a root made much more sense to me than head-hunting or the ceremonial starving and torture of animals. The lad who originated this ceremony used it as a method of co-operating with an accident-prone enemy force inside himself and of socializing that force.

However, those who inherited the ceremony would be acting as though this particular enemy force were also inside them. Here, it seemed to me, was the fatal error of these inherited ceremonies. We who went with Igun to appease the spirit of the crooked root did not, in fact, have inside ourselves his enemy force and pattern.

As we left our tobacco at the crooked root and visualized Igun's bent old man, we created the spirit of the crooked root inside our own minds, the graven image of a god who would attack us if we did not make sacrifices to him in the future. We were creating a payment deity, like the Bayiads of the Ifugao. This deity might well keep all kinds of accidents in bamboo tubes, and uncork them on us if we did not give him bigger and better sacrifices. In the West, when children watch their mother throw salt over her shoulder, they are being saddled with this kind of payment deity. They believe that this deity will visit future calamity on them if they do not make him such a sacrifice whenever salt is spilled. If only the essence of the salt were given to the god and the material salt were given to a salt priest, the priest would have a vested interest in keeping the ceremony alive and might even announce, obtaining his information through the diviners, that people often spilled salt when they did not realize they were doing so, or that a pinch of salt was not enough to appease the gods.

The lineage head who was ordered off the land by the earth demon at the funeral feast in Bataan, might have been directed in his dream to propitiate the earth demon as Igun was directed to appease the demon of the crooked root. If the earth demon had demanded my head as sacrifice, the Matungulon—the Pay-backable type of deity—might have been created in the minds of all the rest of the Negritos and functioned like the Pay-backables of the Ifugao.

I could now see that all of the other orders of Ifugao gods existed in embryo in the ceremonies of the Negritos. When chronic physical or mental illness led the Negrito to become a shaman, or the Ifugao woman to become a *halag*, or the priest to seek possession through his dreams and the ministration of his fellows who had inherited a way of dealing directly with the inner forces which made him ill, the patient often recovered and himself became a healer.

The thing that vexed me was the manner in which the quality of the healing deteriorated, as I traced it up along the rungs of technical progress from the Negritos to the Ifugao. As the societies became less democratic, and as they were able to create a greater surplus of food and goods, healing became more entangled in politics and carried a greater and greater burden of the payment type of deity. And a greater and greater share of the payment went to the leaders who were the go-betweens for the payment deities.

Among the Ifugao, the priest who recovered from illness by contacting his own enemy forces in trance did not receive the creative dividend that Igun had received. The energy released was apparently expended in learning the names of more gods, his obligation to them, their place among the other gods, and their customary way of reacting toward the gods, toward other people, and toward himself. Once he had contacted the messenger deities, his dreams and visions became more stereotyped. The people he treated for their minor ills with the aid of these deities, those who were not driven to seek help through trance possession, also tended to develop the same stereotypes—to see the priests, the gods, and ancestors contending in their dreams.

That is why their answers, in my test collections of dreams, emotional experiences, and fantasies, included endless repetition of their ceremonial experiences. In all the groups men only became well and emotionally mature as they themselves became healers. In all the groups, the dream or trance being which spontaneously appeared to serve the individual who was having the dream or vision became a burden, rather than a helper, to those who accepted the pattern as a spiritual force for their own lives.

My vision, and my work with visions, had made me realize that the images of people in my mind were not people, but things; and that if these images were attached to negative feelings or emotions in myself, such as fear or pain or rage, they had become a liability to me and to anyone else who would accept them as anything but troublesome things which I should be helped to get rid of.

While collecting the dream drawings of the Negritos, I had noted a tendency, especially among the shamans, to put the dreamer's image near the center of the paper and to arrange the other dream characters around it. As I studied the drawings I fell into the habit of thinking of the "I" of the dreamer as the center, and the other characters as the border. Since they depicted the man looking at and interacting with his dream creations, I soon came to regard the two parts of the drawings as the center and the border of the self.

Now it was possible to see how set ceremonies would strengthen the border against the center of the personality as it was depicted in these dream drawings, and how the shamanistic healing ceremonies would strengthen the center against the border, the "I" of the dreamer against the other dream characters.

The dreams of patients undergoing prolonged shamanistic treatment often included the shaman as a dream character working with one or more of the other dream characters in the interest of the central "I," either serving the "I" of the dream directly or opposing other dream characters which were hostile toward the dreamer. The shaman's image and the spirit guides already developed in the course of the treatment worked in the interest of the center, and the central "I" gained power because of this support and because these characters progressively weakened the border characters which opposed the "I."

When the Negrito lineage head responded to the dream in which he was attacked by the earth demon merely by moving off the land as the demon directed, the "I" and all its allies were weakened. The central "I" had withdrawn from the border, and had therefore started or strengthened the habit of withdrawal. Ceremonies which attached a hierarchy of gods to a dream character, all of whom were thought to be more powerful than the dreamer, would still further weaken the "I" in its struggle against the border.

Now I found my mind playing with some of the strange, inexplicable things which had occurred when I had asked sick people in trance what they saw. They had often described colors. Among all the groups in the central mountains, I had noticed the same trends which had showed up among the Negritos. There was a consistency about the colors described which indicated that the color associations were not a feature of any particular culture. If the patient was suffering from a headache, he reported purple or some other combination of red and blue. When the subject suffered from abdominal pains, yellow was always part of the color described—some shade of brown, orange, or dark green, running into black, was selected. I also noticed that the most terrifying images were either black or radiant white, like the moon. This was true of both dreams and trance states.

These findings made me suspect that emotion comes up into the mind of man as color—that red is associated with man's aggressiveness and euphoria, as the Negritos claimed; that blue, yellow, and green are characteristic of the receptive side of his personality, and that purple and brown represent some sort of inner short-circuiting of his aggressive-receptive systems which leads to pain and malfunction; that white and black represent absolutes of good and bad, which cannot be unified with the major personality without the sense of psychic death and rebirth of which the mystics speak, that areas of the personality represented by black and radiant white will usually remain rigidly set off by themselves and inhabited by the gods unless society develops a socially functioning therapeutic mechanism by which the individual can be assisted in the process of accepting these terrifying forces or parts of his inner kingdom.

Of all the dreams and revelations I had heard or experienced, the coming together of the black and the radiant-white images in my own hallucination in the rapids seemed by far the most significant. I could not determine what kind of dance I would do if I were a Negrito to express the freezing, annihilating self-hatred and condemnation I had felt upon seeing the radiantly beautiful cloud image of my mother, when I had charged myself with the greatest of all crimes of which I could conceive—self-murder; when I had known that I was completely and utterly and absolutely bad; when I had felt the rhythm of life inside me freezing, slowing down, and stopping completely.

I would not know how to portray the darkening of that radiant image as it lost its effulgent glow like a burning, white coal turning black on the hearth, and how to show the vague animal-like expression in the bulging eyes of the starving José's mother, determined to say something, determined to say with mute gestures and sheer force of emotion that I was not completely and utterly bad, that my whole life had not been wasted, since through my efforts her son had come back to life. I could never dance the bursting of that inner ice jam and the crazy, weird journey through the whirlpool to the Mother of Fountains. No dance or ceremony of which I could conceive would suffice to express the conviction which was now settling upon me that the human being, having been saved by his mother from the whirlpool of birth, could never get away from the sense of guilt until he had again tasted of or accepted death.

Like all men I was guilty of wishing to live my own life, to exercise free agency. I was facing what I accepted as certain death, yet all the fear the situation released had at first stayed inside my viscera and my nervous system and found no way out to my muscles, as though I had never been born, as though I had never learned to use my body at all. The sense of guilt had not helped me to solve any problems; it had paralyzed me; it had made me in no way good or useful there in the rapids. Could this be what the mystics described as the coming into consciousness of original sin?

The radiant mother who had made me feel I was utterly bad because I had exercised free agency, and the brown woman who had said I was deserving of worship, adoration, tears, and moans of gratitude, also because I had exercised free agency, had come together in that moment of shock and had created a tremendous emotional release.

Perhaps the pent-up destructive impulses of the head-hunters were released through the torture of a dog or a chicken and the taking of heads, because the ceremonial identified these sacrifices with the black or white nightmare characters in each individual. Perhaps the beating of dogs and the taking of heads enabled these people to release their intense self-hatred by destroying images which, while the ceremony was performed, symbolized in their minds the unclean or unacceptable things inside the self.

These ceremonial outlets, however, all fell short of therapy. In a sense they created the very problem which they solved. They perpetuated infantile tendencies and animistic ways of thinking, and attached the individual's sense of guilt to every object in the environment or every name in the hierarchies of ancestors and gods.

As I thought about it, I was seized with the conviction that Christian ideas had bridged the gap in my mind between death and rebirth, enabling the image of the Filipino woman to start my heart beating again. Perhaps it was my knowledge of Christian revelation and my experience with shamanistic healing which had broken down the inner deadlock. Without this bridge, perhaps I would have sunk like a stone, dead of fear, before I ever reached the whirlpools. Then I would not even have had the satisfaction of knowing that it was fear which was killing me, because that lethal fear had been twisted by my mother's image into self-hatred and condemnation.

Among the Ifugao, whose primitive caste system split society into layers comparable to those of Hindu and nondemocratic Western societies, the crushing sense of guilt which I had felt in the whirlpool, apparently operated on the leaders of society whenever any change in the social structure was envisaged. The Ifugao could not plant two crops of rice a year. The balance of forces inside themselves would be destroyed if they looked at the unknown, as the balance had been destroyed in me when I peered at the whirlpool over the silver-crested ripples of the rapids. Because their ceremonial attached all the layers of society to the layers in their own socially structured minds, anything that threatened to change the structure of society would release panic, concealed by hatred, in them; just as the change from stones to water under my feet had affected me. The fear and hatred released would be directed toward the graven images of unclean things in the minds of the leaders, which, in this case, would represent threatening authority, such as a powerful foreign country, or the socially inferior elements of their own society who were fomenting change in the social structure. Their hatred in the teeth of the unknown would not be directed at their inner selves, as mine had been, or at their own bodies, as was the hatred of the Negritos in the typhoon, but at the liberal members of society, or at the members of the alien society who pointed out that two crops of rice a year would give them more to eat.

These thoughts were depressing. I could not envisage any basic social change in any society until its methods of psychotherapy or emotional education had created a wide sprinkling of individuals who were no longer dependent on the type of ceremonial that divided the personality into parts and released the emotions, as did the bloodletting of the Negritos, the chicken-beating ceremony of the Bontocs, the head ceremony of the Ilongots, and the rice-increasing ceremonies of the Ifugao.

Since my earliest childhood, I had heard that there should be no strata in society, that all men were brothers, but as I grew up, I had come to regard this as a view based on religion, not psychology and sociology. My experience with the Ifugao was giving to this old religious doctrine the validity of a new scientific principle, applying both to the structure of the personality and to the structure of society. The radiantly white graven image of my mother had worked against me in the rapids, just as the Ifugao priest, with the help of the gods, worked against rationally guided change in his society. The image of the stupid old black woman, no higher than a slave in the social scale of my mind, had worked for me, once the radiant image of my mother had lost its power to keep her down in the underworld of my personality, where I had, since childhood, discarded the images of people whom I considered socially inferior to myself.

As an individual, I had not discovered and accepted these graven images and discarded models until I was faced with what I thought was certain death in the whirlpool. Some inner wisdom had brought the white, radiant mother and the black, ridiculous, witchlike image together in this supreme moment of crisis in a way which did not happen in the ceremonially guided adaptations to crises in the various societies I had observed.

The society did not become more adaptable in moments of stress. The Negritos tore out their hair and stabbed their thighs. The Ifugao had more rice-increasing ceremonies, in which they used up their slender store of animals and paid higher fees to the priests. The Ilongots took more heads. In times of stress they worked together better, but this working together was not guided by the inner wisdom of the individual, nor could it be unless the leaders, at least, were encouraged by the patterns of culture which they received from the past to look at and solve an outer problem in the present, instead of using past ceremonies to release their emotions against people and animals who were not responsible for their troubles.

The simplicity of the Negrito social structure made the psychological processes which created ceremonies stand out clearly. The dream-trance revelations threw light on the origin of the emotional needs which the ceremonies satisfied. The difference between the spontaneous ceremony and the inherited ceremony showed how the individual could build dreams and ceremonies to fit his needs, and how that same type of need could be related to, or built into, fixed ceremonies which were already established.

The startling thing to me, as I walked along the jungle trail, so shaded by interlocking branches that the afternoon sunshine changed to twilight, was the way in which the spontaneously created patterns reinforced the integrity of the individual as he projected himself into the group, like sunshine filtering through a tree, whereas the set ceremony sapped away his individual integrity as it related him to the group, and made him more and more dependent on forces which he, as an individual, could not control. It progressively undermined that divine balancing quality which produced a self-regulating, self-determining individual, taking away, rather than building up, what the mystics had called free agency.

Now as I walked along through the cathedral-like columns formed by the giant trees, I felt the world had grown larger. The experience in the whirlpool had broken things up in my mind and allowed them to fit together in a new way, which attached them more firmly to my feelings. Suddenly I realized that I was released from a lifelong suspicion that the worst that could happen was about to happen at any moment. In its place was the feeling that the best that could happen was already taking place. Now I was giving a different answer to the question, "What is the best thing that could happen?" than I had given in Manila. I was filled with the conviction that the best thing that could happen was to be alive.

And there was no end to life which I could picture. Long ago I had accepted annihilation at death as a probability—absolute, complete, utter annihilation. But now annihilation no longer had its old meaning. I had experienced annihilation as I looked at the gleaming, twisting, convulsive monster which writhed beneath the scarred face of the cliff below me in the rapids. And what was annihilation? Now it was a miraculous symphony of surging thought and feeling, a rebirth. What was life after death? It was perhaps still annihilation, but the void of annihilation was now filled with something that had the quality of joyous life.

# TWENTY-THREE

# Universal Man

THE months of work and thought since I had left Manila had increased my feeling of religious awe at the vastness and intricacy of the kingdom inside man's skin, the universe which was man himself. And I had made other advances. At least I was now convinced that there was a universal man, that the children of all races could be safely credited with my own childhood motives, feelings, and emotions. In every group there would be some who thought faster than others, and who developed a greater or smaller capacity than the average to deal with abstractions. But everywhere the results of the individual mental tests would arrange themselves on the same normal curve of distribution which had been observed in the West.

Now, knowing there was a universal man, I would have to admit that I was he. I was the Negrito, the Ilongot, the Ifugao, and the American. At the *center* I was the same in all these groups. The tests had shown that. Soon I would be back in Manila. The test results would convince my friends that the "I," the universal man, was the same in childhood in all the groups I had visited. How could I depict the ways in which the universal man in the various groups evolved with the help of the dreams, the shaman's ceremonies, the séances, the crooked root, the typhoon, the dog-starving, the chicken-bleeding, the head-hunting, and the rice-increasing? How could I explain to Mrs. Hartendorp what the various cultures did to my universal man? How could I explain what culture had done to her, to the universal being beneath the images she had built up inside her skin since she was conceived? She and the others had understood or appreciated the account of my preoccupation with the egg, of how my feeling of unity, of oneness, of identity, gave me the power to imagine what the egg felt as oneness or identity and what the egg felt as it created a secondary conflicting individual or center inside its skin in response to the biologist's beam of light. Probably they would also be able to go with me on this further voyage, when I said, "I, Negrito dreamer, see an earth demon who tells me that I and my fellows must cease to change the surface of the earth."

This would mean that I, the dreamer, plus all of the images built up by the individuals of the social group I have known, do not have power in my dream to outface or control the earth-demon individual or image of the dream. Since the Negritos had, in fact, moved off the land they were clearing, and abandoned the project because of this dream, it would mean further that I, a social chief of the Negrito horde, plus all the individuals who accept my guidance in the workaday world, do not have, or at least do not exercise, the power to undo the memory of my dream and to do what we wish even while we are awake.

This would indicate that I, the Negrito, do not own the images of the ordinary things and people with whom I work from day to day, to the same extent that I, the American, own them; I, the Negrito, do not own the images of the trees, the land, the streams, and the rocks well enough to be able to rearrange them in my abstract thinking, draw a map of the way I have rearranged them, and then set out with confidence to change these features of the environment to correspond to my plan and my map. I, the Negrito, do not own the images, the living photographs, which I have built up inside my skin. They may block me at any point in my reflective thought, in the drawing of the plan, or in its execution. I, the Negrito, do not even own the images in my mind of the blades of grass and the shrubs, and must ask their permission if I wish to spit. They are not powerful as individuals, but these little men

## UNIVERSAL MAN

of the ground are numerous. It is easier to change the crust of the outside earth than it is to change the image of the earth's crust which resides inside my skin.

I, the Negrito, have no right to sit down on a rock or lean against it, or even to disturb its solitude. I have no right to kick, even accidentally, the root of a tree with my bare toe. The pain I create, along with my whispered apology to the tree, may not persuade it to forgive me for my clumsiness. Perhaps the image of the rock I have leaned against or disturbed, or of the root I have kicked, will appear in my dream and demand that I return on awakening and leave material payment. Perhaps it will even demand that the group join me in sacrificing time and things of value to release the pressure it exerts in my psyche.

This would indicate that the rock and the tree own me, at least that part of me which is occupied by their images. It would indicate that I, the Negrito, get smaller and more impotent and more hemmed in each time I add another of the images of outside things which I build up inside my skin. Instead of learning to think as I grow older, I learn how the tree, the rock, the snake, and the bee behave, and how people behave. I learn to respect the images of all these things, to fear their power, and to govern my actions according to their individual tendencies, rather than to manipulate them as facets of my own psyche.

I can remember how my living photographs behave well enough to be under the tree when its fruit ripens or when its crevices are full of honey, to be on the ground at a certain place when the tubers ripen, to be on the pig runs when the piglets are half grown. I am propelled about my territory by my memory of these things. I cannot rudely shuffle them about and rearrange them to answer questions of foreigners about this time layer or that time layer of my mind, so foreigners say I have no memory.

I, the Negrito, have learned to protect myself from the earth, plant, and animal spirits by finding out in dreams and visions what they wish me to do and then doing it. Then, if they still punish me, I have learned, with the help of the shamans, to attack and destroy or transmute them in my dreams and visions.

I, Ilongot branch of universal man, am like the Negrito in many ways, but I have learned to till the land and to build wooden houses. The earth demon allows me to change the earth, and the tree demon allows me to use the wood, because for the life I take from the earth and the tree, I give back human life in the form of blood and heads. This practice separates the images of men in my mind into blood kin, who do not turn against me, and the remainder of the human family, any of whom I may use as sacrifices, but who at any moment may kill me.

I, the Ilongot, am somewhat dependent on the food I obtain through cultivating the land, but I cannot protect myself by attacking the earth and plant demons. To till the soil, I must ring the trees and burn them for my clearings. I must plant and harvest. The earth, tree, and plant demons do not like this, but my ancestors discovered that they will accept sacrifices of human life in exchange for the life-giving substance which I obtain from them.

I, the Ifugao, cannot protect myself by doing what the earth, plant, and animal spirits tell me to do. I must change the face of the earth. I must plant the seeds and use the fruits of the plants. I must breed the animals for food, regardless of what the spirits think about it. I am completely dependent on these activities. My ancestors learned how to do these things from the powerful spirits of the sky world. And I will be protected from the earth and sky spirits if I do what my ancestors tell me and make the proper sacrifices. When I get sick in spite of my efforts to respect and obey my ancestor spirits, I can find out in dreams and trances what more I must do in the way of vengeance, magic, prayers, and sacrifices to get my ancestor spirits to put forth greater efforts to protect me from the earth and sky spirits.

I, the Kalinga, the Bontoc, the Kankanai, am moving toward the great miracle of human thought which has established the high god, the only god, at the center of the mind of the Christian, the Buddhist, and the Taoist, where it is one with the heart. I am moving toward the concept of the blood brotherhood of all humanity, of loving my enemies, of opposing them with good will so that their images in the border of my mind will work for, rather than against, the center. I, universal man in all these groups, am moving away from the old Negrito type of thinking which makes the image of the tree belong to the tree, rather than to the man who created the image of the tree in his mind as he looked at it. Gradually I will learn, as Western man did, that the images by which I am surrounded in my dream are part of me, are mine to use in my thinking, to rearrange into a blueprint for a future better than the present which I observe when I am awake.

I, Western man, can examine the nonscientific groups and see where their therapy is better than my own and why it is better. I can see how Western man has gained in the control of his environment as he discovered that the images of his dreams and visions were not the outside world, that they belonged to him rather than to the things which his mind had photographed. I can see how he has erred in failing to recognize that these emotionally charged images of things and people are, nevertheless, real things, things which both reveal and determine his inner state of being—the universe which he is himself.

I, Western branch of universal man, do not have to do what the earth, plant, animal, or sky spirits tell me to do in my dreams and visions, or to make sacrifices to them. I profit by the sacrifice of Jesus Christ, who accepted the knowledge of the wise men from the East and the shamans of Israel. I do not protect myself by giving way to, or compromising with, earth, sky, or ancestor spirits, but relentlessly attack them. I profit by the religious tradition of breaking up the graven images of the authority of the past.

Western man is protected from the Ifugao tendency to multiply gods by the example of Jesus Christ, who refused to become a graven image in the minds of His followers, and said, "There is none good but one, that is, God." He set up the tradition of asking His followers to destroy His image periodically by symbolically eating His flesh and drinking His blood.

Western man is also protected from the ancestor gods by this type of tradition: "I came not to send peace, but a sword. For I am come to set a man at variance against his father, and the daughter against her mother, and the daughter-in-law against her mother-in-law."

Western man is protected from the Negrito type of demon by the religious tradition, established by St. Peter, of killing and eating the unclean things of dreams and visions. He is encouraged to simplify constantly the border of his mind, to recreate the unity it had in the beginning, before the images of the earth and sky forms were animated with his spirit and emotions and became tenants in his psyche, quarreling individuals which use up his force and refuse to help him with his reflective thought. I, Western man, also profit by the research of the paleontologist, who traces the creation of my body through some seventy-five miles of sedimentary rock, and of the zoologist, who shows me how my body is related to the animals which stopped evolving and changing their structure at various stages along the trail my body took, or which branched off and changed according to a different plan.

I profit by the research work of the biologist and the physiologist, who demonstrated to me that my physical body began as an egg. They showed me what happened when the egg was attacked by the beam of light. They showed me that in the nine months between conception and birth my body dramatized or re-enacted the hundreds of millions of years of development of my ancestors. I profit by the work of the philosopher and the psychologist, which indicates that there is a psychological as well as a physical aspect to this development.

I profit by the work of the sociologist and the historian, which enables me to trace the growth of my mind from the Negrito type of thinking up to the present.

This perspective, which is included in the self-consciousness of Western man, gives me a point of vantage from which I can see the other members of the biological family and of the human family as points on a scale in my own development. In twenty-one years and nine months I am supposed to complete the physical, mental, and spiritual growth which the race has taken eons of time to attain, and to be in a position as a free agent to carry it forward. From the point of vantage of Western man I can see that I, universal man, go through a stage of prenatal development where I am everything of which I am conscious, through a stage where, like the Negritos, I create images of things and people from the outside world in the border of my psyche and regard them as my masters, my allies, and my enemies, and through a further stage where I learn that these images are a part of me, that if they are not well arranged they can turn me against the group as a criminal or against myself as a neurotic or a sufferer of chronic physical illness, or can wall me in to the point of insanity. On the other hand, if they are well organized, they can serve as avenues for thought and feeling leading to a past, present, and future which daily become more vast and more interesting.

I, Western man, can so educate my offspring as to produce the type of maturity in the individual and in the group which I think is best. I can take responsibility as parent, teacher, priest, or friend for the behavior of my image in the border of the minds of my associates. At last I know that it is my words and actions which determine how my image will function toward the center of the mind of the child, and which expand that center into a self-created, self-reliant, self-regulating individual or turn it into a slave or enemy of my image.

I, Western scientist, can look at the gods of the Negrito and of the Ifugao as they express themselves through the entranced shaman and priest, and through the folk tale, the origin myth, and the ceremonial procedure in the various groups. I can compare the behavior of these gods with the behavior of the child at various ages and with the behavior of the unborn child or of the animals which correspond to the various stages of development of the unborn child.

Certainly not all of the inspirational revelations I had collected were valuable as blueprints or plans for social action. Some of them blocked social change and therefore social progress. Some even blocked technical progress and the utilization of natural resources by either the individual or the group. Some led to the relatively harmless waste of luxury resources, such as a little tobacco and betel nut, and to relatively harmless attacks upon the body of the revelator and his followers, such as the pulling out of hair or the tattooing of the skin, while others led to serious self-inflicted physical mutilation. Still other dreams and revelations led to the torture of animals and to the taking of the lives of slaves or of men who were of another lineage or community.

Other revelations did make valuable social contributions to the individual or the group. The dance and song of Igun enriched the artistic heritage of the Negrito, and the revelations from Lumawig gave to the Bontocs a code of ethics and an economic system.

I concluded that man can safely say that all dreams and revelations come from the central wisdom which builds up his body and his personality—from the God who is One with man's heart, his central mind. But man must regard dreams as having two purposes which are often contradictory—the purpose of purifying and simplifying the total self, and the purpose of rearranging the images of the units of society in such a way that they work better both inside and outside the self, and therefore make a blueprint for a better social future. But since one man's image is another man's body, since, indeed, his dream or thought pattern may include the body, mind, and spirit of every member of his group, each pattern for the future, whether drawn from dreams or from reflective thought, must be judged on its merits by the revelator's contemporaries and descendants, and accepted or rejected by the process of consensus in a democratic framework, if man wishes to make consistent social progress.

I arrived at this conviction because the dreams and revelations which could not be accepted as a model for social action, even those which would lead to disaster if followed out on a social level, still seemed to have value in simplifying, unifying, and reorganizing the border images in the minds of the individuals who expressed them. In all the groups people recovered from both physical and mental disorders by telling their dreams and by following out the policies acceptable to their group which were recommended or suggested by the dream characters. This was true even though the systems of dream interpretation were different, in some respects contradictory. As healing devices, some were much more efficient and effective than others.

I became convinced, finally, that all dreams and revelations, all reflective thought and spontaneous creative thinking, might safely be regarded as revelation from God by those who believe in religion, and as revelation from the gargantuan intelligence which creates and maintains the physical body by those who do not have the conviction that their own heart is one with Him who creates and maintains the universe.

The Western branch of universal man can safely adopt this attitude and free the creative indwelling wisdom of the body because, at last, we can understand why obsolete, contradictory images or centers in the border of the mind of the individual must be destroyed by the process of annihilation or unification as though they were disease germs.

We can at last differentiate between the spontaneous mental activity which breaks down and recreates the self, and that which might serve as a model for a new and better machine or a better way of doing things in the social world. Man's spontaneous mental activity could not be regarded as always good until he realized that the images of his father and his wife were integral parts of him, just as his lymph and his blood were parts of him, and until he further realized that the spontaneous movement of these images in his dreams and creative thought was ruled by the same inner wisdom which caused his lymph and blood to circulate. Until then he could not realize that the coming together of these images in his dreams did not constitute a breach of the law of incest, for which he had to murder his wife or his father or both in order to save the social group from the rage of the high god, or to kill himself or go insane because of the conflict between the law of incest and the law of the blood feud.

Man could not allow his indwelling wisdom to work on the images, which are photographs of the elements of the social group, as it did on food and water and oxygen, until he realized that the elements of his mind were unclean once they had been associated with his negative emotions, and therefore had to be destroyed before he could become socially knowledgeable and wise.

The mystics who created the great religions have understood this for a long time. They have warned their disciples that psychological wisdom is often the opposite of social wisdom, that the wisdom of God is foolishness to man. But religious organizations, like other social institutions, must be perpetuated by the average man.

Until Western science discovered the all-wise king inside the egg of the frog, the average man could not believe he had such a king inside himself, and could not credit his neighbor who drove the garbage truck with such an indwelling king. The average man could not believe in the wisdom of his own body until thousands of physicists, chemists, and mathematicians had worked together for generations and changed the face of the earth, without, at the same time, being able to do any one of a million things that the body of anyone of those scientists or of the average man can accomplish while he is asleep. The bestiality, sodomy, sex perversion, murder, cannibalism, and witchcraft to which various individuals and societies have been led through dreams could have been avoided if the dreamer had been encouraged to express freely his dreams and fantasies to authorities who could help him decide where the indwelling wisdom of the heart was bringing about a unification of the border images of the mind and where it was inventing social policies—perhaps better than past ways of doing things—which should be presented for approval to the group involved.

The tensions and chronic illness in all the groups I had visited, and the amuck of the Ifugao, well demonstrated the fact that failure to express dreams and fantasies which would be antisocial if acted out did not protect the individual or the group from the spontaneous activity of the border images of the mind.

As Westerner, I had looked at the shamans' dramatizations of many of the animals which were among the unclean things which St. Peter saw in the famous vision which changed Christianity from a Jewish sect into a world religion. In his vision St. Peter was told to kill and eat these unclean things, much as the Negrito patient was told to attack and destroy the animal spirits which would not co-operate in the healing process. Knowing that the wisdom in the egg had built the physical body of the Negritos, I knew that these trance expressions might be providing information which even my Western mind was not yet able to comprehend.

Knowing the pattern of man's development from the egg and of his way of modifying his original pattern as he built inside his body the record of the outside universe, I was aware of at least two different types of things which might be happening in the trance. The clam god of a shaman's dream might represent the return of the shaman's adult mind to an event in childhood when he was told by an older sister that he must shut up like a clam; or it might represent a return to a much earlier incident, to an accident—like the scientist's beam of light—which occurred when his body had developed no further than what might be called the clamlike stage of prenatal maturation.

I had collected both trance and dream expressions which had relieved people of physical and mental symptoms, and which seemed to fall into these categories. At least, I could account for them as easily in no other way. I had heard the turtle demon speak to the shaman in the spirit cave on the subject of arthritis. Was it the wisdom which created the body speaking when the shaman heard the demon say that because of an agreement entered into before his birth, he must speak up in the councils of the old men when their decisions enraged him, and he must fight it out with his nagging wife and become the man of the family if he wished to stand up on his hind legs like a man who was a healer and cease going around on all fours with his back as stiff as a turtle? It seemed fantastic, yet the question persisted: Had some stimulus, like the scientist's beam of light, penetrated his prenatal world at a time when he could best protect himself by throwing out a substance which was like a turtle's shell and which would serve him for a skeleton on the outside rather than the inside of his body?

Did all men tend to become stiff in gristle and in muscle, to regress to an earlier stage of body development, when they protected themselves by building up inner tensions rather than through creative or aggressive action on the things or people surrounding them?

The Negrito trance and the Ifugao gods of arthritis and rheumatism seemed determined to warn man that it was dangerous for him to return to animal methods of solving problems when his life as a human being became difficult. Even though man can react to his problems like a reptile, a turtle, or a clam, it is not a good idea for him to solve them in any other way than as a complete man using all his adult resources.

The trance states made it appear that accidental stimulation in any stage in man's development resulted in the building up of extra resources in that area, as though the scientist's beam of light had caused the organism to create an extra center or head at that point. Once a man gives up his adult human way of doing things and reverts to a more simple or more primitive pattern of reaction, he is likely to go back to the points where his normal growth has been disturbed. Once he has employed the extra heads built up there, they tend to hold him at that level, as though they wished to solve all his problems in a subhuman fashion and thus to pull him away from his social group and his human way of doing things.

All the primitive psychologists I had met in the jungle seemed to say that, with the aid of his fellows, a man can travel back to find what, inside him, is destroying his life in the present. But their attempts at healing showed that the forces which are discovered must be brought up to the present and given social expression if the individual is to profit by the experience. The ghouls, spirits, and gods of illness could use both the individual and the group, if the man who was ill, or his associates, did not have both the knowledge and the will to either destroy or transmute them.

Man must express his excess energy either in reorganizing himself or in changing the outside world. If he acts destructively toward a dream character, he is opposing and trying to destroy a troublesome fragment of himself, but if he acts in the same way toward human beings, he is attempting to destroy what is equal to himself. Since he can only know other human beings as he credits them with his own self-feeling, any destructive social policy to some extent turns him against his own center. This point had been emphasized with the monotony of a turning wheel during the past few months. Man must have no social policy which condones turning his aggression toward other men, as the head-hunters did. Otherwise, he will always be turned against himself.

It seemed to me that in science, religion, and politics the Westerner had found a possible solution to this problem. Every man is my brother. I will contend with him only within the framework of good will, as I do in sports, in scientific research, and in democratic assembly. But through my education and my psychotherapy I must develop to a point where even when life becomes difficult I will not regress, as an individual or as a group, to the head-hunter or the ghoul stage of reaction.

Ahead of me on the trail back to the village, the twilight void was now filling in with something living. Soon the amorphous mass broke into jogging, sweating, running human beings and horsemen. The lads had reached the village and spread the news of my fate. The whole populace was hurrying down to the Mother of Fountains, to get my body from the water, lest it should serve as crocodile bait and build up the wrong kind of appetite in the reptiles which frequented the ford of the river. Seeing me, the cavalcade froze into immobility. There was terror in their faces, horror in the eyes of all who looked at me. Their expressions protested that I was a ghost, that I had brought them face to face with the supernatural.

It was astonishing that people could be afraid of me, when seeing them gave me such joy. I was especially glad to see the lads who had been with me in the river, and Julio, who at last had arrived from the north and had come with them. Now as I looked at them staring at me, their ribs rising and falling, their mouths opening as though to speak, without making a sound, as I looked at their disheveled hair and their bodies gleaming with perspiration, I knew that the feeling I had had for them before had been mainly intellectual—that I had only been thinking about them before and was now letting myself be with them for the first time.

"You must have had a much harder time getting down here than I did," I said at last. The fear that I had left my body in the whirlpool with the queen of the water fairies, and that my ghost had come to punish them for something or other, was melting now. Their expressions were changing from horror to incredulity, to curiosity, to joy.

I was glad they were laughing and crying, that they were people who could express themselves freely, for the fluttering, sobbing aliveness in the middle of myself had started up again the moment I had seen them. The bubbling ripples which flowed up were no longer sobs, but neither were they laughter. This was an action feeling for which I had no name, with which I had had no experience. Again and again it was set in motion as the villagers swarmed about me, examining the vine which held up my banana leaf, touching me to reassure themselves that I was really solid flesh.

The most trivial details could start it all over again: the curious angle a girl's elbow made as she tucked a hair in the bun at the back of her neck, the whites of the eyes of a lad as he looked up at me, the flaring arch of the nostril of an old man, the bulging eyes of a pony, which looked as though he were still certain I was a ghost.

Something had changed since I had last seen these people. I had lost some of my dignity or stability, my sense of detachment or rigidity, but I had not lost contact with reality. That was reassuring. These people were more real to me than people had ever been before. I no longer expected that something or someone would punish me if I allowed myself to feel toward them and express my feelings. I no longer expected them to let me down and hurt me if I allowed myself to like them and to trust them.

One of the boys was still staring at me, openmouthed, not saying a word. I could see that he did not share my feeling of mutual trust. Perhaps I was no more than a ghost. He would have to see for himself. At last he extended his hand, brushed it across a trickle of blood from the scratch on my ribs, and examined it.

By now the others were demanding what charm I had used against the water fairy. I thought that the boy with the staring eyes was going to ask me for the blood as a talisman. When he spoke there was a note of anger in his voice, of one who is convinced of something against his will.

"Well, anyway," he said, "the water fairy got your half-soled pants."

# Index

Abra province, 119
Abra River, 253–254
  gorge expedition, 3–14
  Stewart's experience in rapids of, 9–14, 260–261, 265–270, 282–283
Adolescence:
  circumcision, 57
  dreams of, 61
  racial, 25
  scarification, 57
  sexual education during, 178–179
  teeth chipping in, 103–104
  test results in, 61–62, 111
Adultery, 33, 73, 179
  high gods and, 32
African pygmies, 24
Agreement trance, 49, 92, 111–112
  description of, 41–42
  Ilongot, 141
Ainus, 130
Airplanes, Negrito reaction to, 112
Alfonso, King, 59–61, 89
Amambay, 217–218
  recital of Ifugao gods and ceremonies, 218–239

Amuck, Ifugao tendency to run, 199, 207–209, 233, 238
Ancestors:
  calling of sick people by, 183
  eating of crops by, 139
Ancestor worship, 134, 139–140, 168, 209–210, 234
  spirit possession in, 241–242
Andaman Negritos, 24
Angaki, 253
Animal life, 63–68, 250
  bats, 108
  buffalo, 32, 213–214
  chicken beating, 182
  dogs, 83, 85, 127–128, 164–165, 168, 202
  dreams of, 207
  earthworms, 32, 33
  horses, 163–165
  insects, 35–38, 63–64, 104–106, 176, 180–181, 219
  monkeys, 33
  pigs, 62–63
  snakes, 4–6, 35–36, 38, 188
  souls of, 219

Animal life (*continued*)
  torture of, 164–165
*Anitos*, Ilongot beliefs about, 134, 137, 138, 141, 183
Annihilation, meaning of, 270
Anopel, 254
Ants, as food, 104–105
Arthritis, 240
Asin River Rest House, 244, 249

Bamboo, uses of, 38, 151, 154, 155
Banaue, 193, 199–211
Bangued, Stewart's stay in, 120–131
Barton, Dr. Roy Franklin, 209
*Basi*, 134, 143
Basic man theory, 16, 26
  central and border aspects of, 20–21, 265
  research methods, 20–27
  trinity in unity, 17–18
  universal man, 271–283
  *see also* Man
Bataan Negritos, 32–38, 40–58
Bataan peninsula, 30
Bats, fruit, as food, 108
Bayombong, 129, 130, 132, 133
Bees, 37
  dances of, 63–64
Beliefs, 141–142, 187
  ancestor worship, 134, 139–140, 168, 209–210, 234
  blood brother, 34, 95
  Bontoc, 170–174, 181–191
  Ifugao, 168, 195–196, 221–248, 263, 264
  Ilongot, 134, 137, 138, 141
  Kankanai, 164
  Negrito spirit, 65–66, 68–69
  tattooing, 163
  *see also* Dreams, Religion, Spirits, etc.
Betel-nut chewing, 102–103, 104
  taboo of, 176
Betrothal:
  child, 166
  *see also* Courtship
Beyer, Dr. H. Otley, 29–31, 129, 192, 209
Binet Test, 22

Black magic, 26, 39, 41, 255
Blood brother belief, 34, 95
Blood feuds, 40, 95
  Bontoc, 179–180
  Ifugao, 198–199
  Ilongot, 137–138
  Kalingan fines to replace, 144
  marriage taboos and, 33–34
  Negrito, 33, 40
Blood sacrifice, 118, 142
  *see also* Head-hunting
Bokai, 3, 192, 254–261, 282–283
  Stewart's journey to, 249–255
Bolo, 7–8, 124
Bontoc (city), 162
  social patterns in, 170–174
Bontocs, 24, 30, 168, 269
  code of ethics, 173
  culture and characteristics of, 173–190
  high god of, 172–173, 185
  emergence of political rites among, 171
  emergence of political law among, 171
  emergence of primitive economics among, 173
  origin myth of, 172
  sexual life of unmarried, 172
  significance of development, 274
  social institutions, 170–174
  war against the United States Army, 193
Brown, Dr. Radcliffe, 24
Buffalo, 32
  sacrificial, 213–214
Buguias, 162
Burial customs, *see* Funeral ceremonies

Caliat, 133
Camps, Negrito, 38, 103
Caterpillars, 36, 106
Caves:
  Pinatoba spirit, 63
  treasure, 5–6
Centipedes, 38
Central mind theory, 16, 21, 67, 69
  dream drawings and, 265

# INDEX

inherited ceremonies and, 265
spontaneous ceremonies and, 264
Ceremonies:
  ancestor-worship, 134, 139
  birth, 223-224
  Bontoc, 171, 181-186
  courtship, *see* Courtship
  food gathering and preparing, 63-68
  funeral, *see* Funeral ceremonies
  healing, *see* Healing
  head-hunting, 140-146, 152, 156-157, 184-185, 267-268
  Ifugao, 195
  Kankanai, 166
  magical dances, 63, 64, 65
  man's inner balance affected by, 262-270
  psychological aspects, 64, 225-226
  puberty, 57
  taboo-cleansing rituals, 77-78
  typhoon-placating, 116-118
Cervantes, 253
Child, Dr., 17
Children, 25
  Bontoc, 173, 178, 185
  Ifugao, 207-208
  Negrito, 60-62, 69, 90-91, 108, 111
Chirp, 211, 217, 229, 244, 249
Christianity, 268
  Bangued people's attitude toward, 122, 126, 128
  Kankanai beliefs and, 164
  Negrito attitude toward, 95
Cigarettes, 37, 81
Circumcision, 57
Civilization, stages in evolution of, 23, 129, 162, 186
Clappers, Ifugao, 219
Clothing:
  Bontoc, 178
  Ifugao, 199, 205
  Ilongot, 135-136
  Negrito, 34-35
  sacrificial, 134, 241
Cogon grass, 34
Color, trance significance, 42, 55, 78, 266-267
Copper, 133, 163-164

Councilors, 144
Councils:
  Bontoc, 170-171
  Kalingas, 144
Courtship:
  "American way," 86-96
  Bontoc customs, 174-180
  dances, 72, 79, 94
  Filipino, 128
  Ilongot customs, 150, 154
Cowrie shells, 135
Creativeness:
  dream-induced, 25-26, 63-64, 264
  Negrito, 46-47, 109-110
Cyst incidents, 51-54, 112

Dance:
  courtship, 72, 74, 94
  Filipino, 152
  food gathering and preparing, 63-68
  Ifugao, 214-215
  Ilongot, 151-152, 155-158
  shaman's, 124
  spirit-placating, 116
  *see also* Ceremonies
Death:
  Bontoc beliefs, 183-184
  gods of, 247-248
  Ifugao attitude toward, 229-231, 233-234
  loss of head, 185
  Negrito attitude toward, 99-100, 231
  suicide, 248
  *see also* Beliefs *and* Funeral ceremonies
Deer hunt, Negrito, 62, 107
Disease:
  deities controlling, 229-230
  Ifugao and, 240
  Kankanai and, 166
  mental, 241-243
  Negrito chronic, 48
  sopot-sopot, 120-127
  trance-state treatment of, 40-58
  tropical, 31-32, 42
  venereal, 179
  *see also* Healing *and* Medicine

Divination, egg, 210
Diviner deities, 235
Dogs:
  Filipino, 127–128
  as food, 164–165
  Ifugao, 202
  Negrito, 83, 85
Drawing:
  action, 207
  Ilongot, 136
  Negrito, 111, 265
Dreams, 26, 207
  adolescence, 61
  balance in, 65
  dead parents, 91
  death and guilt aspects, 11, 91–92
  drawings in, 265
  falling, 108
  food, 168
  food-gathering, 65
  head-hunting, 184
  healing effect of, 278
  impact on group life, 45–47
  Kalingan priestess', 140
  Negrito, 45–58, 61–64
  nightmares, 68–69
  Ogong's father-spirit, 54–57
  purpose of, 277
  reflection of life patterns through, 18–21
  reflective thought in, 64
  shaman, 91–92, 115, 262
  Un's baby-spirit, 51–54
  Zog's earth-spirit, 66, 68
  *see also* Beliefs, Myths, *and* Trance
Drinking:
  Bontoc, 174
  Ilongot, 155–156
  Kankanai, 165
Drums:
  Ifugao, 243
  Kankanai, 165
  Negrito rhythm for, 43
  shamans, 124
Dumagates, 136
Durian trees, 108

Earthworms, 32, 33
Egg ceremony, Lumawig, 184

Eggs:
  divination by, 210
  as food, 180
Egg story, 17–18
Emotional Response Test, 22, 27, 41, 184, 211
  Ilongot, 137
  Negrito, 61, 111
Evans, Negrito work, 24

Farm schools, 31, 101
Feasts:
  funeral, 55–57, 59, 62–70, 80–86, 89–92, 166, 183
  Ifugao, 199–200
  rice-increasing, 212–219
  *see also* Ceremonies
Fertility:
  Bontoc rock battle, 168
  egg related to, 184
  gods and, 221
  head-hunting related to, 146
  reproduction gods of, 223
  return of souls, 219
  rice priestess, 168
Filipinos, 88
Firearms, 32, 34, 193
Fire-kindling, 103
Fish, 165
  Bontoc spirit food, 184
  taboo, 78
Fogs, mountain, 105, 107
Food:
  Bontoc, 180
  ceremonial, 167, 168
  dream, 168
  high god, giver of, 172
  Ilongot, 154–155
  inheritance tax, 166
  Kankanai, 164–165
  meat preparation, 82
  Negrito, 104–105, 108, 110
  taboos surrounding, 78
Funeral ceremonies:
  Bontoc, 183
  burials, 98–100
  death requesting, 247
  Ifugao, 246–247
  Ilongot, 168

# INDEX

Kankanai, 166
Negrito, 55–57, 59, 62–70, 80–86, 89–92
post-burial, 247
reburial, 242

Gabriel, 130, 143–153
Gallman, Captain Jeff, 209
Game-owning deities, 236
Ghosts, 100
  Bontoc, 188–189
  as gods, 233
  Ogong's father's, 55–57, 81
  return of, 247
  stories, 189
Ghouls, as gods, 247
Giles, Lieutenant, 209
Girdles:
  Bontoc, 178
  Ilongot, 135
Glin, 78–81, 85–88, 94, 96
Gloc, 115
Gods:
  Bontoc high, 172–173, 185
  Ifugao, 208–210, 221–248
  Kalingan high, 139
  Kankanai high, 164
  Negrito high, 32, 33
  possession, 228
  significance of effect on man's inner balance, 265
  see also Beliefs, Myths, and Religion
Gold, 146
  Kankanai and, 164, 166–167
  ornaments, 167
  prospecting for, 162
Gongs, 144, 166
Goodenough Draw-a-Man Test, 22, 27
  Ifugao, 207
  Ilongot, 136–137
  Negrito, 61, 62, 110–111
Granary idols, 219
Group experience, 99
  individual inner balance and, 262
Guilt, sense of, 10–11, 266–267, 268
  expiation of, 117–118
  fear and, 266–268

*Halag*, 241–244
Hapao, rice-increasing festival at, 212–219
Harpies, as gods, 230–231
Hartendorps, the, Stewart trip and, 15–28
Hawaii, University of, 22
Headache myth, 239
Head-hunting:
  ceremonies associated with, 140–146, 152, 156–157, 184–185, 267–268
  dreams associated with, 138–139
  fertility related to, 146
  Ifugao gods and, 222
  Ilongot beliefs and, 137–138
  influence of firearms on, 193
  reasons for, 160–161, 167–168
  see also Bontocs, Ifugao, and Ilongots
Healing:
  Bontoc, 181–183
  Ifugao, 239–244
  José incident, 255–258
  Kalingan, 139–140
  Negrito, 36–38, 40–58, 255–256
  trance, 46–49
  witchcraft, 122–125
Heaven:
  Bontoc concepts, 185
  center of earth, 32, 33
  Ifugao, four, 195
Honey, 64
  Negrito use of, 36–38
Horsehair, 133, 150
Horses, 163–165
Hot-head justice, 171
Houses:
  Bontoc, 171–172
  Ifugao, 199
  Ilongot, 130, 150
  Kalingan, 134
  Kankanai, 163, 165
  Negrito, 38, 103
*Hudhud* myths, 223
Hungduan, 217
Hunt, Dr. Truman K., 192
Hunting, 62–68, 236

Hymns, effect on primitive peoples, 152–153, 158
Hypnosis:
  agreement trance and, 40, 42
  Negrito reaction to, 40, 42
  self-induced, 241–244
  trance-like, 228
Hysteria, 144

Idols:
  granary, 219
  inner, 65–66
  phallic, 171–172
  property-guarding, 227
Ifugao, 23, 24, 191–196
  customs and characteristics, 195–205, 207–221
  gods and religious beliefs, 221–224, 225–237, 244–248, 263, 264
  healing and charm-activating ceremonies, 238–246
  religious beliefs, 168, 195–196
  significance of development, 274
  social structure significance, 268–269
Igorots, 162, 168
Igun, 108–110, 263
Ijah, 147, 148–149, 152
Iloko, 192
Ilongots, 23–25, 129, 130, 134
  culture and characteristics, 151–152, 167–168
  eating customs, 154–155
  emotional make-up, 141–142
  fears of, 137
  friendliness, 150
  memories, 137
  physical characteristics, 135–136, 150, 158
  reactions to testing program, 135–143
  significance of development, 274
  wars with Lowlanders, 133
Incest:
  ceremonial, 77
  dreams and, 279
  first ancestors, 172
  high god and, 33
Indians, American, 19

Indonesian mountaineer children, 129
Infancy, racial, 25
Inner balance, man's effort to achieve, 63–68, 231, 261–270
Insects, 35–38, 63–64, 104–106, 176, 180–181, 219
Isabella province, 134

Jabon's people, 102–113
Jenks, Ernest, 30, 192
Jewelry, Kankanai, 166–167
Jew's-harp, 176
José, cure, 255–258
Journey, charms to guard, 245–246
Juan:
  Bangued and witch-doctor incident, 120–127
  healing sessions and, 39–58
  journey with Stewart, 29, 31–38
  testing program aid, 60–61, 102
  wife-acquiring incidents, 31, 71–81, 85–88, 92–96, 126–127
  Zambales Negritos and, 101–119
Julio, 254
  Ifugao experiences, 191–200, 204–207
Jungles, hazards of travel in, 35–36, 38, 249–253

Kabunyan, 139, 140
Kalingas, 134
  characteristics of, 142–143
  significance of development, 274
  spirit beliefs, 226
  testing results, 138–142
Kankanai:
  culture and characteristics of the, 162–167
  significance of development, 274
Kinga (village), 244, 246
Kinga River, 244

Lace panties incident, 87–88, 92–93
Lango, courtship dance, 72, 79
Language:
  man's development and, 18
  Negrito, 30
  sign, 203–204
Larvae, honeycomb, 38

# INDEX

Leeches, 35
Lice, 177
Locusts, 176, 180–181
Loincloths, 35, 135, 177
Loo, 252–253
Love:
  Bontoc attitude toward, 179
  Christian, 95
  charms for, 244
  *see also* Courtship
Lowlanders, 33
  Ilongots and, 133
  language, 30
Lucas, King, 59–60
Lumawig, Bontoc belief in, 183–187
Luzon, 129, 162

MacGregor, experiences of, 159–169
Magat River valley, 162
Magic:
  black, 39, 41, 255
  dances, 63, 68
  egg divination, 210
  hunting, 236
  love charms, 244–246
  spirit-placating, 109
  witch doctor's, 122–125
  *see also* Beliefs *and* Ceremonies
Malaria, 42
Malaya, Negritos of, 24
Man:
  basic, 16, 20–27
  central mind theory, 21–22
  Ifugao gods and, 234
  inner balance and outer relationships, 261–270
  Lumawig and, 172
  universal, 271–283
Manolo, trading post of, 134–135, 143–147
Marriage:
  blood kin taboo, 33–34
  Bontoc customs, 179, 184
  Kankanai customs, 166
  native-white, 161
  Negrito customs, 71–81
  *see also* Courtship
Meat-eating, 235
  *see also* Foods

Medicine, 39–40, 48, 49
  constant-state-of-body theory, 20–21
  free distribution of, 31–32
  honey as, 63–64
  sopot-sopot treatment, 121–122
  *see also* Healing
Messenger deities, 228
Metal Maze test, 22, 27, 61, 62, 111, 137
Ming jars, 5
Mining, Kankanai, 163–164
Money, 80, 133, 163–164
Monkeys:
  joke incident, 90–91
  myths about, 33, 187–188
Moon myths, 39, 128, 184, 222, 235
Mormonism, 17, 20
Mountain province, American influence on, 192–193
Music, *see* Dances *and* Songs
Musical instruments, 124, 151, 165, 166, 176
Muzzle, gold, 167
Myths:
  headache, 239
  head-losing, 184–185
  *Hudhud*, 223
  lizard, 187
  monkey, 33, 187–188
  moon, 39, 128, 184, 222, 235
  origin, 172, 208
  rice bird, 180, 187–188
  rock-demon, 105–106
  root, 109–110, 263
  salt, 263
  serpent-eagle, 184–185
  snake, 4–6, 188
  stiff-neck, 239–240
  thunder, 43–44, 117
  water fairy, 3–14
  *see also* Beliefs

Negritos:
  attachment to land, 30, 50, 58
  Bataan groups, 32–38, 40–58
  beliefs, 65–66, 68–69
  chipped teeth, 103–104
  Christianity and, 95

Negritos (*continued*)
  communities of, 103
  culture of, 16-17, 23-25, 129-130
  eastern groups, 129
  food taboos, 78
  friendliness response, 100, 101, 107
  gourmandizing, 84-85
  head shaving, 101
  healing methods, 40-58, 255-256
  original endowments, 62
  personality characteristics, 30, 50, 67, 98-100, 107-108, 111
  physical characteristics, 31, 37-38, 73-76, 101-104
  pregnancy taboos, 66-67
  racial mixing, 129-130
  return of dead, 91
  scarification, 57
  shaman dreams, 91-92
  significance of personality-environment reactions, 261-266, 269-270, 271-273, 277, 280-281
Neuroses, 21, 46, 69
  lata, 144
  starvation, 255-258
Nonliterate peoples, 19, 25
Nueva Vizcaya, 129, 130

Ogong, 81
Olan, marriage project, 71-81, 126-127
Omens, 171, 188, 194, 222

Palali Mountains, 129
Pana, treatment and testing of, 41-49
Pangat Guhlu, 143-144
Patterns, growth, 18-21
Pay-backable deities, 218-220, 240, 263
Perez, Dr. Gilbert, 16, 17, 22, 23, 25
Peter, St., 275, 280
*Philippine*, 16
Philippines, primitive peoples in, 23-25, 30, 216
Philippines, University of, 29
Photographs, primitive reactions to, 175-176
Pig hunts, 62-63
Pili, property-guarding god, 227

Pinatoba, spirit cave on, 43
Plant life:
  cane, 155, 250
  cogon grass, 34
  durian trees, 108
  food plants, *see* Foods
  rice, *see* Rice
  souls of, 65
  tubers, 110
Population figures, 30, 216
Porcupine, as food, 155
Porteus Maze Test, 22, 27, 61, 110, 137, 138, 150
Pregnancy, taboos, 66-67
Priests:
  Bontoc, 170-171
  Ifugao, 210, 220-221, 228, 247, 264
  shaman, *see* Shaman
  *see also* Religion
Private ownership and enterprise, 186, 226-227
Progressive Fantasy Test, 22, 61, 111, 137
Prospecting, 162
Psychology, *see* Psychotherapy *and* Testing
Psychotherapy:
  Bontoc, 182
  creativeness in, 47
  cultural development of man and, 271-282
  deteriorating influence of technical progress, 264
  dream calling to, 140
  group, two types of, 45-46
  group aspects, 99, 108
  Ifugao approach, 228
  José incident, 255-258
  Kalinga, 140
  meaningful nature of whirlpool experience, 260-262, 267-270
  Negrito healing and, 41-58
  priestcraft and, 243-244
  priesthood and, 247
  shaman practice of, 115
  social institutions and, 268
Puberty:
  scarification, 57
  *see also* Adolescence

# INDEX

*Pudung*, 226–227
Pygmies:
  African, 24
  Philippine, *see* Negritos

Raft accident, 254
Rattan trade, 134
Religion:
  Christian idea significance, 95, 122, 126, 128, 164, 268
  cultural development and man's inner balance, 271–282
  primitive, *see* Beliefs *and* Ceremonies
  science and, 20–21
Reproduction, gods of, 223–224, 234
Revelation, 262, 277
  Bontoc, 173
  Pana, 44
  Smith, Joseph, 17, 20
Rheumatism, 240
Rice:
  ceremonies surrounding, 169, 212–219
  as food, 180
  priestess, 169
  significance to Ilongots, 152, 153, 158
  terraces, 198–199, 201–205, 215–216
  test for guilt by, 171
  wine from, 165
Rice bird myth, 180, 187–188
Ringworm, 37
  treatment of, 40, 49, 50
Roads, 174
  Bontoc trail, 191–196
  jungle, 32–38, 249–253
Roberto, 32, 34, 94
Rock myth, 105–106
Root myth, 109–110, 263
*Runo* loop, 226–227

Salt:
  gift, 102
  myth, 263
Salvadors, the, 121–131
Samoki, 162, 168
Santiago, Julio, 191–200, 204–205, 254
Sari, at the funeral feast, 89–91

Scarification, at puberty, 57
Schebesta, Father, 24
Science:
  knowledge and, 26
  point of vantage and, 277
  religion and, 20–21
Schools, 31, 101, 132–133
Sex:
  Bontoc customs, 172, 174–180
  Ifugao attitudes, 223–224
  impotence in, 236
  license in, 194
  masculine-feminine spirits, 51–53
  test experiences in, 136
  *see also* Courtship *and* Marriage
Shaman, 91–92, 114–116, 228
  Jabon, 102–113
  Negrito healing by, 40–58
  training for, 115
  *see also* Healing
Shrines:
  Ifugao, 227
  Kalingas' anito, 134
  Kankanai, 161
Silk threads, for currency, 133
Skirts, bark cloth, 93
Sleep:
  god of, 20
  men's psychology and, 20
  new patterns and, 18
Smoking habits, Negrito, 37
Snakes, 35–36, 38
  myths about, 4–6, 188
Snow, 50
Social reality, 243
Social relations gods, 225–226
Society:
  Bontoc, 170–174
  dreams and, 66
  Ifugao, 268–269
  influence on emotions and mental growth, 21–26
  Kalingan, 144
  Negrito, 45, 60, 108
  reaction to stress, 269–270
  western man's new concept of, 278–282
Songs:
  Ifugao, 200

Songs (*continued*)
  Ilongot, 151–152, 155–158
  Kankanai, 165–166
  Negrito, 83–85, 98, 102, 109–110, 116
Sopot-sopot illness, 120–127
Spanish influence, 163–164
Spear, Bontoc anti-*anito*, 190
Spiny caterpillars, 36, 106
Spirits:
  Bontoc belief in, 181–191
  ghosts, 55–57, 100, 233
  ghouls, 247
  Negrito beliefs, 65–69, 109–110, 238
  possession, 108–110, 243, 246–247
  shaman struggles with, 115–116
  *see also* Beliefs
Spitter deities, 231
Spoon, magic, 227
Squirt guns, 146–147
State Training School, Utah, 20, 22
Stewart, Kilton, *passim*
  background of expedition, 15–28
  whirlpool experience and interpretation, 3–14, 260–270, 282–283
Stiff-neck healing ceremony, 239–240
Storms, jungle, 116–118, 250–251
Sugar-cane, 155–156
Suicide, 248, 266
Sweet potatoes, 165
Sympathy Test, 61, 111, 137

Taboos:
  betel-nut chewing, 176
  eating, 78
  gambling, 176
  group support against spirits by, 69
  isolating, 117
  marriage, 33–34
  pregnant woman, 66–67
  property-guarding, 227
  sex, 77–78, 223
Tajo, 174–182
Talisman:
  guardian spear, 190
  love charms, 244–246
Talisman-activating gods, 234–235
Tapon, 174–190

Tattooing, 57, 163
  Bontoc, 163
  Ilongot, 135
  Kalinga, 142
  Kankanai, 163
Teeth, chipped, 103–104
Testing program, 21–22, 27
  Bangued High School, 121, 129–130
  Bokai incidents, 253–255
  death dreams, 91
  Ifugao, 207–211
  Ilongots, 135–143, 150, 154
  loss of records, 254
  Negrito, 39–58, 60–62, 75, 110–112
  shaman reaction, 114–116
  *see also* separate tests
Thunder:
  gods of, 226
  Negrito beliefs about, 43–44, 117
  typhoon, 116–118
Ticks, wood, 36
Todas, 130
Tolandian, 32–34, 45, 65, 77–78, 117
Trade, 59, 134, 135
Trance:
  agreement-type, 41–42, 49, 92, 111–112, 141
  creativeness in, 47
  healing through, 46–49
  Jose incident, 256–258
  Kalingan and Ilongot reactions, 138–142
  shaman use of, 114–115
  significance of response to, 265–270
  spirit contact through, 106–107
Tree demon incident, 105–107
Tree snakes, 36
Tubers:
  as food, 110
  trance mention of, 143
Twins, Ilongot custom concerning, 161–162
Typhoon, 116–118, 261, 262

Un:
  marriage-making incident, 71–77, 87, 92–96

trance-treatment of, 50–54
United States:
  Americans as colonizers, 192–193
  Ilongots and, 133
  Negritos and, 59, 60
Universal man, 271–282
  *see also* Basic man *and* Man
Utah, 42
Utah, University of, 19

Venereal disease, 179
Villiar, 101

War, 133, 170, 193, 222
Water fairy myth, 3–14
Weapons, 135, 142–147, 157
Weaving, gods of, 219
Whirlpool experience, 9–14, 260–270, 282–283
Wind deities, 229
Witch doctor, sopot-sopot treatment, 122–125

Women:
  Bontoc, 174–179, 185
  funeral ceremonies performed by, 83–84, 85
  Ifugao, 205, 216–217
  Ilongot, 151
  labor ceremonies, 223–224
  marriage customs, *see* Marriage
  musicians, 165
  muzzled, 167
  Negrito, 32, 116
  priestesses, 139–140, 181, 241–244
  pregnancy taboos, 66–67
  reticence of, 50
  virtue attitudes, 128
Writing, automatic, 47

Young, Brigham, 145

Zambales Mountains, 30, 129
  Negritos of the, 102–113, 114–118
Zog, dream of, 66, 68

LIBRARY OF DAVIDSON